IMAGES
of America

BOSSIER CITY

On the Cover: This photograph is of a group of servicemen from Barksdale Air Force Base and librarian Irma Beck, taken in the reading room of the Bossier Branch Library located in Bossier City's city hall on October 2, 1941. The servicemen are all wearing Army uniforms, as the Air Force was not yet a separate branch. (Courtesy of the Bossier Parish Library Historical Center.)

IMAGES
of America

BOSSIER CITY

Kevin Bryant Jones

ARCADIA
PUBLISHING

ISBN 978-1-4671-1321-2

Published by Arcadia Publishing
Charleston, South Carolina

Printed in the United States of America

Library of Congress Control Number: 2014942666

For all general information, please contact Arcadia Publishing:
Telephone 843-853-2070
Fax 843-853-0044
E-mail sales@arcadiapublishing.com
For customer service and orders:
Toll-Free 1-888-313-2665

Visit us on the Internet at www.arcadiapublishing.com

To my parents, Richard and Jane Jones, for all their help and dedication toward my education, and my wife, Robin, and children, Megan and Gavin, without whose support, encouragement, and help this endeavor would not have been possible

Contents

ACKNOWLEDGMENTS

This work acknowledges the people whose love for Bossier City keeps the tight-knit community spirit alive and well. I would like to acknowledge the help of the Tubbs family and the employees of Tubbs Hardware, Joe Maggio and the Maggio family for all their help and stories about Bossier City, Mickey Capuano and the Peters family, the Cobb family and the fine people at Joe Cobb's BBQ, George Fritze and Red River Chevrolet, the Noel Memorial Library at LSU-Shreveport, Gene Barratini, the Trinity Presbyterian Church, Clifton Cardin and the late Col. Neil Yarbrough for all their accomplishments and help, and countless others who have helped in my effort to memorialize Bossier City.

Special thanks to the staff of the Bossier Parish Library Historical Center and for the help of Marisa Richardson, Ann Middleton (director), Ann Toellner, Pamela Carlisle, Crystal Ogilvie, Tina Williamson, and Phillip Martin.

Introduction

When compared to other cities in the South relative to its size, Bossier City is a very new city. Although Bossier City can trace its roots to 1839 and the Elysian Grove plantation, it was in the 20th century that the city really boomed.

Bossier City has been known by many different names. In the 1830s, it began as the Elysian Grove Plantation. Shorty before the Civil War, it began to be known as Cane's Landing, named after James and Mary Cane, who owned the land where steamboats began docking across from Shreveport, Louisiana. As early as 1884, the area around the Elysian Grove Plantation and Cane's Landing was being called Bossier City.

In 1843, the parish was named after a famous Louisiana militia general and planter, Gen. Pierre Evariste John Baptiste Bossier. In the 1840s and 1850s, hundreds of people a week were migrating through Bossier City on their way west. Many of them were attracted to the area's natural beauty and decided to stay in the region on the east side of the Red River.

Confederate batteries were placed at Cane's Landing to protect the Red River's crossing, and Fort Kirby Smith was erected in the area where Bossier High School is now located to protect Shreveport from eastern advances.

Most people in the area at this time were making a living from agriculture. Subsistence farmers grew enough food to feed themselves and their families, while a few plantations sold cotton or other cash crops. Social life revolved around the churches, mostly Baptist and Methodist. Life began to change after 1877, when the Union army stopped occupying the area. Residents enjoyed more leisurely activities and events, and life remained unchanged for the area around Cane City for most of the late 19th century. In the 1880s, Cane Plantation began selling off its lots for new residences, and a town of a few hundred people started to form across the river from Shreveport.

In the 1870s and 1880s, some major changes in transportation had massive impacts on what was known then as Cane City. First, Shed Road was built to cross the swampy bottoms that separated Cane's Landing from the rest of Louisiana. It was an instant success and ran from 1874 to 1886, charging people tolls to use it. This nine-mile stretch of covered and raised road allowed farmers from the outlying hill country to bring their cotton and crops to Shreveport. The construction of dams and levees to help control the Red River began about the same time. In 1884, the Vicksburg, Shreveport & Pacific Railroad Bridge was built over the Red River and brought rail traffic east to Bossier City. As all Bossier City residents know, it is a major convergence of rail lines. The decision to run those lines through the area played a huge role in Bossier City developing much faster and greater than its sister cities around Bossier Parish. The businesses and residents began settling on the western end of Bossier Parish after the rail lines were laid down.

In 1907, another rail bridge was built, and in 1908 oil was discovered in Bossier Parish. Several mills and a brick factory sprang up, and a charter was granted for the village of Bossier in 1907. Hamilton Cotton Oil Mill was built in the area where Hamilton Road now runs. It made a variety of products from cottonseed and the oil the seeds produce. Between 1910 and 1930, the population of Bossier City tripled.

In 1925, a catastrophic fire raged through Bossier City, causing over $100,000 in damages. It began on Cane Street, which is now Barksdale Boulevard. All along the south side of the street, businesses burned, including the post office and movie theater. When this fire was finally extinguished, another fire started on the north side of Bossier City that burned through many residential homes. The great fire of 1925 burned significant portions of the business district of Bossier City and forced the town to establish infrastructure and public safety. A municipal building was constructed in 1927, and Bossier City was here for good.

The plans for Barksdale Air Force Base began as early as 1924. In 1933, the field was officially dedicated amidst a huge crowd as well as aerial displays and activities. By World War II, the base had become almost exclusively for bombers. In 1949, an estimated 8,500 Air Force and civilian personnel were working at Barksdale Air Force Base. Currently, it is home to the 8th Air Force and the global strike command. The base had an immediate economic impact on the Shreveport-Bossier region and still continues to benefit the area. When the base opened, the only way for cars to cross over the Red River from Shreveport to Bossier City was over the Traffic Street Bridge, and traffic was immediately an issue. The Texas Street Bridge opened soon after, but it was not until the Shreveport-Barksdale Bridge was opened in 1952 that traffic was brought under control.

The population of Bossier City increased from about 5,800 in 1940 to over 30,000 in 1960. This population boom was the catalyst for many new neighborhoods and supporting schools popping up south of the base and east of downtown Bossier City. The Bossier Crossroads and Heart of Bossier shopping centers at the end of Benton Road sprang up during this time.

Part of Bossier City's expansion after the war included the Bossier General Hospital, which was built in 1963. In 1973, the Louisiana Downs horse-racing track broke ground on the far east end of Bossier City. The Eisenhower Interstate Highway System changed the landscape immensely when I-20 began construction in the 1960s. The interstate plowed through the middle of the city, and many homes south of downtown Bossier were demolished in the process. The tornado of 1978 came through the heart of the city, leveling many buildings, but in doing so it opened the area up for the development of Pierre Bossier Mall.

During this postwar era, Bossier City expanded its municipal footprint as well. Originally, the city's 1927 municipal building housed the courthouse, jail, police station, city hall, fire station, and even the library. In the early 1950s, the city began expanding those entities to separate locations. The Bossier Parish Library's city branch moved to 503 Barksdale Boulevard, a new fire station was constructed in 1952 next door to the city building, and the police station and jail were constructed behind city hall. In 1974, city hall was relocated to the old Bossier Bank and Trust Building across the street. In 1985, the large municipal complex located off Benton Road was constructed, and it houses all these entities in addition to the city's convention center and the Bossier Parish Library Historical Center. These developments, along with the Century Link Center built in 2000, will ensure Bossier City's success for years to come.

One

The Core of Bossier City

Notable People, Families, and Businesses

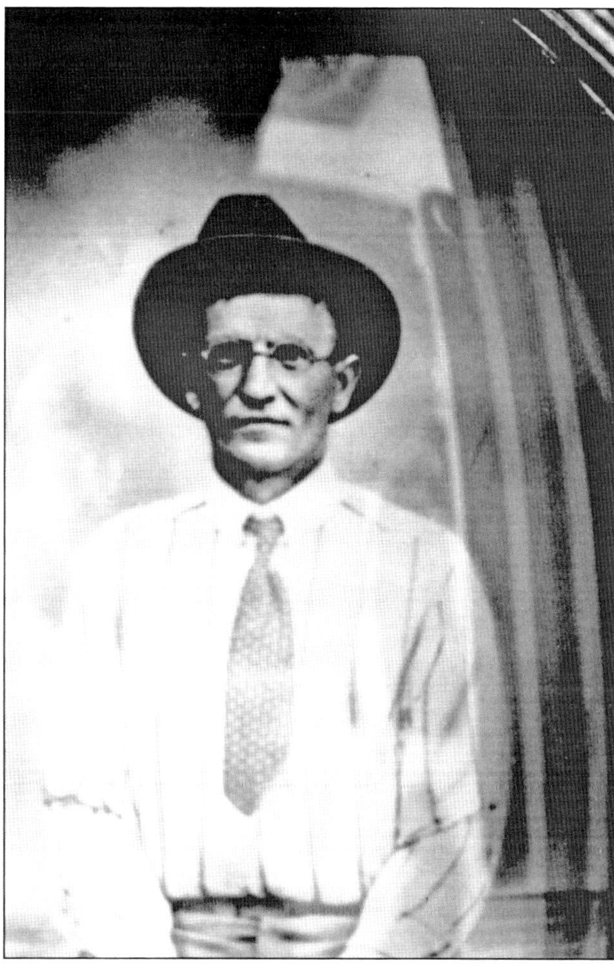

Prentis Martin McClanahan was born in Fillmore, Louisiana, in 1876. He was one of the charter organizers of the Masonic lodge in Bossier City, founded in 1910. The lodge on Benton Road is named the McClanahan Lodge after Prentis, who died in 1916. (Courtesy of Bossier Parish Library Historical Center.)

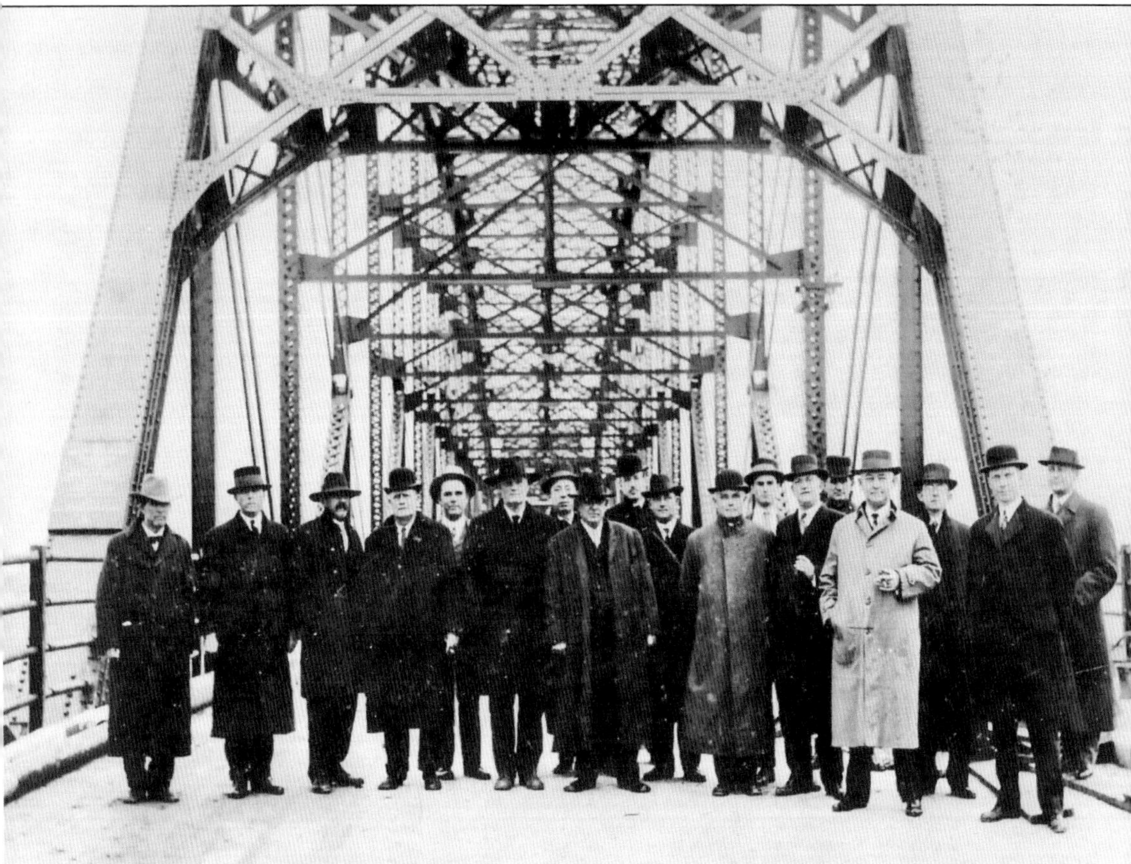

This photograph was taken during the dedication of the old Traffic Street Bridge on January 11, 1915. It was funded by Shreveport and Bossier Parish at a cost of $350,000 and was the first bridge built across the Red River exclusively for automobile traffic, hence the name. The bridge was torn down in the 1960s when Interstate 20 came through Shreveport and Bossier City. (Courtesy of Bossier Parish Library Historical Center.)

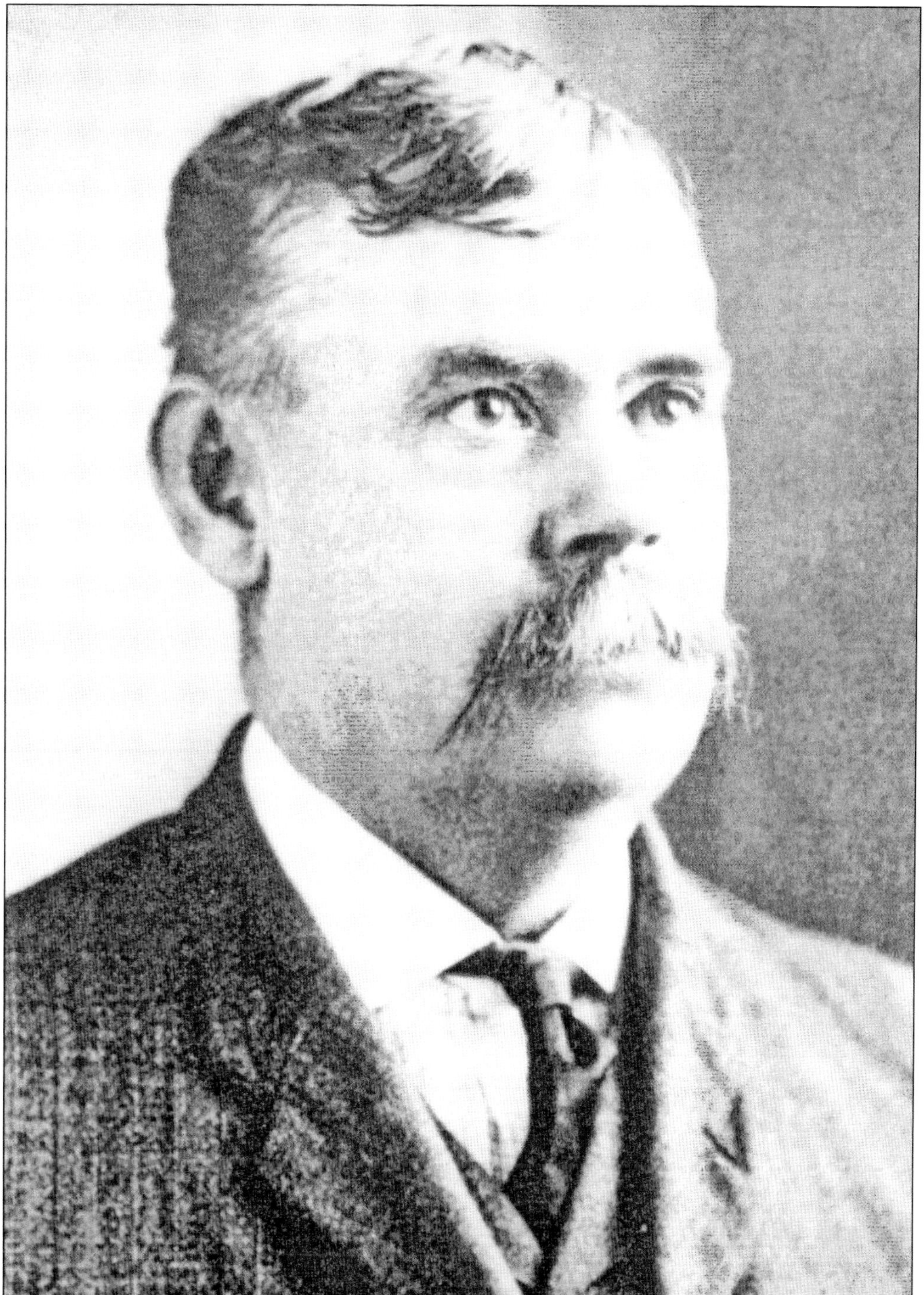

Todd McIntyre Yarbrough was born around Mansfield in 1859, and he married Hattie Eugene Mathews in 1880. He moved to Bossier and had a small farm where Yarbrough Road meets Benton Road. Yarbrough served as a Bossier City councilman and was the third mayor of Bossier City, from 1919 to 1921. (Courtesy of Bossier Parish Library Historical Center.)

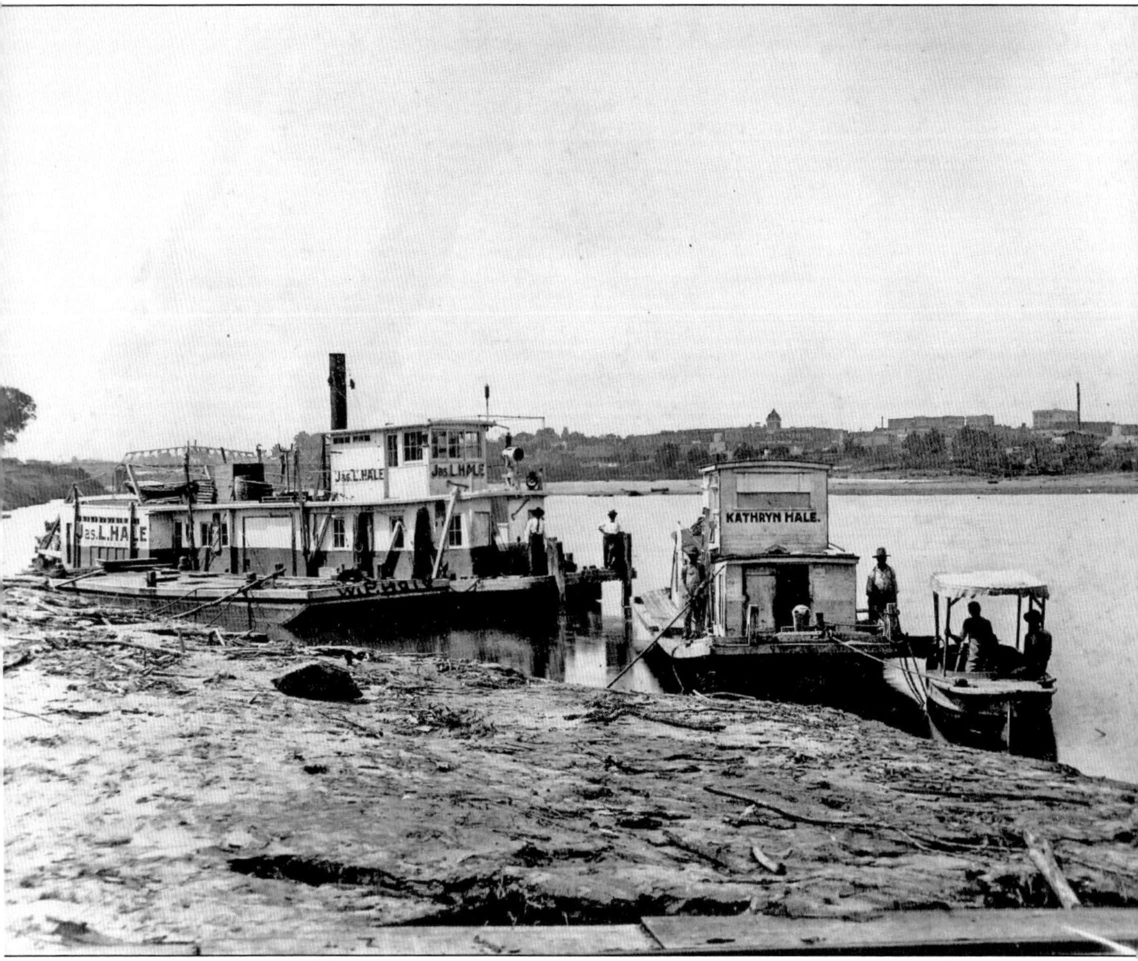

This photograph of the *James Hale*, a stern-wheeler, and the *Kathryn Hale*, a tugboat, was taken on the banks of Bossier City sometime between 1909 and 1912. One can see the Vicksburg, Shreveport & Pacific Railroad Bridge in the distance. (Courtesy of Bossier Parish Library Historical Center.)

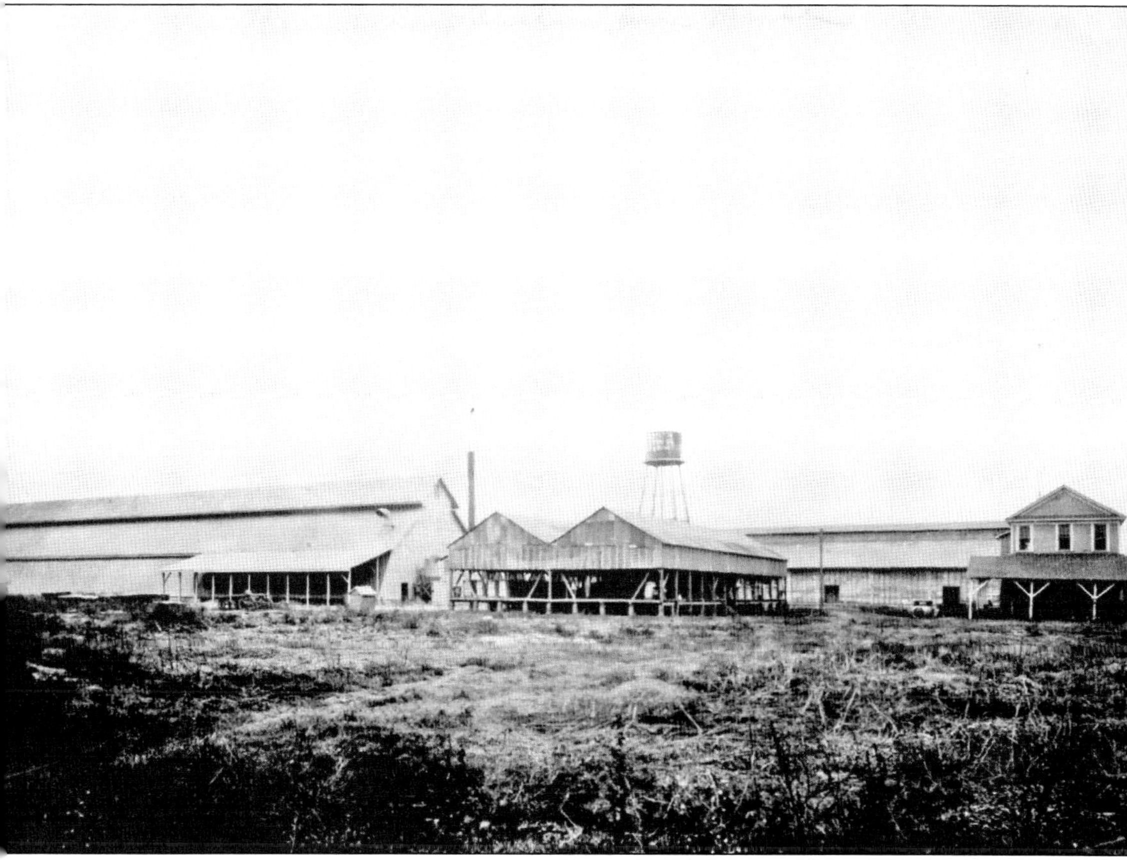

The Hamilton Cotton Oil Mill was located on Hamilton Road in Bossier City. The plant was owned by William E. Hamilton, who was born in Bossier but became a high-profile citizen in Shreveport. The plant turned cottonseed oil into feed, cooking oil, and a variety of other products. (Courtesy of Bossier Parish Library Historical Center.)

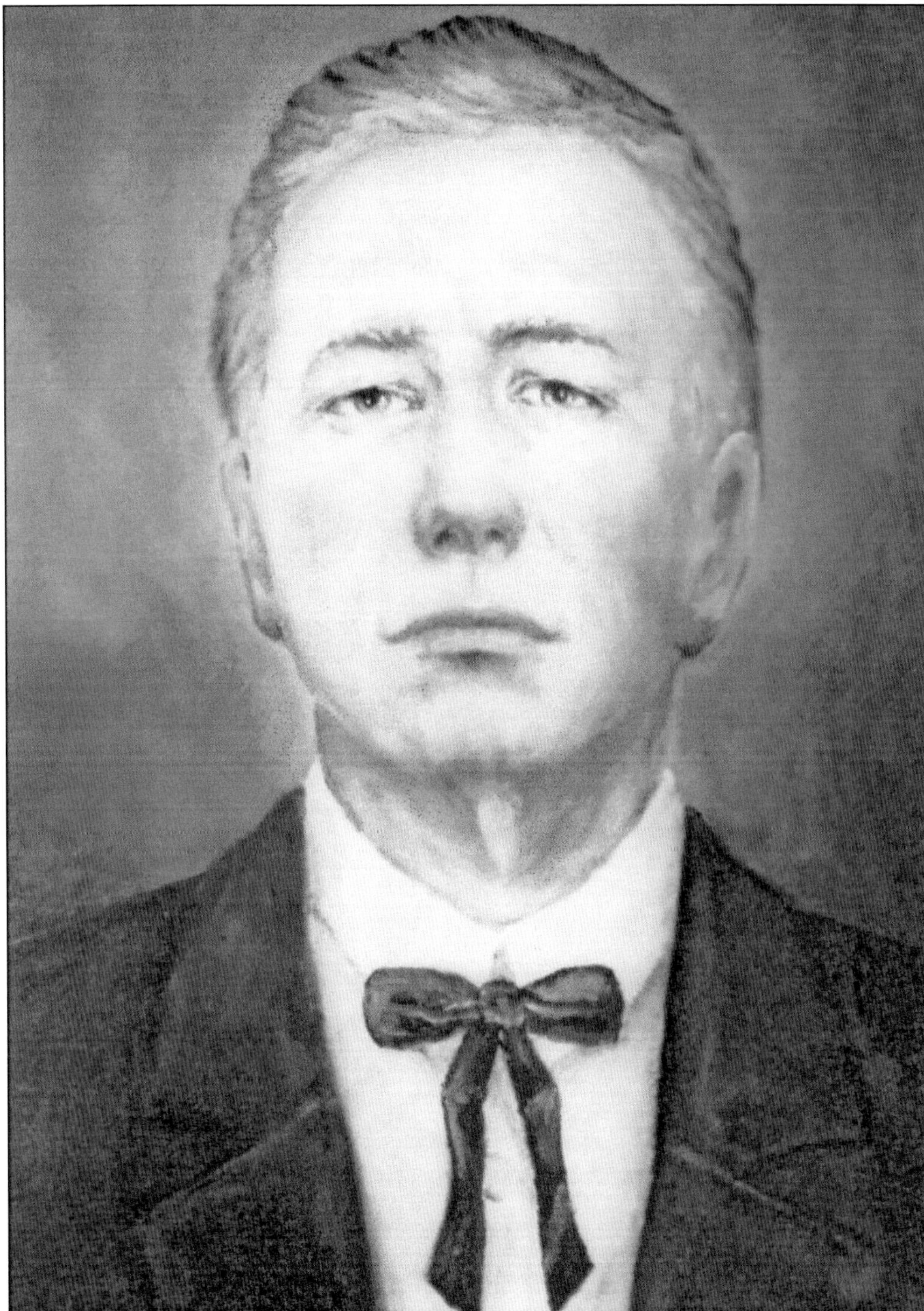

Marco Woodyard was the second mayor of Bossier City, and he served from 1910 to 1919. He was appointed by the city council after Bossier City's first mayor moved to Shreveport. Woodyard also served as the city's judge during this time and was instrumental in getting electricity to Bossier City. (Courtesy of Bossier Parish Library Historical Center.)

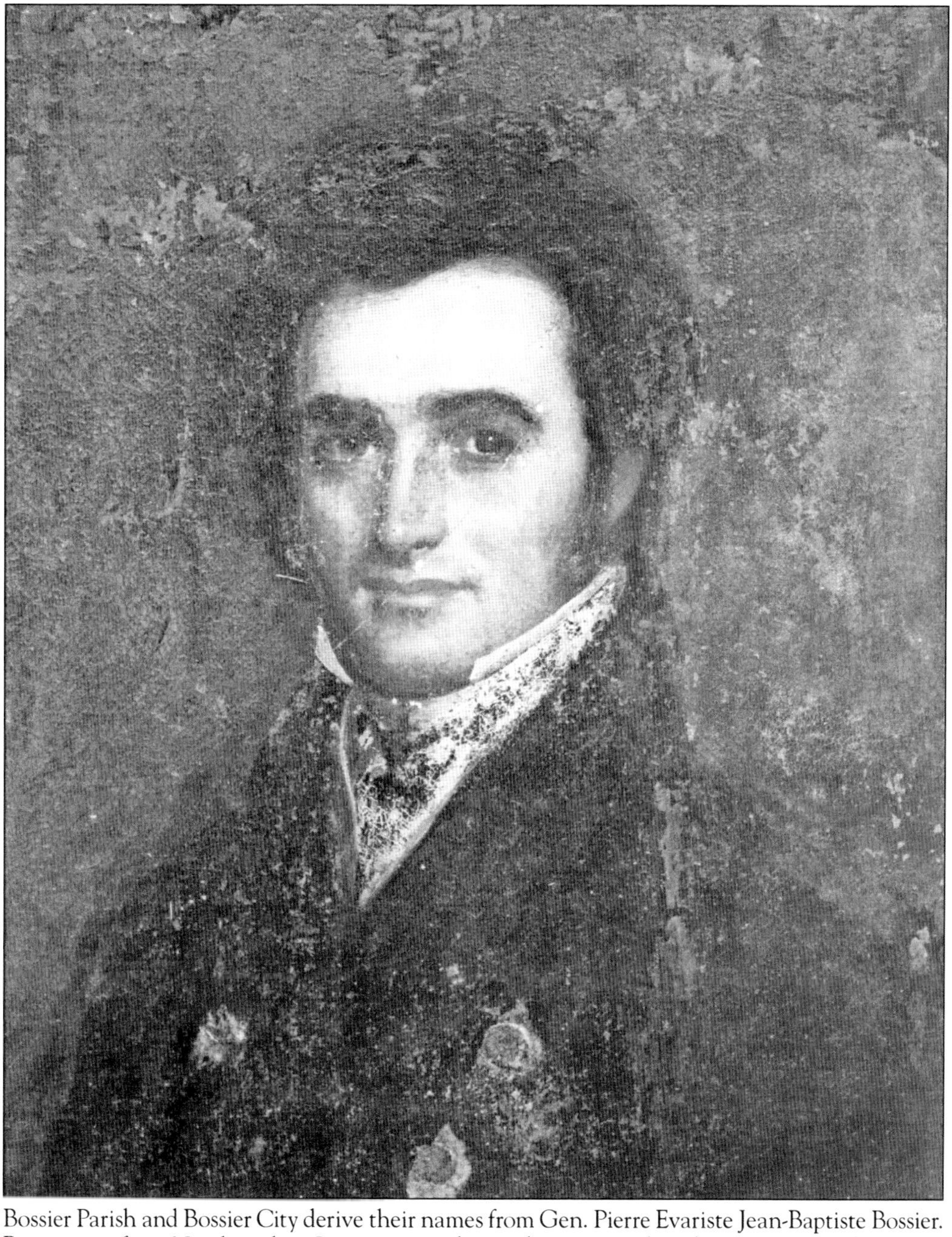

Bossier Parish and Bossier City derive their names from Gen. Pierre Evariste Jean-Baptiste Bossier. Bossier was from Natchitoches, Louisiana, and served as a general in the Louisiana militia. The Bossiers were descendants of French Creole Louisiana families who had been in Louisiana since the 1720s. Bossier served in the state senate and also served as a representative in Washington, DC. (Courtesy of Bossier Parish Library Historical Center.)

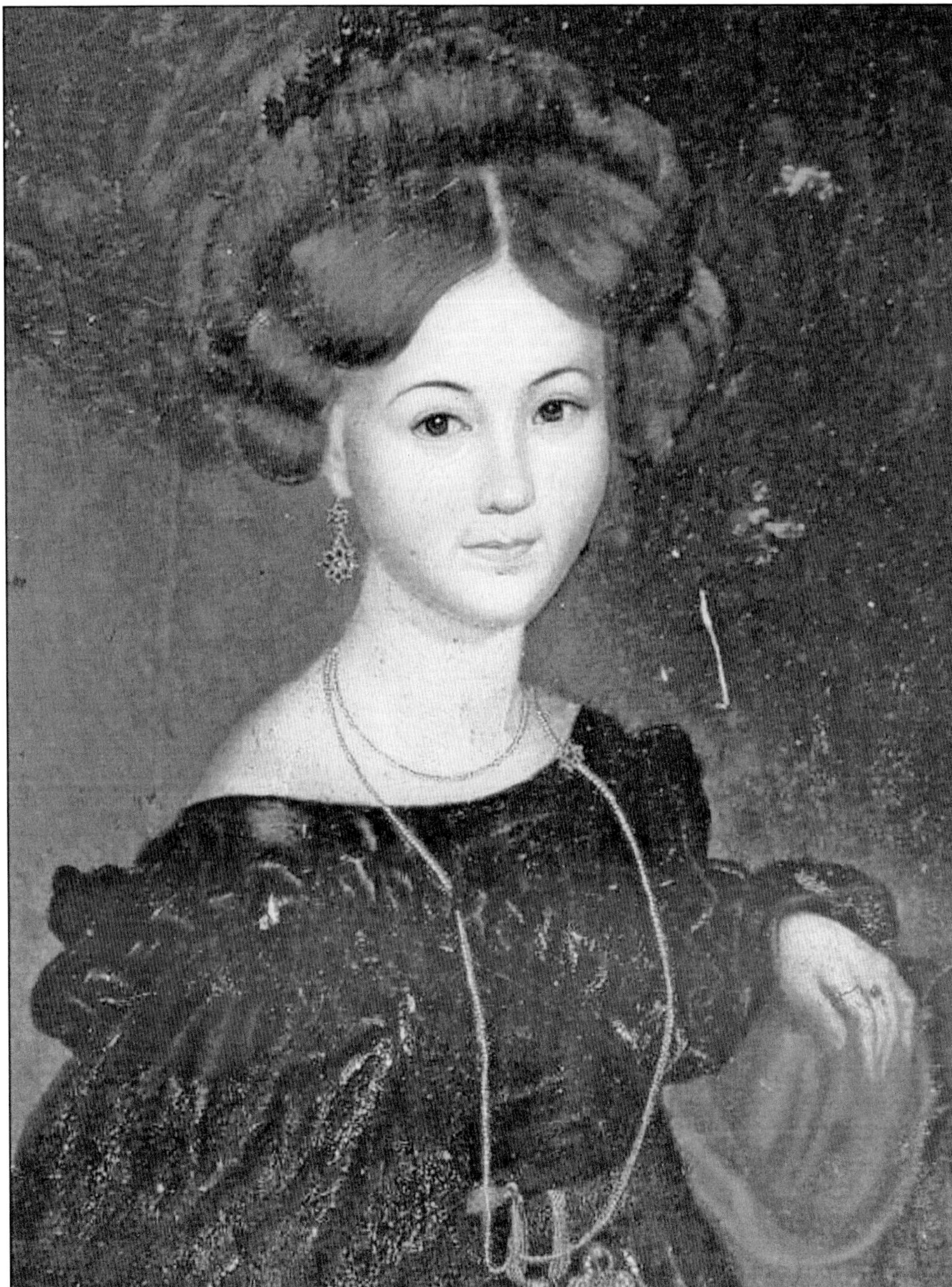

In 1836, Mary Bennett came to Shreveport with her husband, William Bennett. He died a year later, and she married his business partner James Huntington Cane, a recent widower, in 1838. The couple established Elysian Groves Plantation on the east side of the Red River, across from Shreveport, in 1839. From this plantation the first lots were sold in 1882, and Bossier City began to take shape. (Courtesy of Bossier Parish Library Historical Center.)

This is an undated photograph of Anna Brokenbough McCormick Stockwell. She is the granddaughter of Mary Cane Bennett. (Courtesy of Bossier Parish Library Historical Center.)

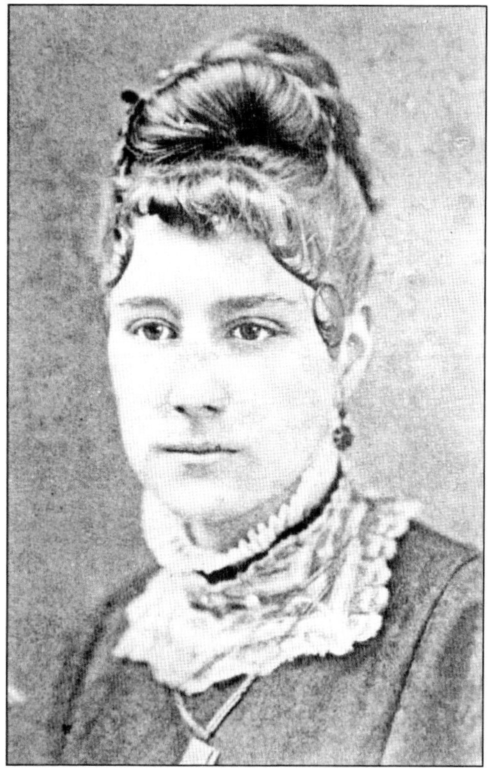

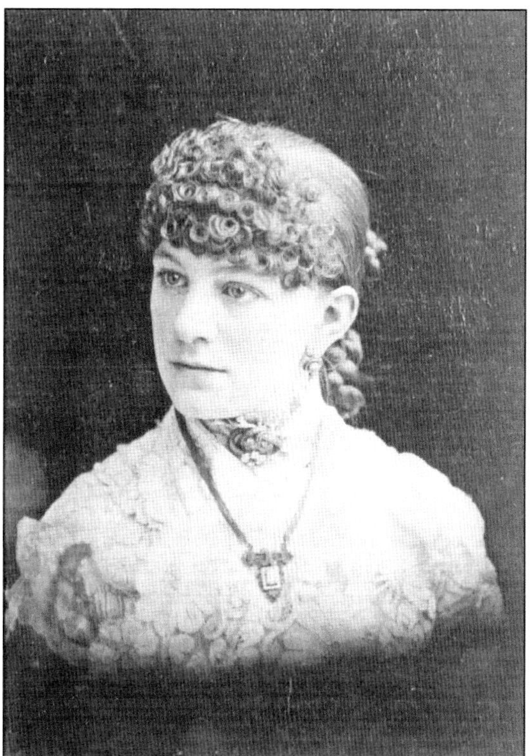

Wilhelminia Bennett McCormick, the granddaughter of Mary Cane Bennett, poses in this undated photograph. It was McCormick and her husband who began selling off plots of land to turn James Huntington Cane's landing into Bossier City. (Courtesy of Bossier Parish Library Historical Center.)

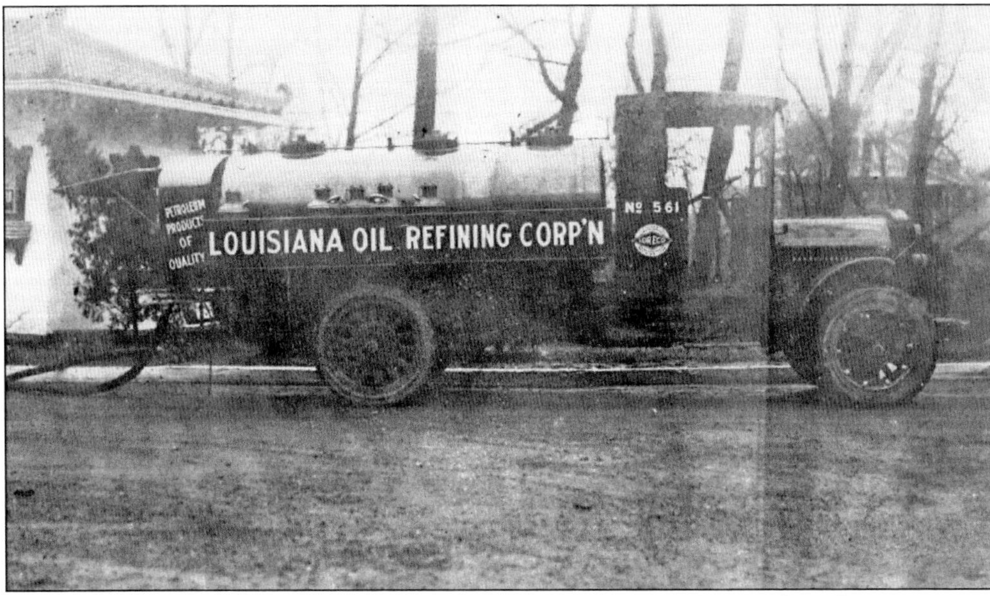

Louisiana Oil Refinery Company (LORECO) became an integral part of northern Louisiana and Bossier City in the early 20th century. By 1930, it employed over 500 locals. LORECO also participated many civic activities. The refinery had its own baseball team and marching band. This truck is at the LORECO filling station located at the intersection of Minden and Coushatta Roads, which is now where Old Minden Road and Barksdale Boulevard meet. (Courtesy of Bossier Parish Library Historical Center.)

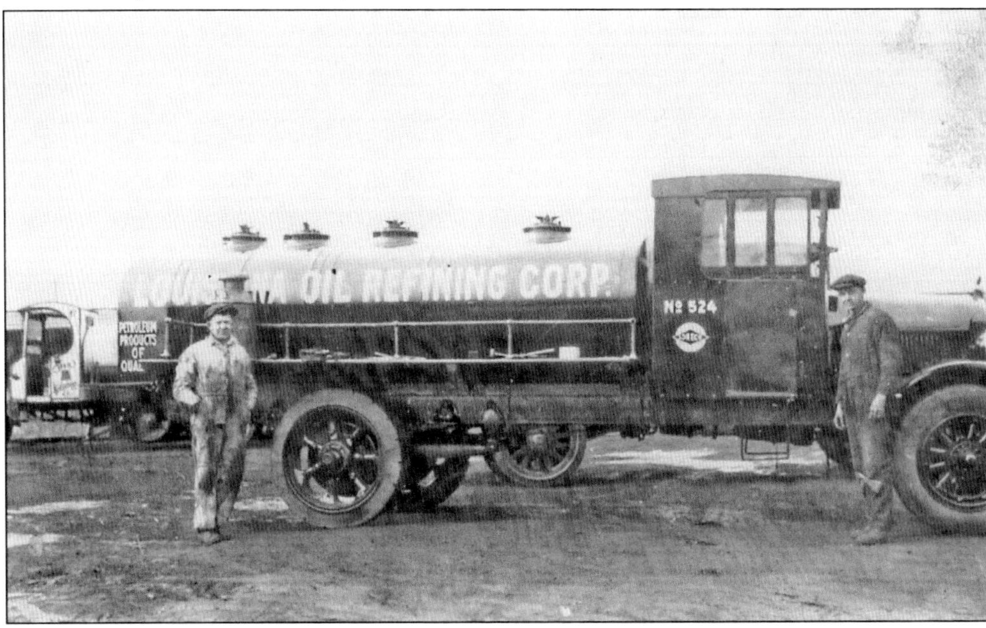

This LORECO Dodge G-Boy truck No. 524 is pictured around 1925 at a maintenance shop at the northeastern corner of Barksdale Boulevard and Hamilton Road. Another portion of the LORECO refinery was located south of Old Minden Road, where First Baptist Church is now located. The refinery stretched from Hamilton Road all the way to modern-day Pierre Bossier Mall and the Waller Neighborhood. (Courtesy of Bossier Parish Library Historical Center.)

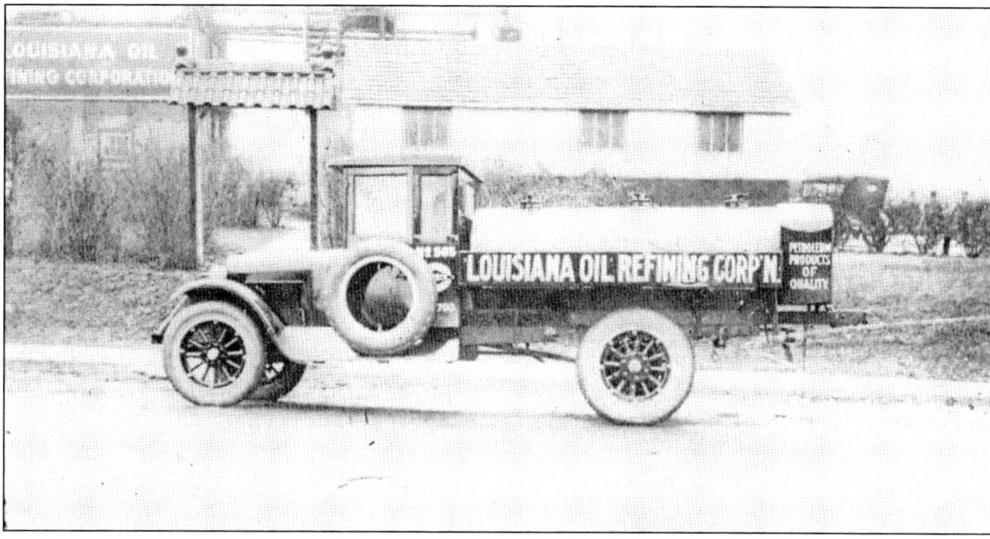

Above, another Dodge G-Boy ready for delivery is featured in a mid-1920s photograph, which was taken in front of the Louisiana Oil Refining Corporation in Bossier City. Below, LORECO truck No. 525 is shown driving down a road on the outskirts of Bossier City around 1926. Unfortunately, a decade later, falling oil prices during the Depression caused LORECO to file for bankruptcy. Before its refineries were acquired by Arkansas Fuel Oil Corporation in 1938, the company lent its name to LORECO Street in Bossier City. The refinery continued to operate until about 1944, when it closed for good. (Courtesy of Bossier Parish Library Historical Center.)

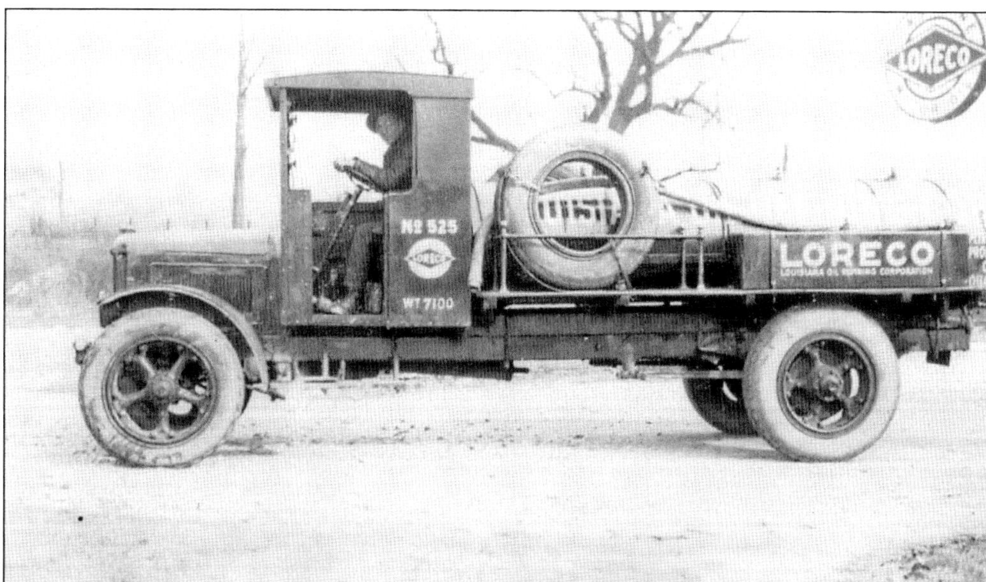

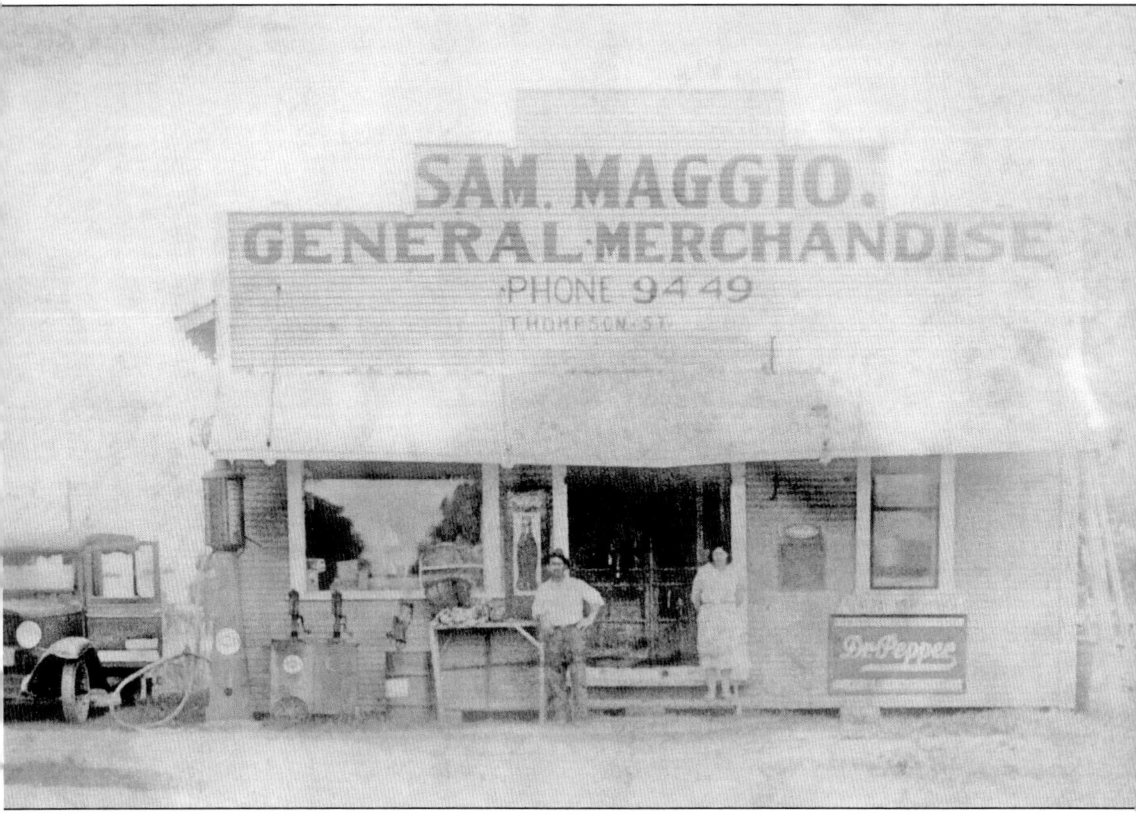

Sam Maggio immigrated to the United States upon the invitation of the US troops he fought alongside in northern Italy during World War I. He met Mary from Terrebonne Parish and established Maggio's Grocery on Thompson Street in 1924, pictured here around that time. The store is still run by Maggio's grandson. (Courtesy of Joe Maggio and family.)

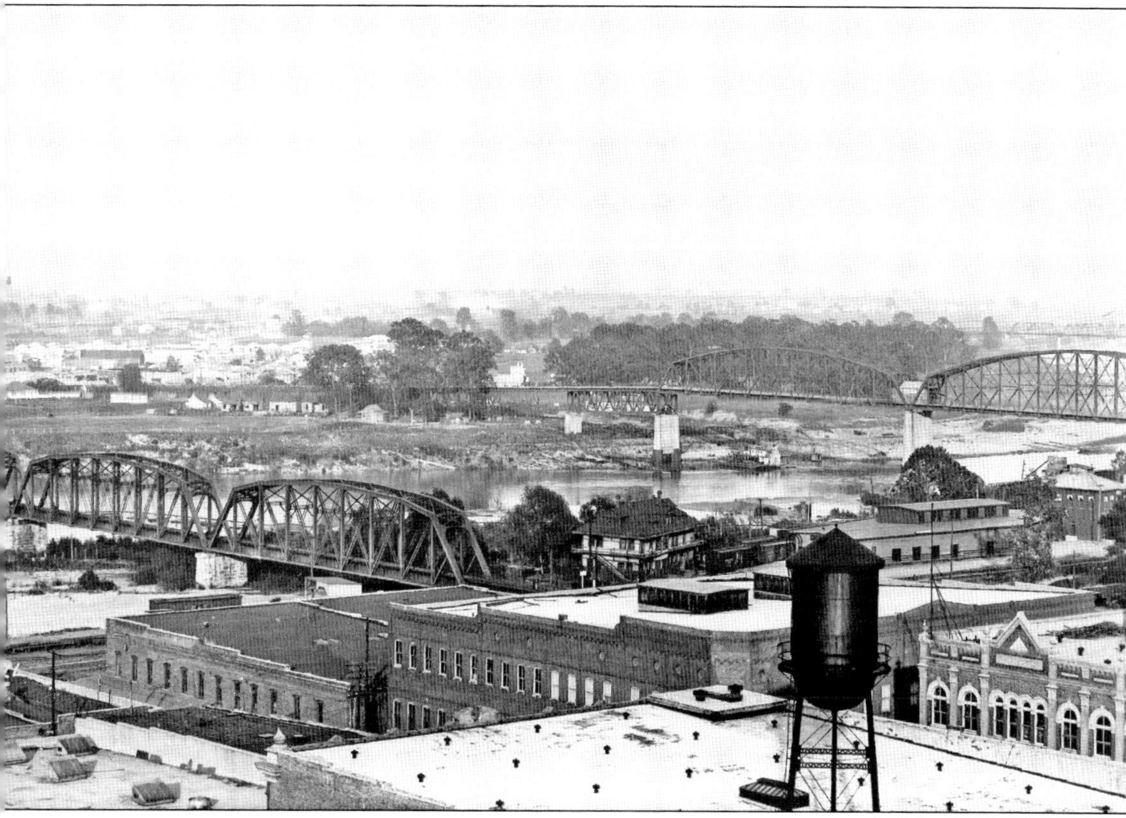

In this 1920s view of Bossier City, taken from the west side of the Red River, the old Traffic Street Bridge and both rail bridges—which are all still in use today—can be clearly seen. (Courtesy of Noel Memorial Library.)

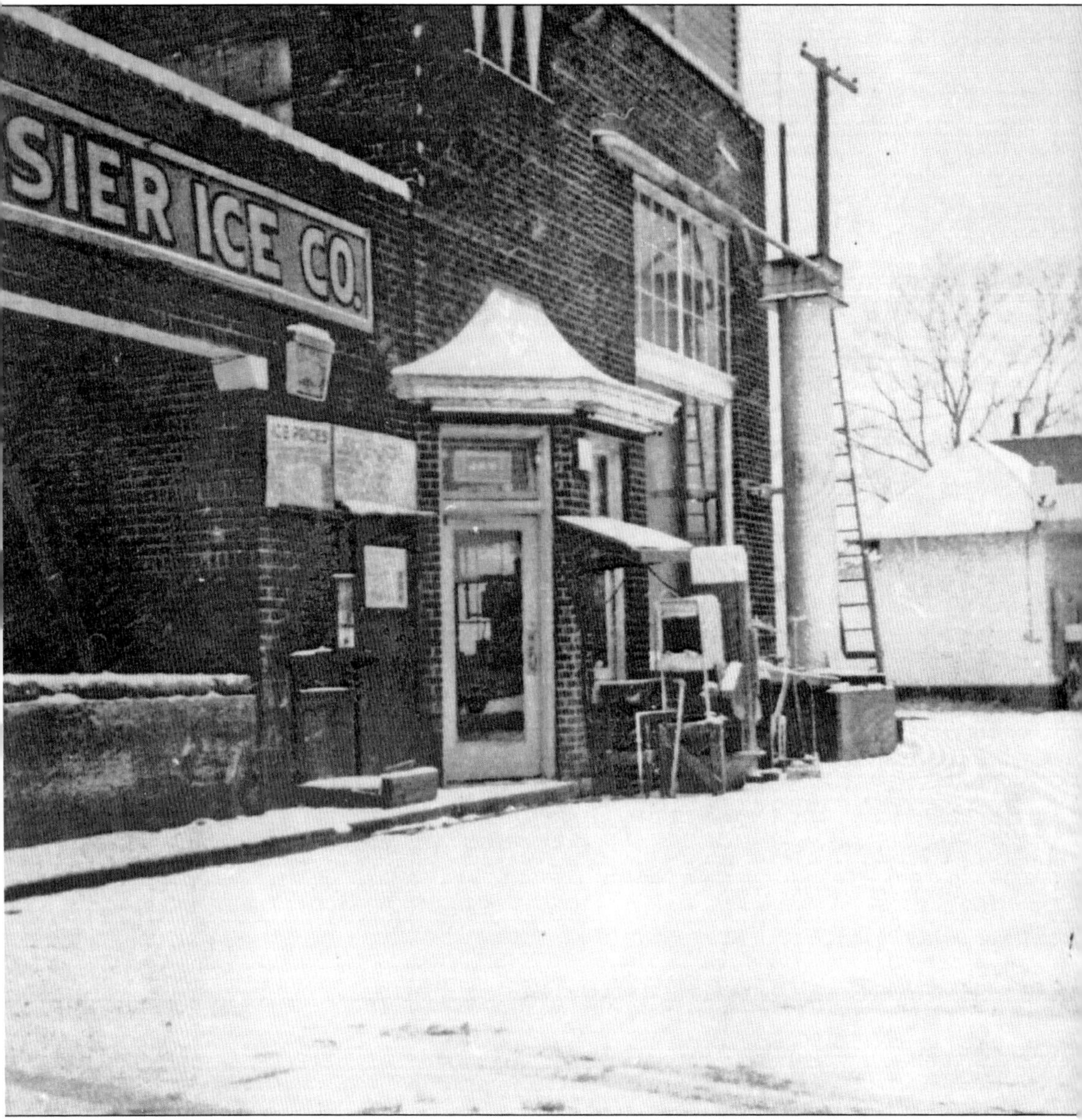

Residents of Bossier City began getting their ice from the Bossier Ice Company in the late 1920s. The company made and sold ice at its building at 600 Cain Street. The plant had commercial trucks and residential delivery methods. The icehouse was an integral part of downtown Bossier City for many decades. It provided home ice delivery as well as a place to get a cool beverage for children and adults. The company was located next to the Bossier Municipal Building until it was torn down in the 1980s. (Courtesy of Bossier Parish Library Historical Center.)

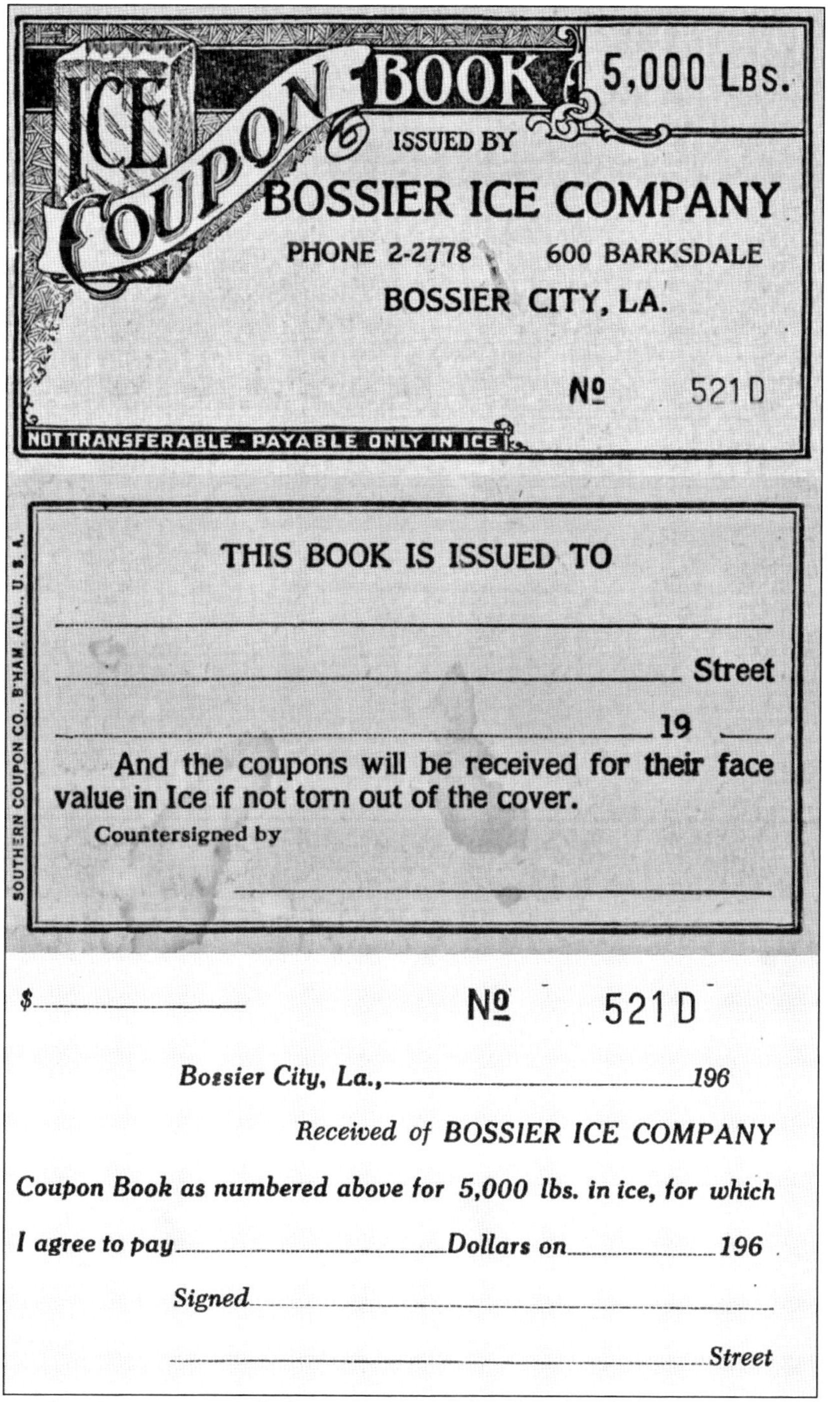
ICE COUPON BOOK

5,000 LBS.

ISSUED BY

BOSSIER ICE COMPANY

PHONE 2-2778 600 BARKSDALE

BOSSIER CITY, LA.

No 521 D

NOT TRANSFERABLE - PAYABLE ONLY IN ICE

SOUTHERN COUPON CO., B'HAM. ALA., U. S. A.

THIS BOOK IS ISSUED TO

____

________________________ Street

________________________ 19 ___

And the coupons will be received for their face value in Ice if not torn out of the cover.

Countersigned by

____

$__________ No 521 D

*Bossier City, La.,*________________*196*

Received of BOSSIER ICE COMPANY

Coupon Book as numbered above for 5,000 lbs. in ice, for which

*I agree to pay*______________*Dollars on*__________*196*.

*Signed*________________________

________________________*Street*

The Bossier Ice Company provided coupon booklets that were redeemable for their value in ice; booklets could include coupons worth 5,000 pounds of ice. Each booklet had an identifying number. This particular booklet was No. 521D. Pictured in this series, from top to bottom, are the booklet front cover, the booklet back cover, and a receipt from the Bossier Ice Company that a customer would receive when purchasing ice. (Courtesy of the Tubbs family.)

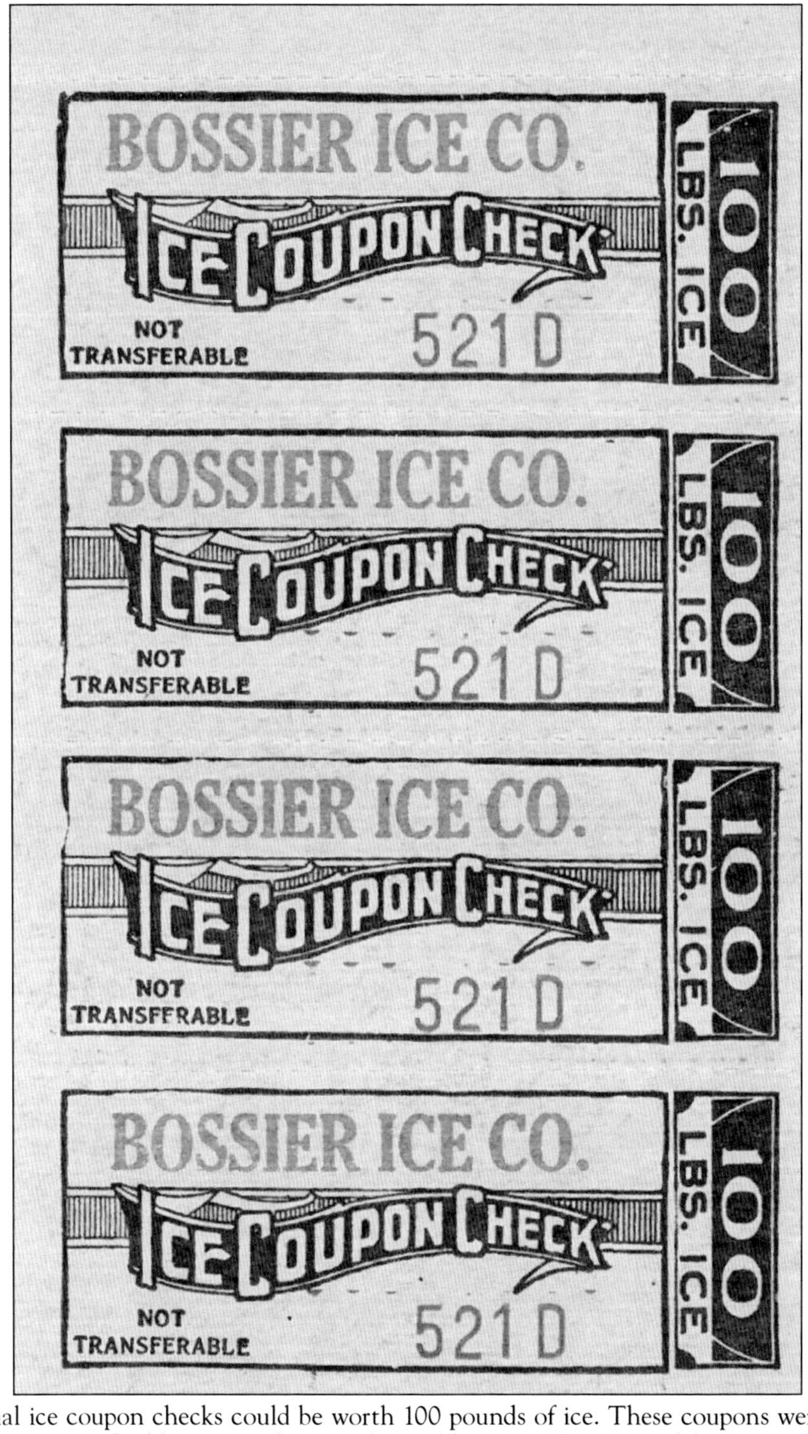

Individual ice coupon checks could be worth 100 pounds of ice. These coupons were clearly labeled as nontransferable items and were only payable in ice. Customers of the Bossier Company would use these to obtain bags of ice, and deliverymen would make home deliveries. Pictured here are the actual coupons that the deliveryman would receive from the customers in exchange. (Courtesy of the Tubbs family.)

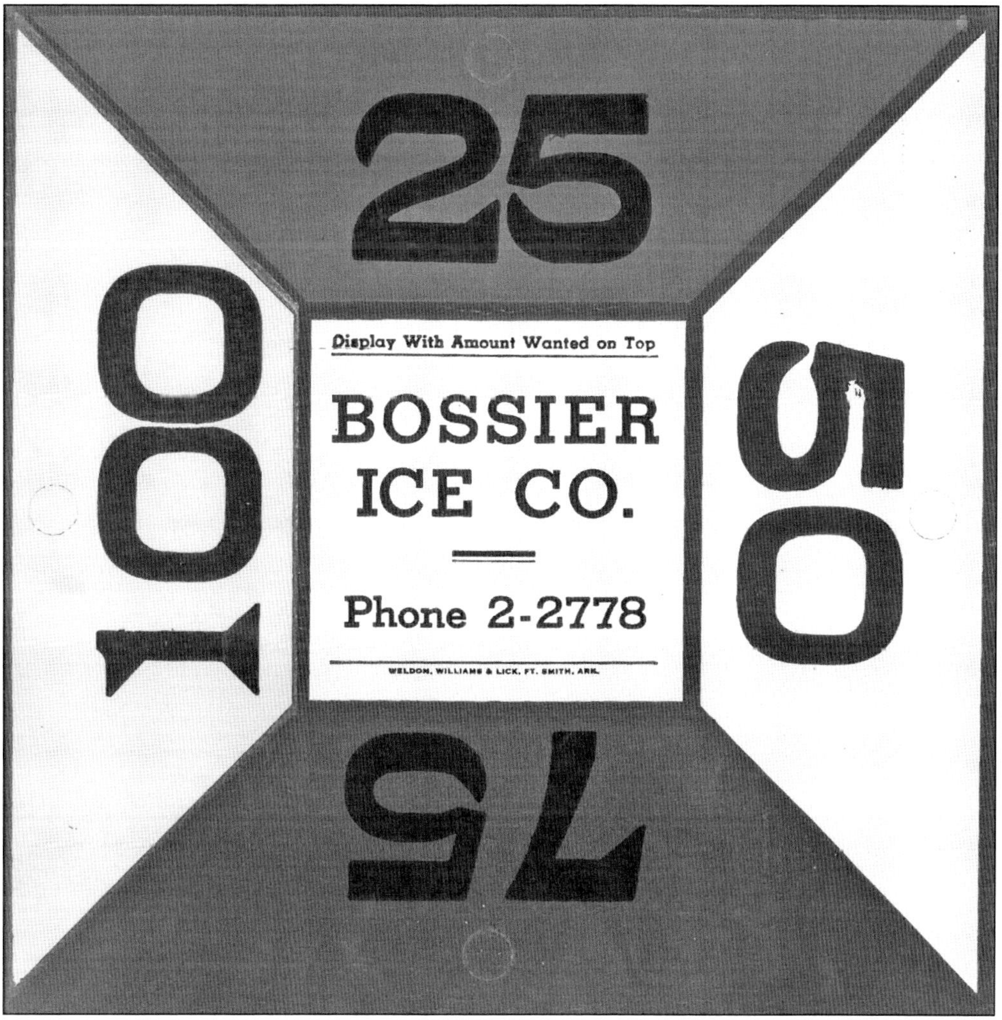

This is the window hanger from the icehouse. This tag was used to indicate the amount of ice that was wanted from any given order. When the deliverymen came, whatever number was right side up would let them know how much ice the customer needed. The options included 25, 50, 75, and 100-pound bags. (Courtesy of the Tubbs family.)

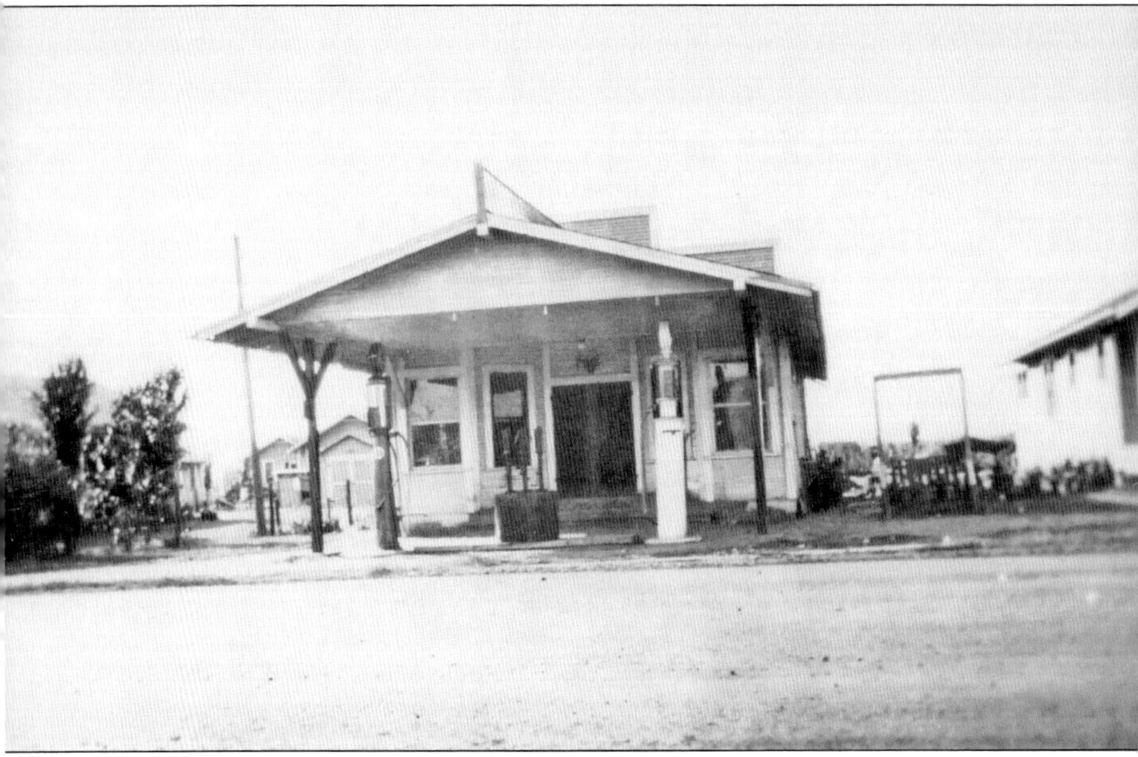

Hebert's Café and filling station was located across the road from the LORECO refinery during the 1920s. Dorothy Hebert frequently prepared to-go meals for the workers for about 35¢. (Courtesy of Bossier Parish Library Historical Center.)

At right, Fred "Pappa" Hebert, owner of Hebert's Café and filling station, is pictured in the mid-1930s on the front lawn of his Bossier City home with his horse Silver. Below, from left to right, Dorothy, Lorena, and Glenn Hebert pose in 1925 in front of a LORECO refinery tank, located across from their home in Bossier City. The Hebert family home was across from the refinery. (Courtesy of Bossier Parish Library Historical Center.)

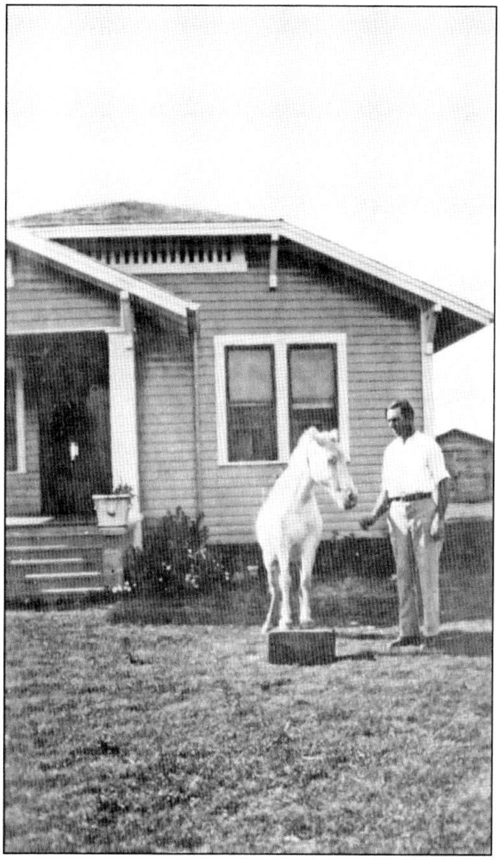

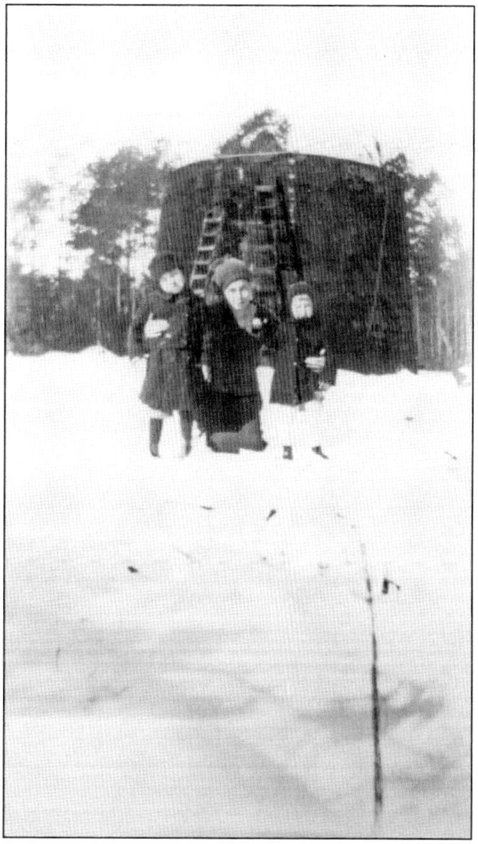

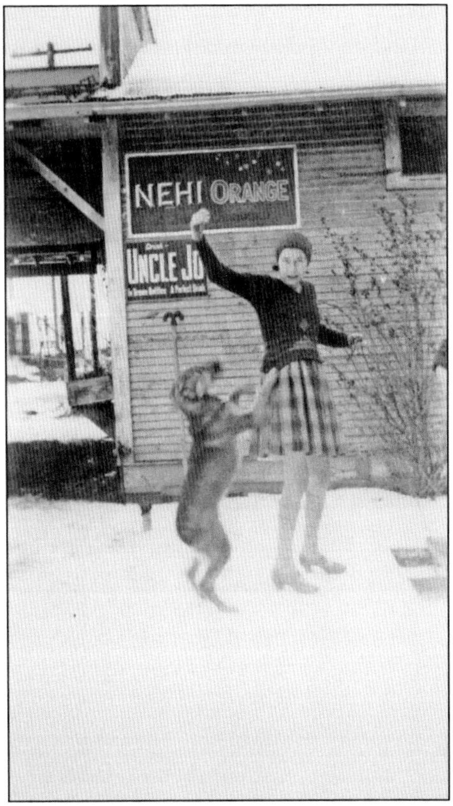

At left, Dorothy Hebert and her dog are enjoying the snow outside Hebert Café on Old Minden Road in 1935. Below, Dorothy (left), Dorothy Glaskil (center), and Glenn Hebert are pictured at LORECO Refinery's employee swimming pool in 1934. At the time, this was the only swimming pool in Bossier City. (Courtesy of Bossier Parish Library Historical Center.)

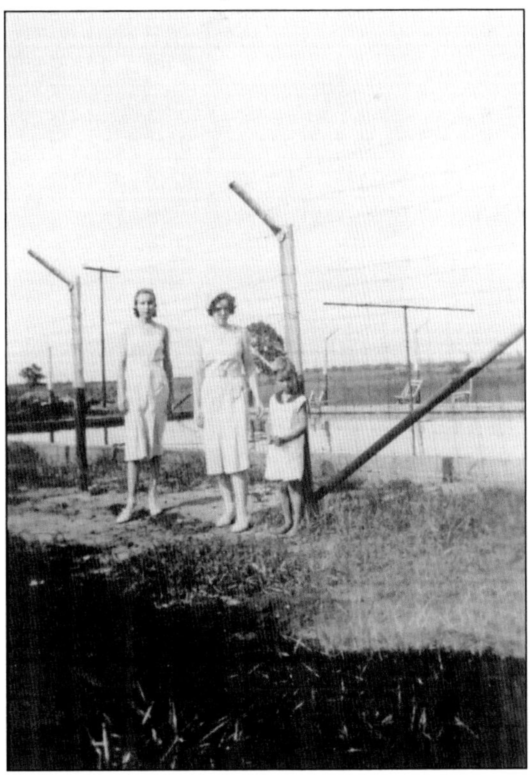

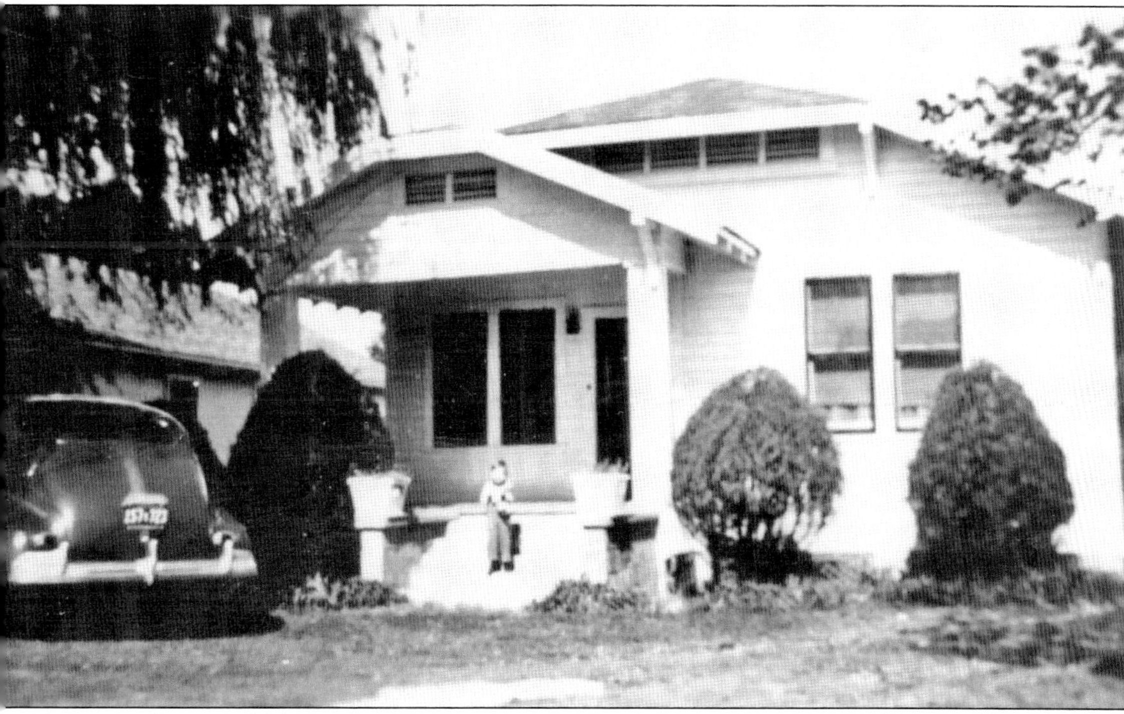

This 1945 photograph shows the entire front of the Hebert family home, located at 2005 Old Minden Road. (Courtesy of Bossier Parish Library Historical Center.)

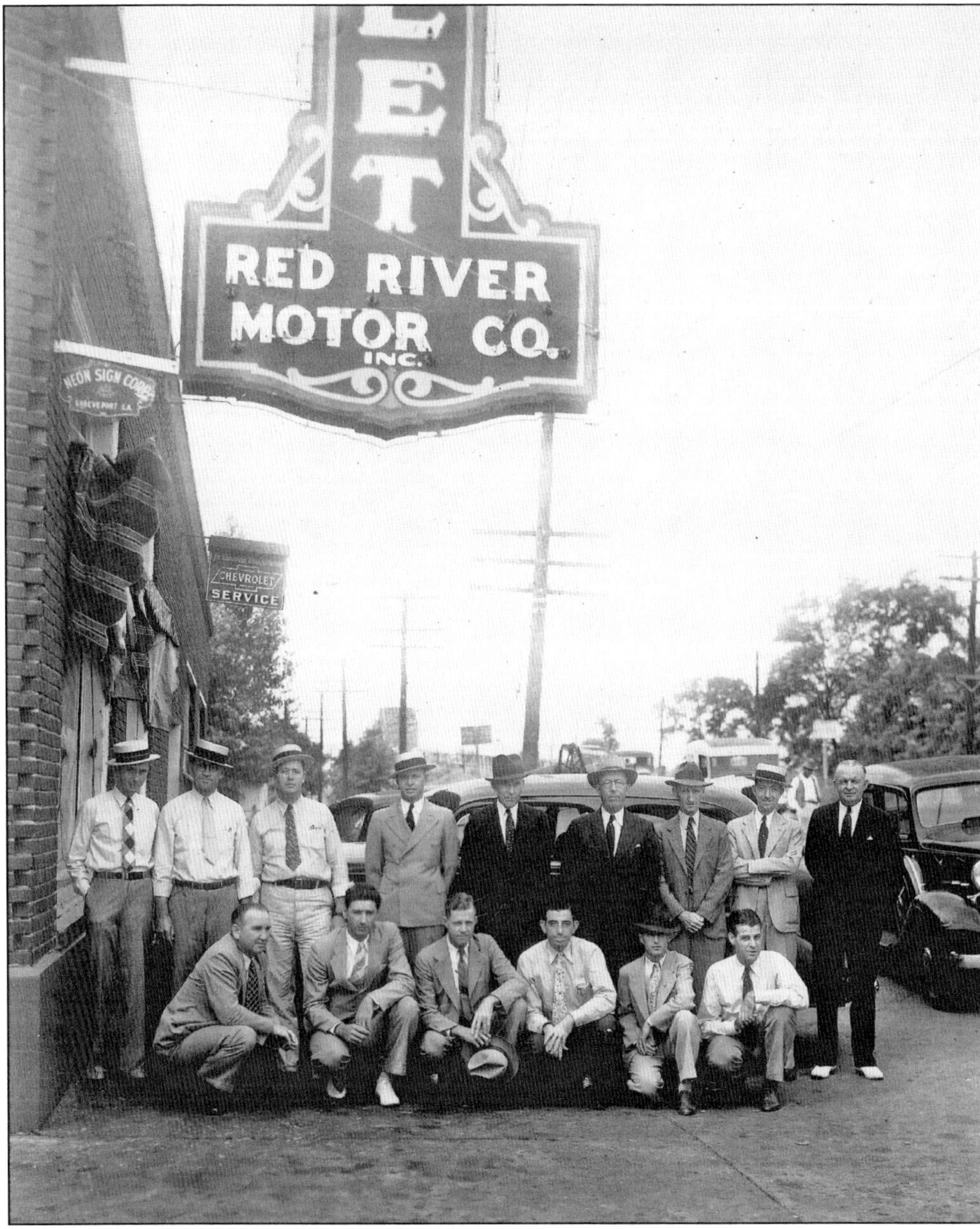

Taken sometime in the 1930s, this Red River Motors Company, Inc. staff photograph includes 15 employees. The gentleman wearing glasses in the back row, fourth from the right, is John Sentel, the dealership's second owner. His family still runs the company. (Courtesy of George Fritze.)

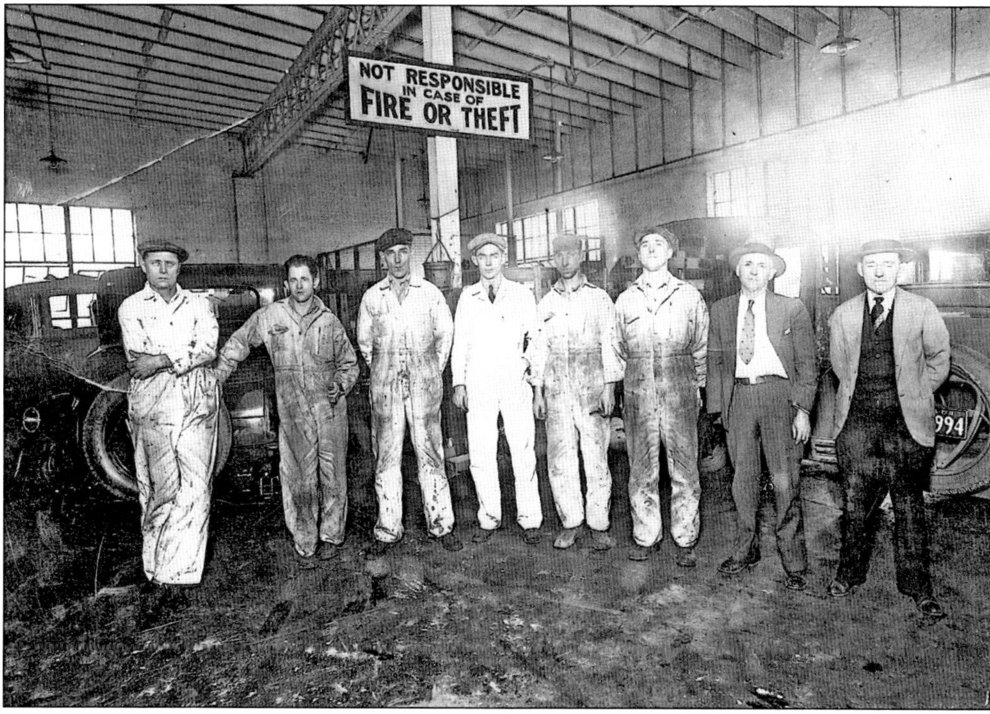

These are early photographs of the service department of Red River Chevrolet and its mechanics. This section of the building is now fully enclosed in the current showroom and offices of the dealership. (Courtesy of George Fritze.)

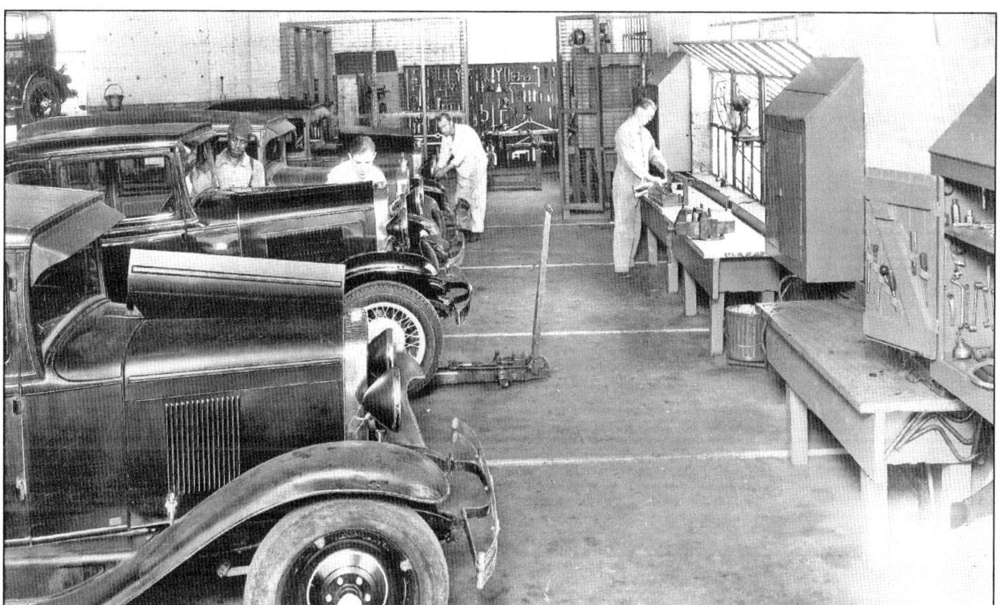

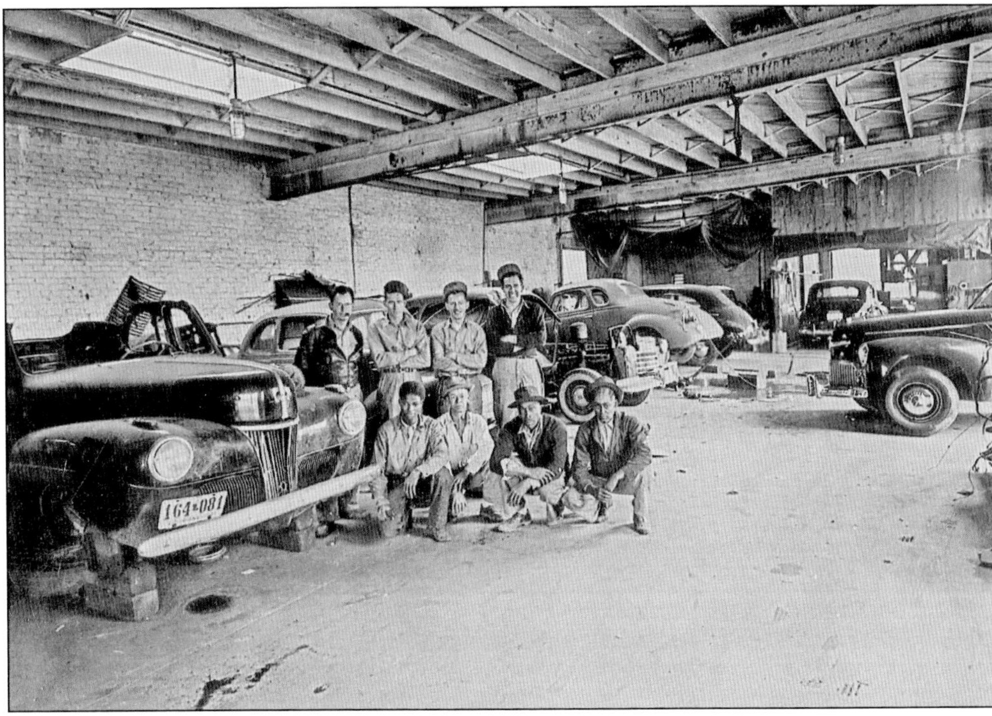

These photographs from the 1940s show the service department employees from Red River Motors. Note that the dealership's staff is integrated, a rarity at that time. (Courtesy of George Fritze.)

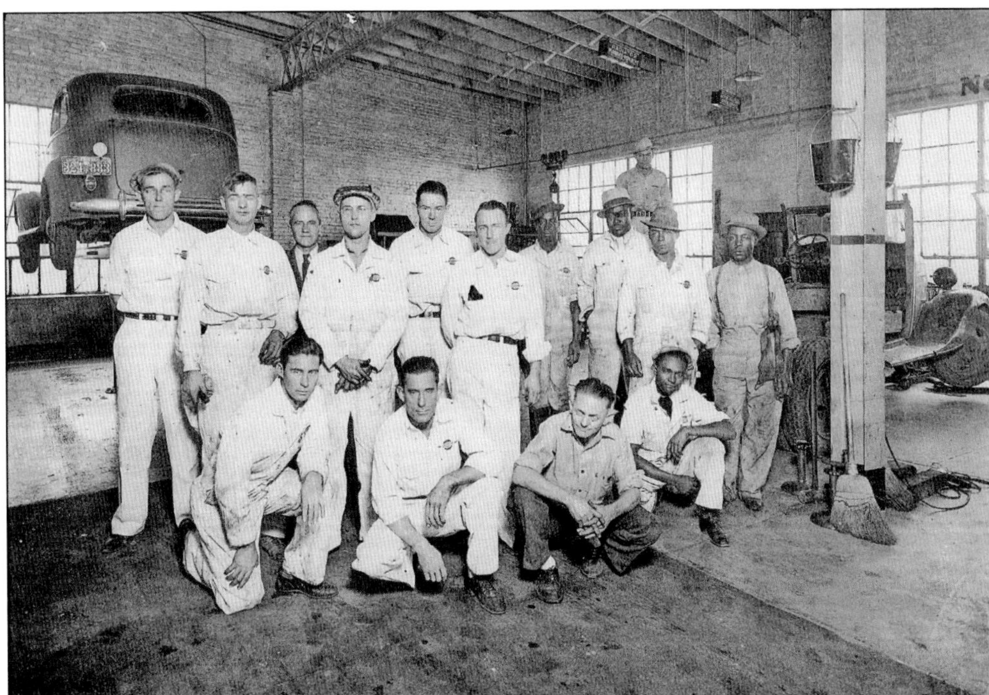

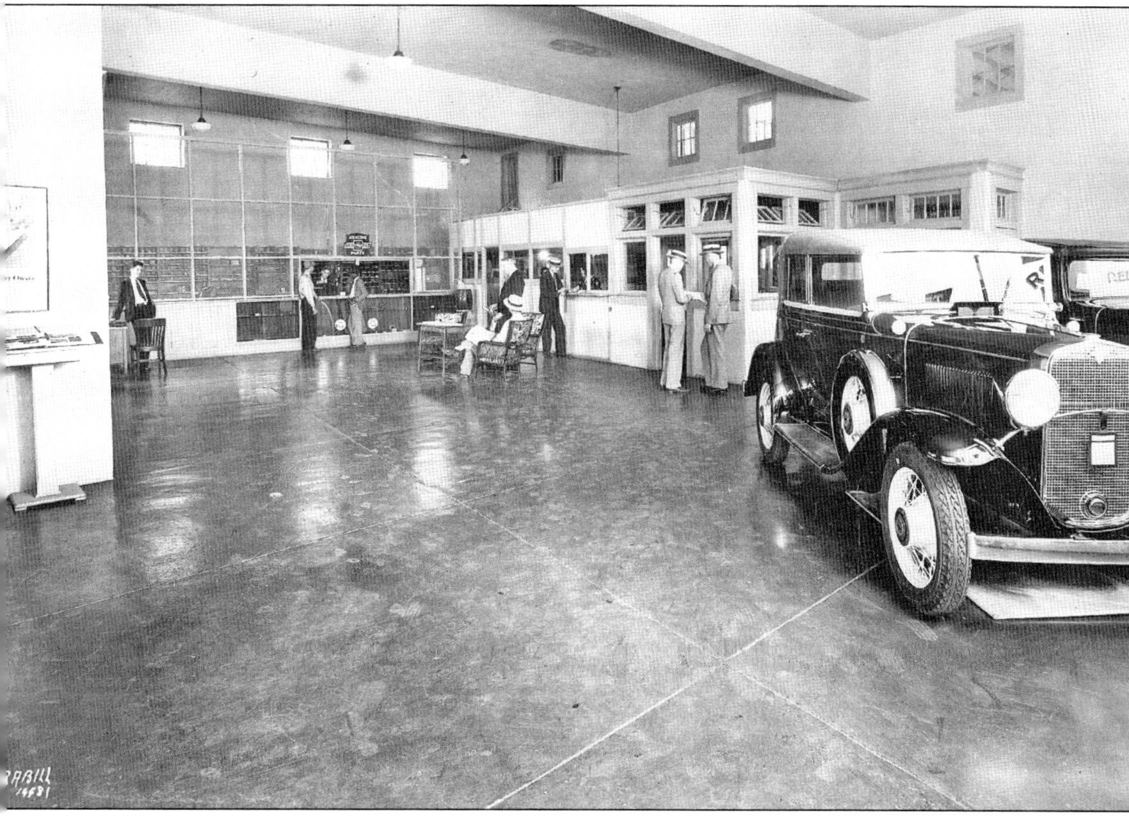

Pictured here is the interior of Red River Motors around 1930, when the showroom, offices, and parts counter were all located in a single room. (Courtesy of George Fritze.)

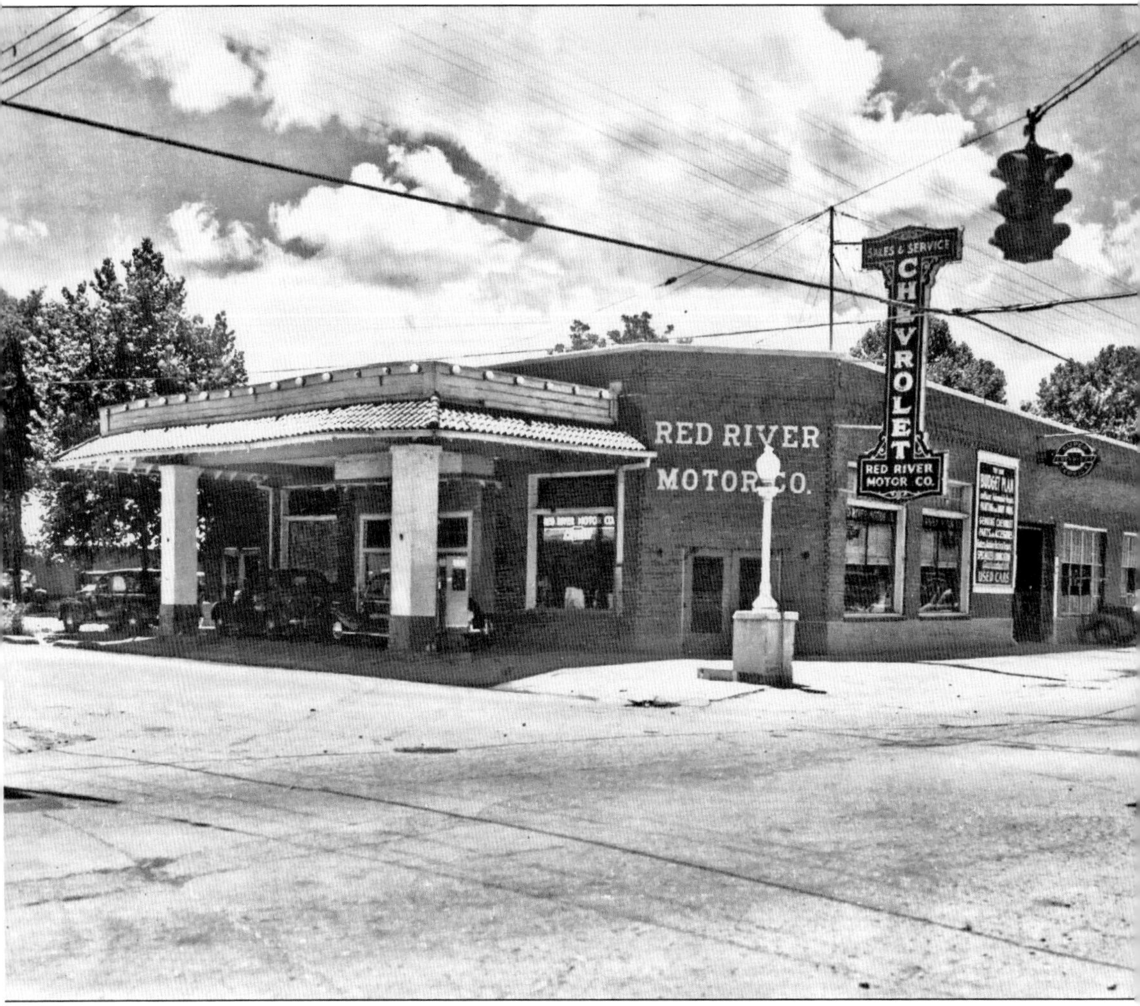

Seen here is the Red River Motors building as it appeared in the 1940s. The showroom was in the front, and the service department was in the back of the building. This was the configuration of the dealership until the company began expanding later in the decade. (Courtesy of George Fritze.)

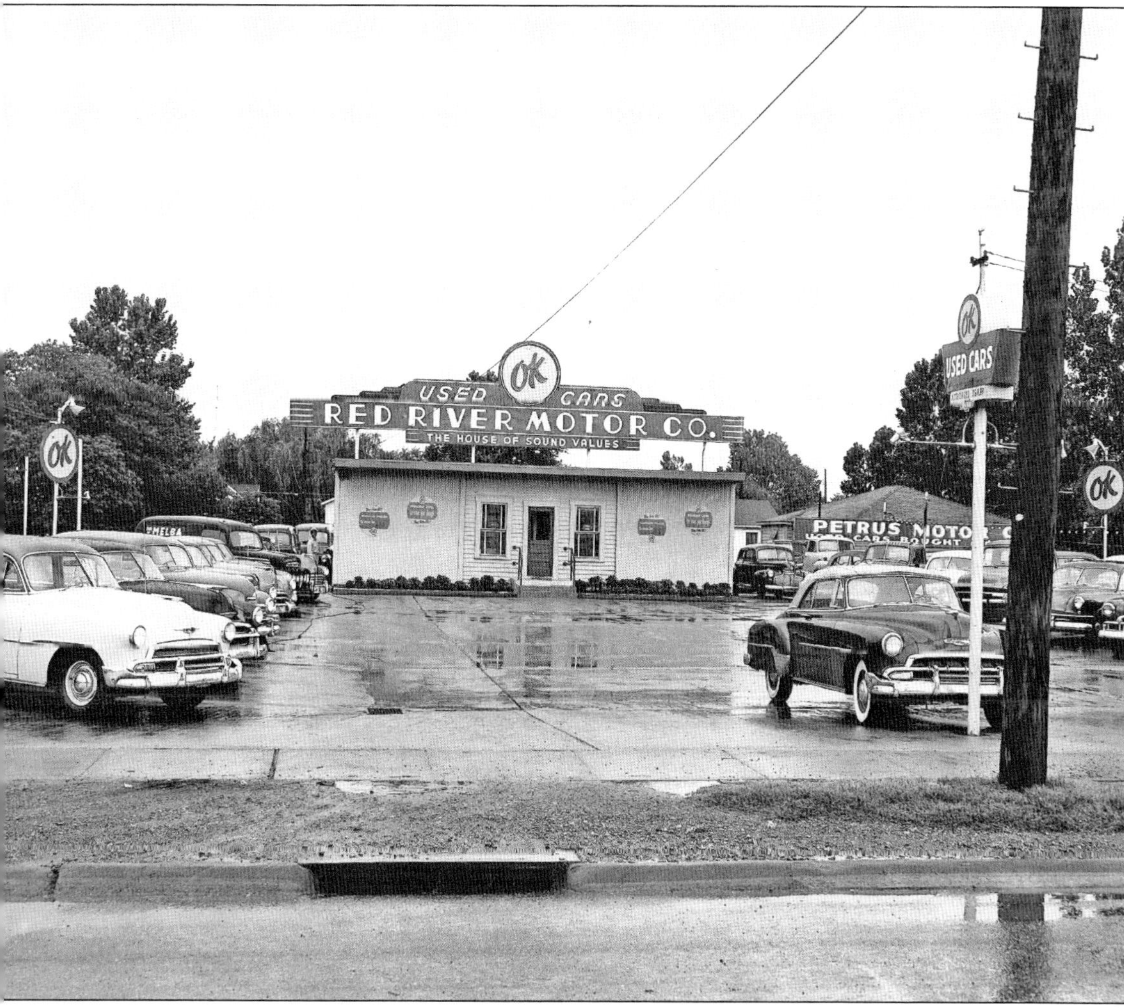

The used car lot, pictured here around 1950, encompassed the area where the current repair and service department building now stands across from the dealership. (Courtesy of George Fritze.)

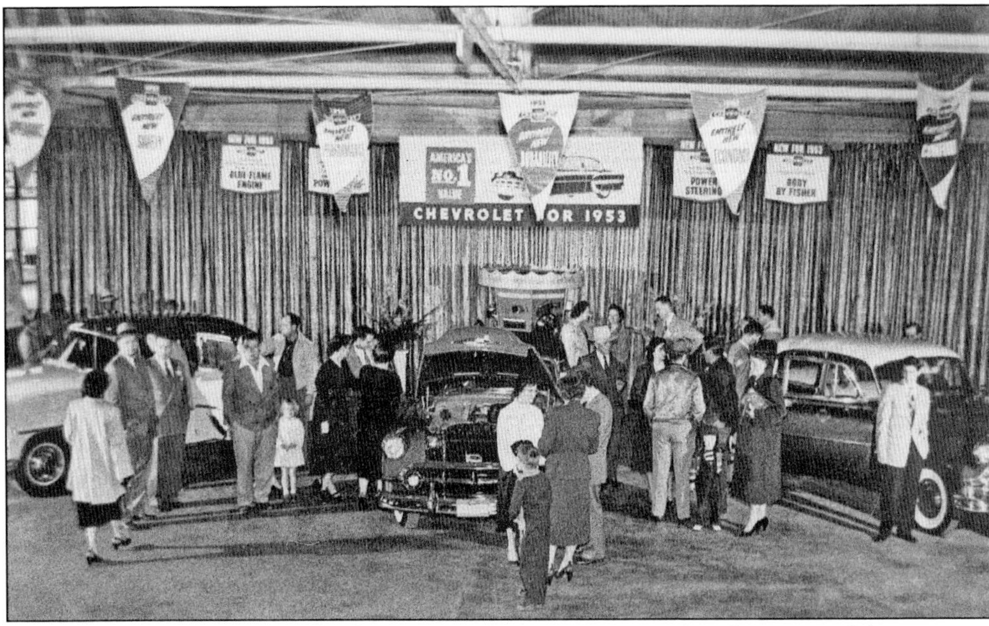

There was a time when people had to go to a release party to see what the new models were going to look like. This was Red River Chevrolet's unveiling party for the 1953 models of Chevrolet cars. (Courtesy of George Fritze.)

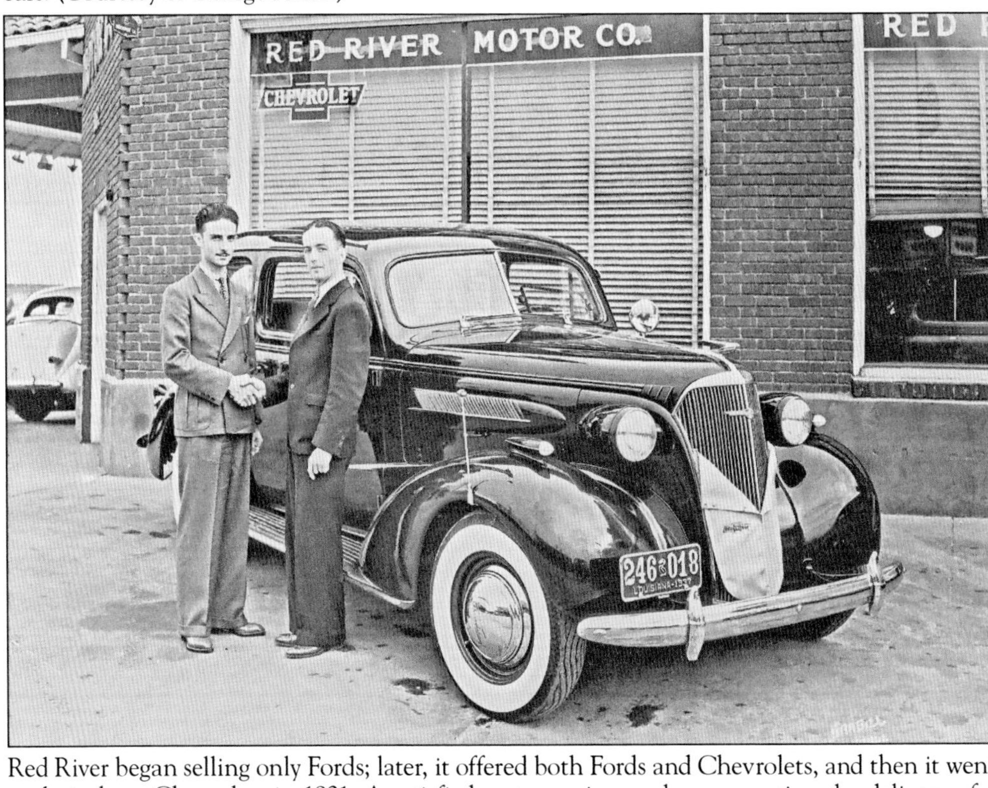

Red River began selling only Fords; later, it offered both Fords and Chevrolets, and then it went exclusively to Chevrolets in 1931. A satisfied customer is seen here accepting the delivery of a new Chevrolet in 1937. (Courtesy of George Fritze.)

At right, a happy family takes the keys to their new Chevrolet; below, another happy customer is handed the keys to his new automobile. White-walled tires were a popular choice for automobiles during this time. (Courtesy of George Fritze)

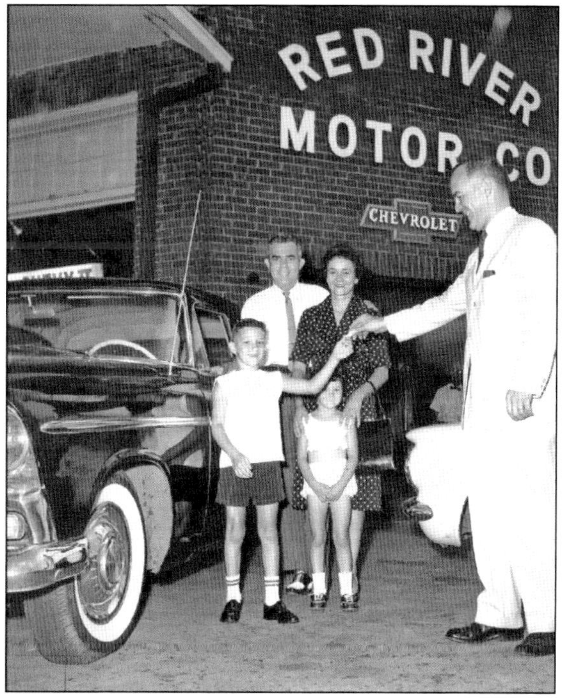

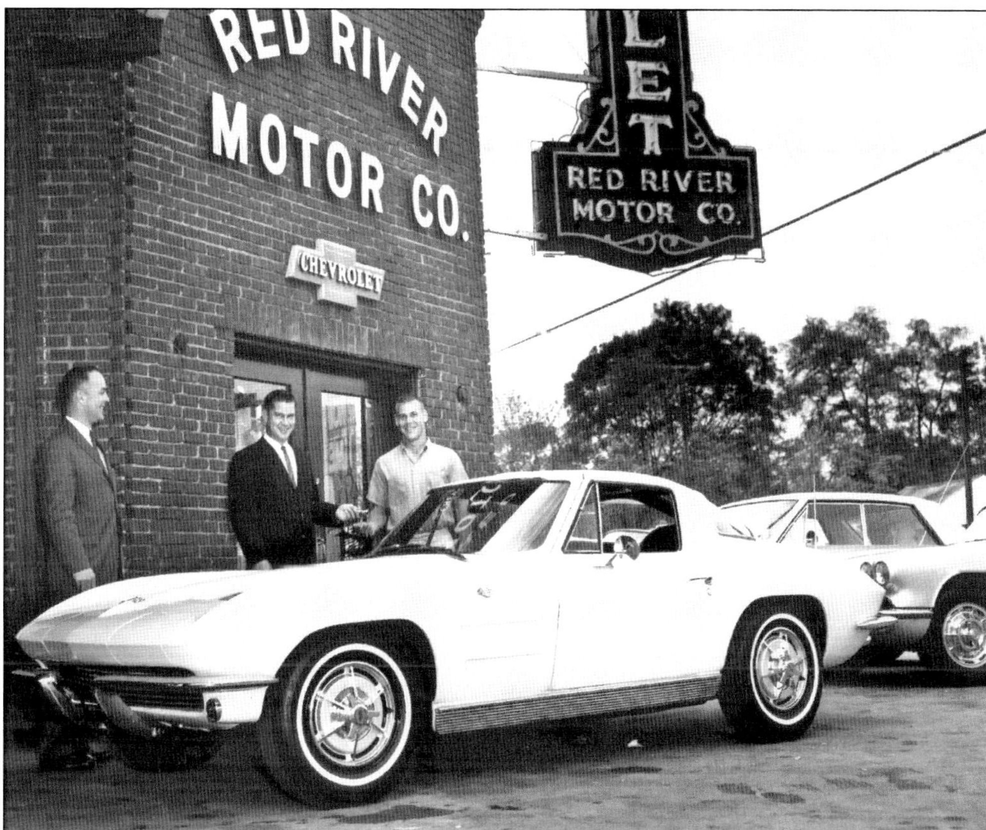

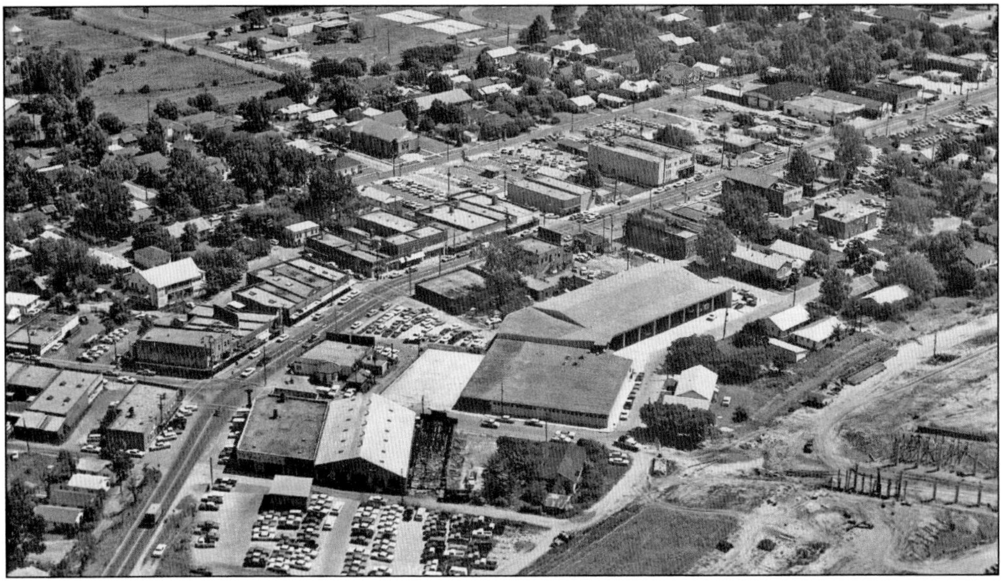

Captured in this early-1960s aerial view of Red River Chevrolet and downtown Bossier City is the Red River Motors building and its brand new service department, which was built across the street. The Bossier Ice Company can also be seen on the far left. (Courtesy of George Fritze.)

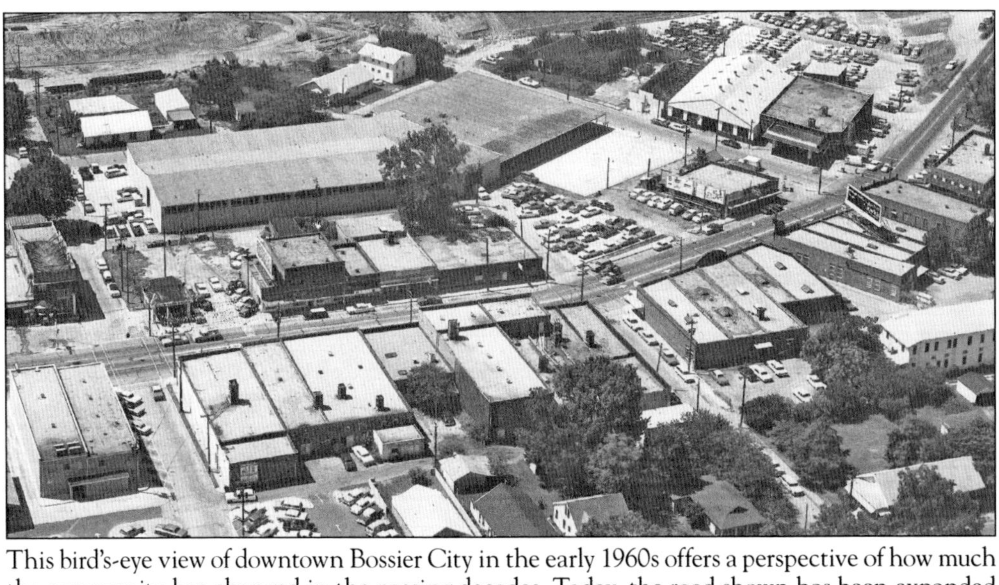

This bird's-eye view of downtown Bossier City in the early 1960s offers a perspective of how much the community has changed in the passing decades. Today, the road shown has been expanded to four lanes, and many of the downtown houses and buildings have since been replaced in the wake of progress. Bossier High School's football stadium is visible at the top of the photograph. (Courtesy of George Fritze.)

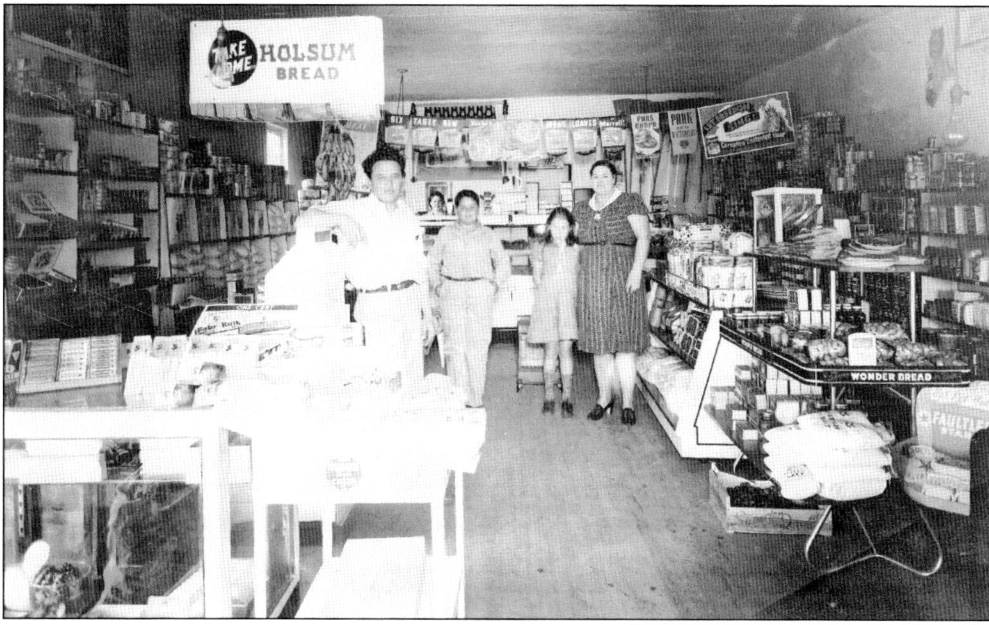

Pictured here in the 1930s is the interior of Adley's Grocery, located at 901 Barksdale Boulevard in Bossier City. Pleasant O'Neal Adley Sr. leans against the cash register, and to the right of him are his son Roy L. Adley, daughter Dorothy Lillian Adley Gleason, and wife Minnie Julie Rambin Adley in a printed dress. Adley's sister Lou Adley Setzer is in the background behind the meat counter. (Courtesy of Bossier Parish Library Historical Center.)

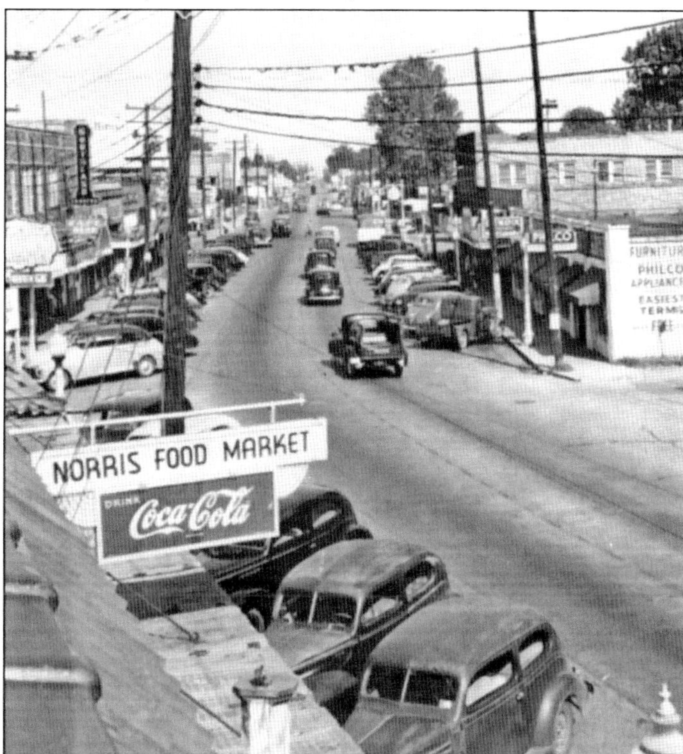

Norris Food Market juts into the foreground of this 1940s photograph of Barksdale Boulevard. Farther down the left is the Southland Theater. The Philco Appliances building, pictured on the right-hand side of the street, is now the home of Red River Chevrolet's body shop. (Courtesy of Bossier Parish Library Historical Center.)

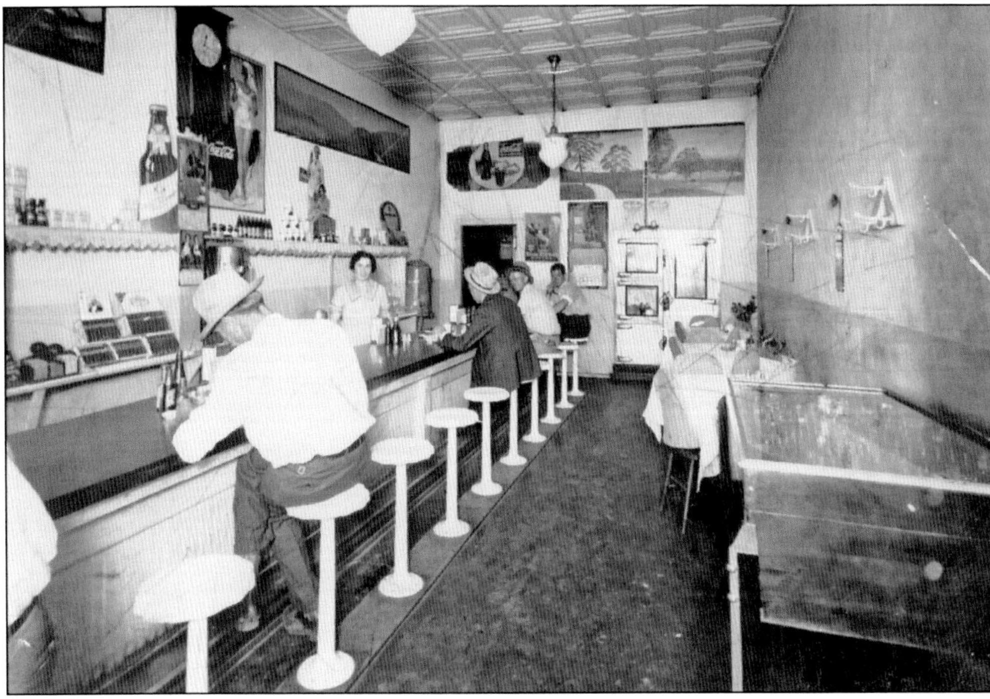

The 1940s photograph above is of the interior of Steve's Café on Barksdale Boulevard. The café was run by Steve Carpenter. The image below is from 1951 after the café was taken over by Johnnie Mae Carpenter. Besides the remodeling, it was also renamed Johnnie Mae's Café. (Courtesy of Bossier Parish Library Historical Center.)

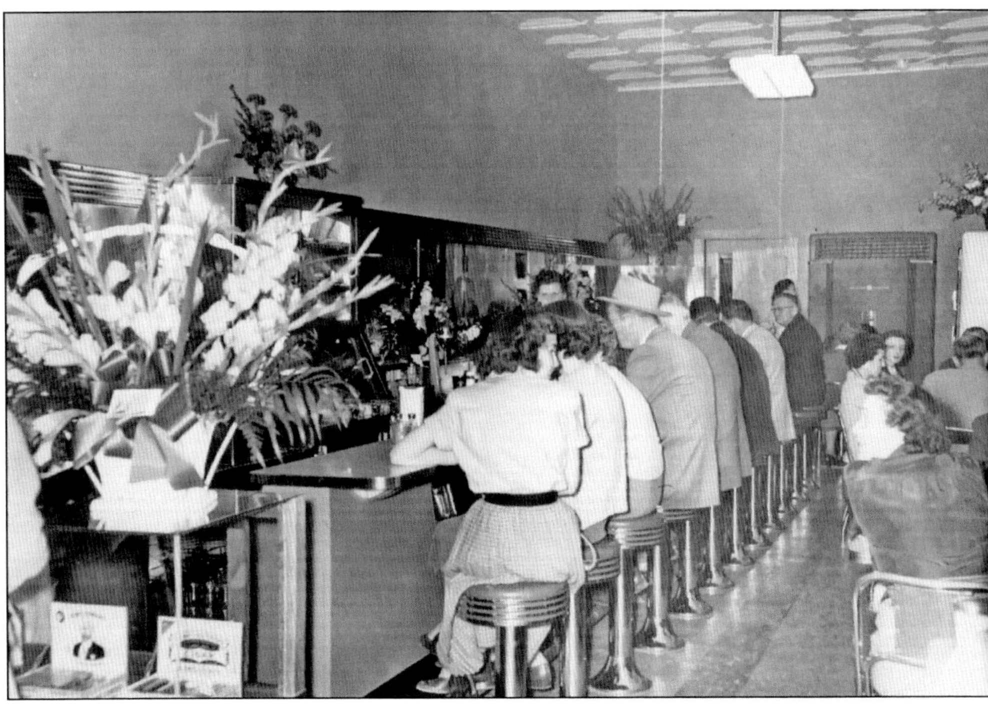

Pictured in the 1940s, at right are Johnnie Mae Carpenter (right) and a friend, while below Johnnie Mae is with her sister Billie in front of Steve's Café. The café was located next to Tibbetts Pool Hall at 504 Barksdale Boulevard. Note the window display, which announces to potential patrons the 25¢-lunch plate. (Courtesy of the Bossier Parish Library Historical Center.)

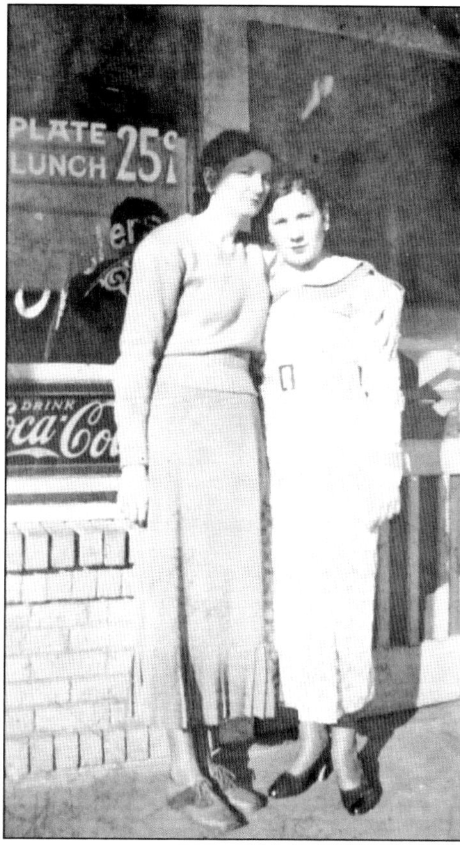

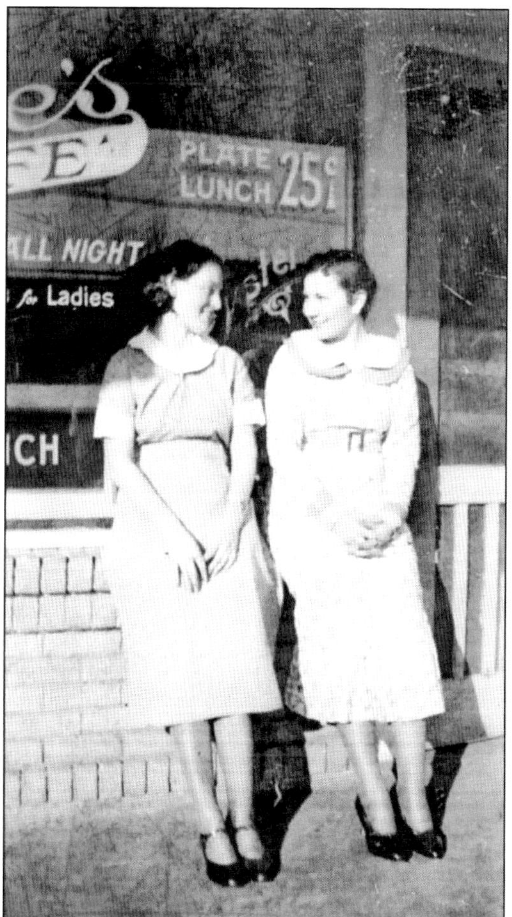

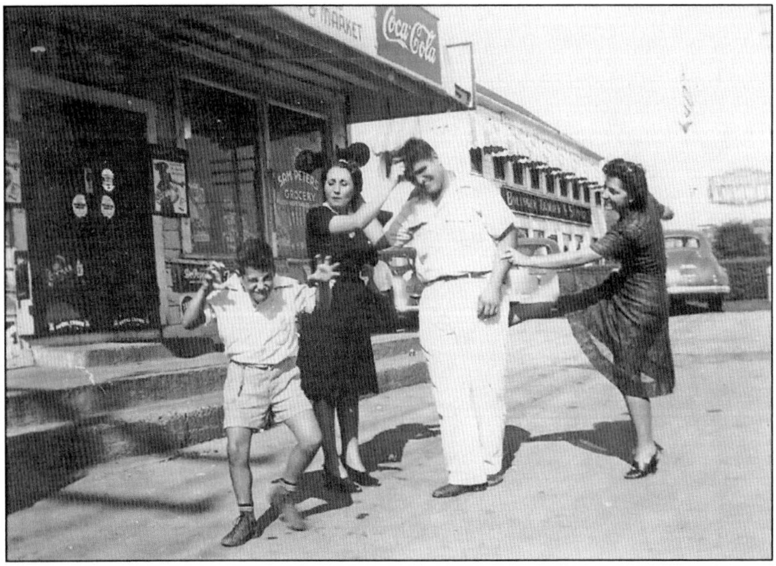

The Peters children play in front of Sam Peters Grocery in the 1940s. The teenager in all white is Sam Fertita, who runs a deli in Shreveport. In the background is Bolinger Lumber Company. (Courtesy of Mickey Capuano and family.)

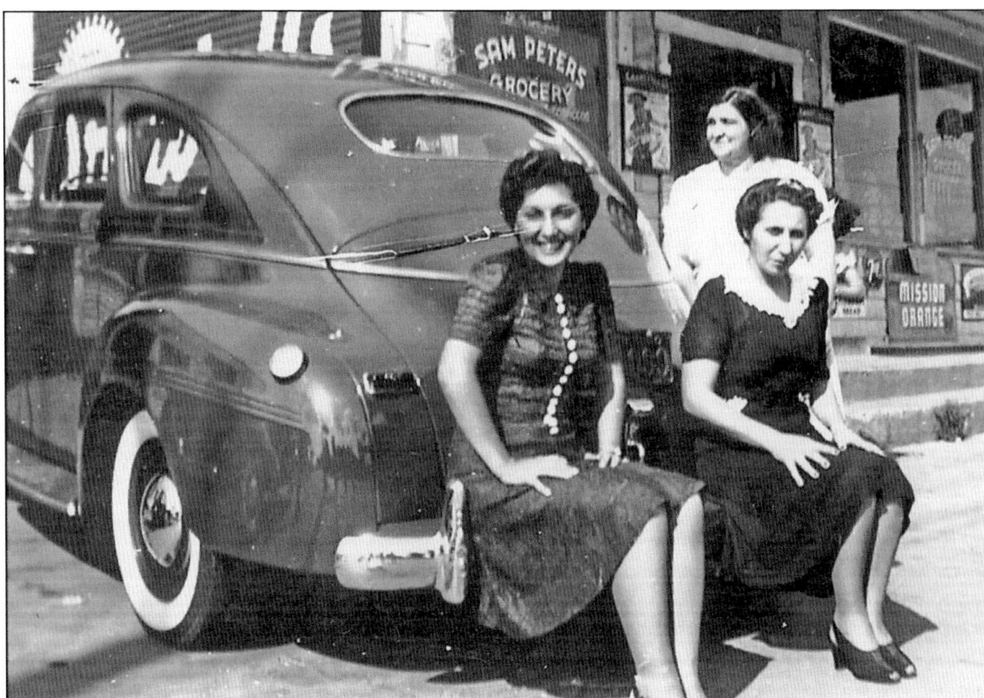

Three ladies pose in front of Peters Grocery in the 1940s. Sam Peters opened his grocery store on Barksdale Boulevard in 1923, and it is still a family-run business. Pictured from left to right are Sadie Peters, Florence Fertita, and Josephine Finley. (Courtesy of Mickey Capuano and family.)

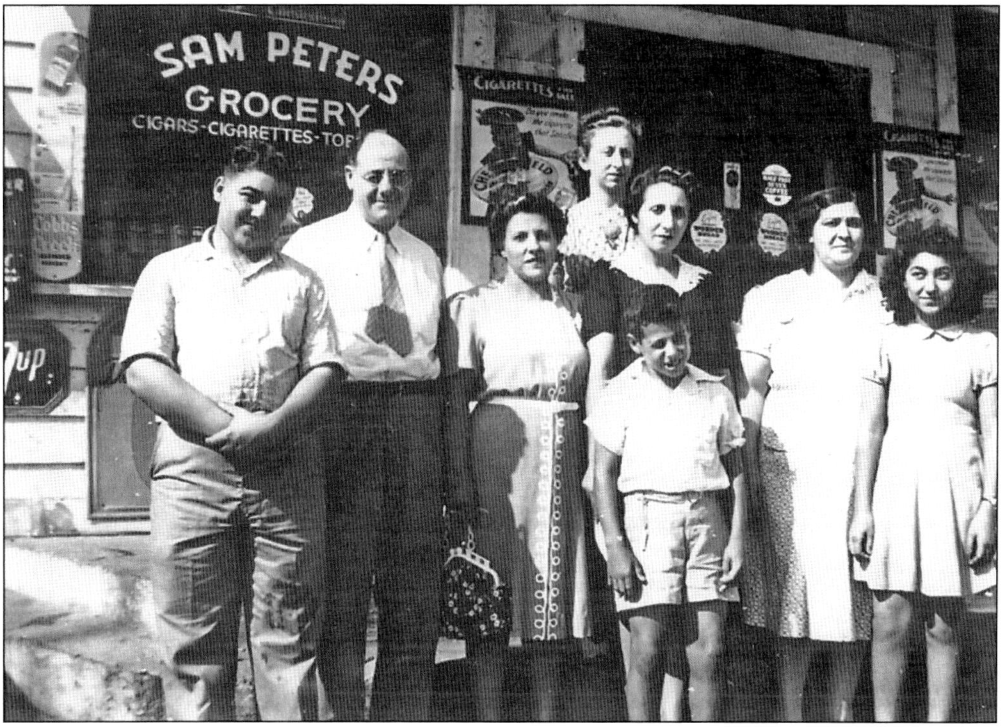

Pictured here in the 1940s, the Peters family poses in front of their store on Barksdale Boulevard in downtown Bossier. Cigars, cigarettes, bread, coffee, and 7up are among the advertisements displayed on the grocery store's exterior. (Courtesy of the Mickey Capuano and family.)

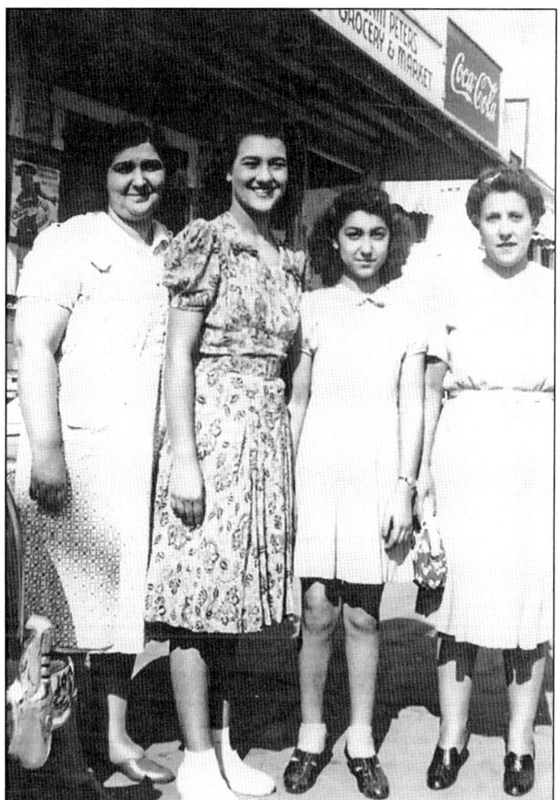

Four ladies pose in front of Sam Peters Grocery in 1940s. From left to right are Sadie Peters, Rose Peters, Connie Peters, and unidentified. (Courtesy of Mickey Capuano and family.)

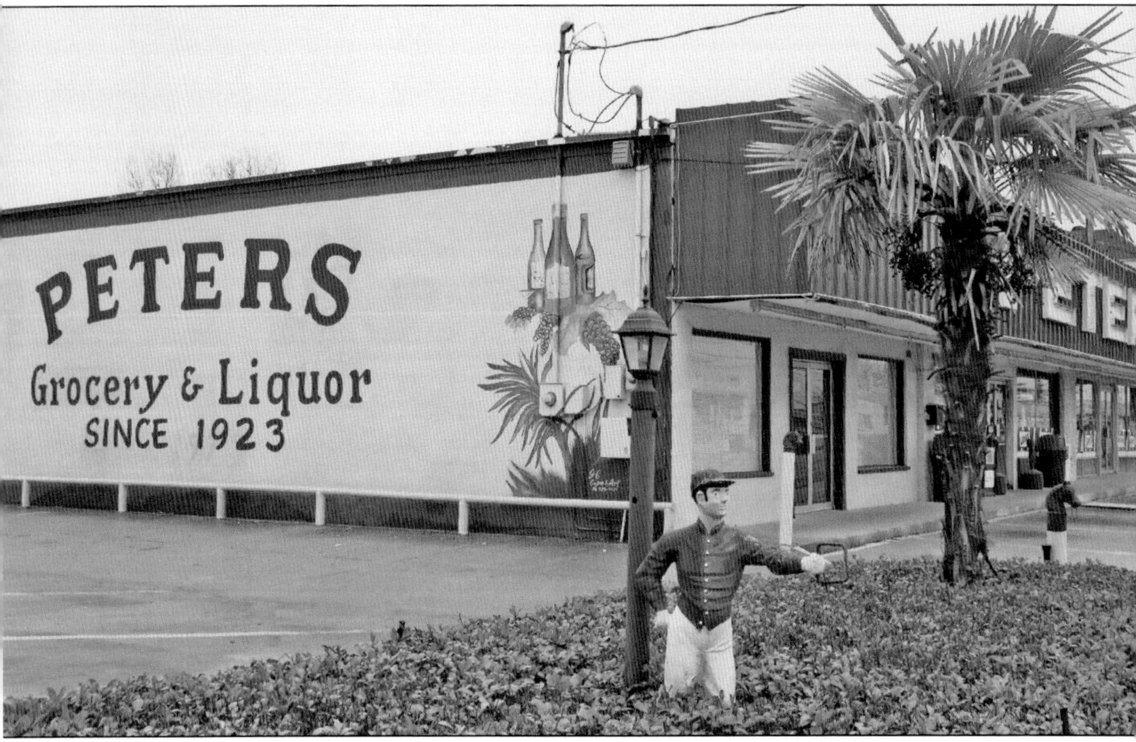

Sam Peters opened his grocery store on Barksdale Boulevard in 1923, and Mickey Capuano and his family are the third generation to run the store. (Courtesy of Mickey Capuano and family.)

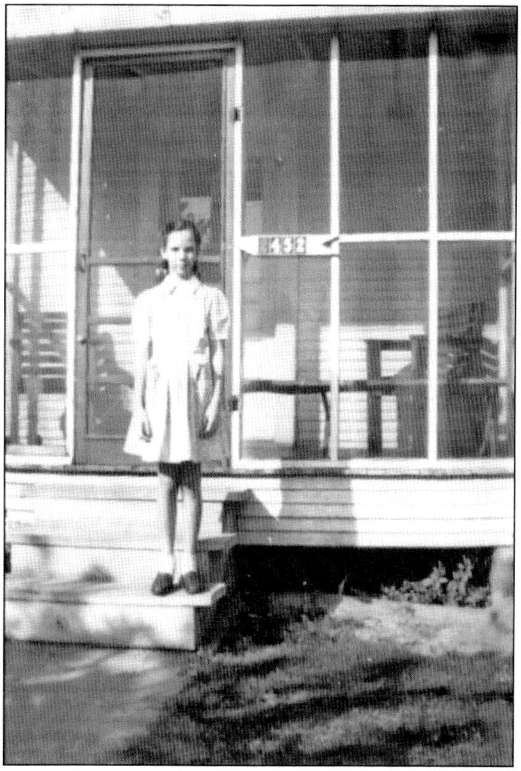

At right, young Joyce Knowles stands in front of her house at 2452 Hoyer Street in Bossier City in 1943. Her mother, Irma Knowles, is pictured below beside the house; she had just emptied some water after washing the dishes in a bucket. (Courtesy of Bossier Parish Library Historical Center.)

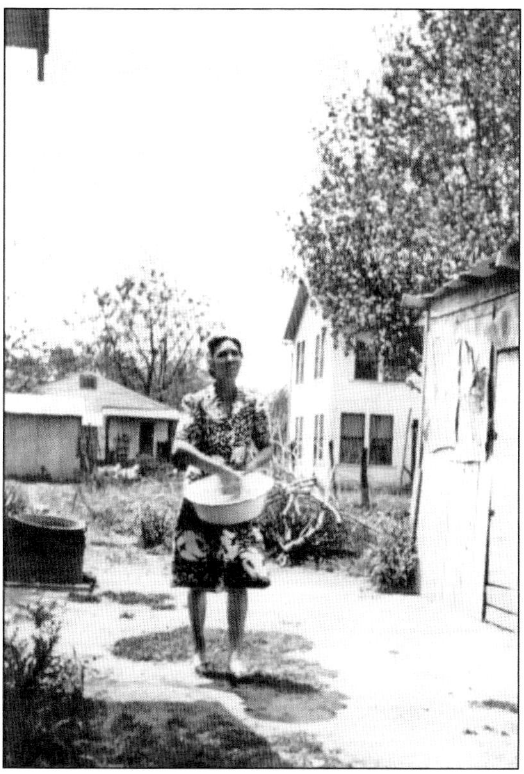

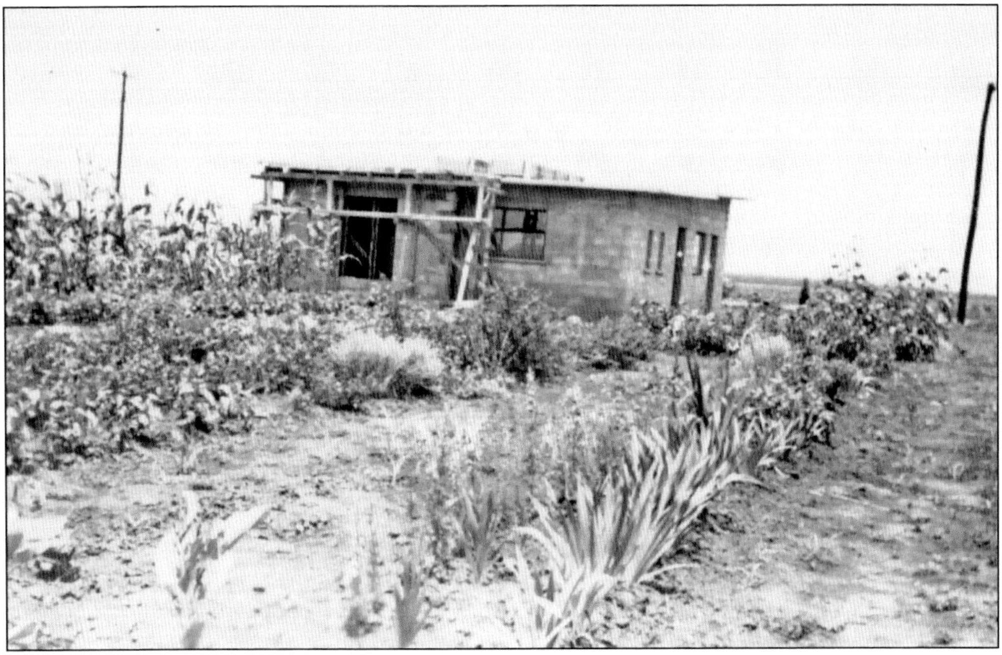

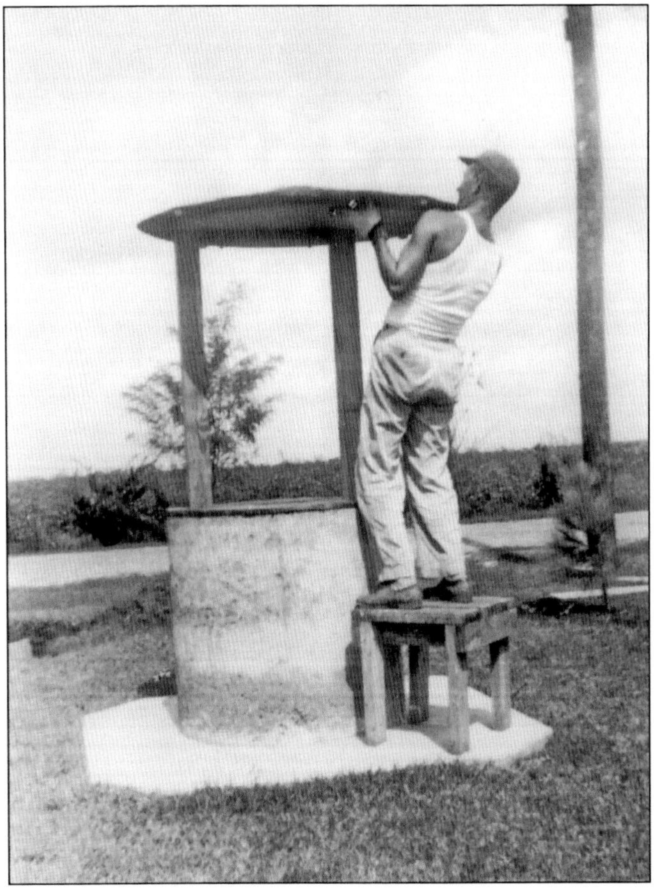

In 1947, Joe Knowles began building his family a new home at 1489 (later changed to 2502) Northside Drive in what was then the edge of Bossier City. Part of the process of building the home included constructing a well, as shown at left. (Courtesy of Bossier Parish Library Historical Center.)

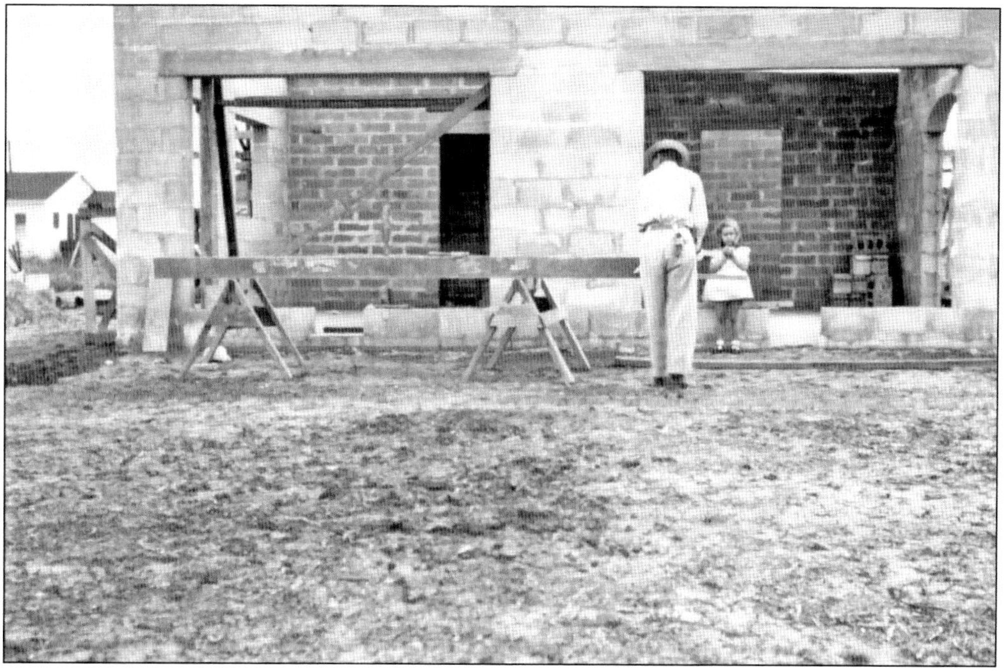

Joe Knowles is pictured above in the process building his family's new home on Northside Drive in Bossier City. The young girl in the photograph is Sandy Hilton. Below, a later photograph shows the Knowles home developing into a more complete structure. (Courtesy of Bossier Parish Library Historical Center.)

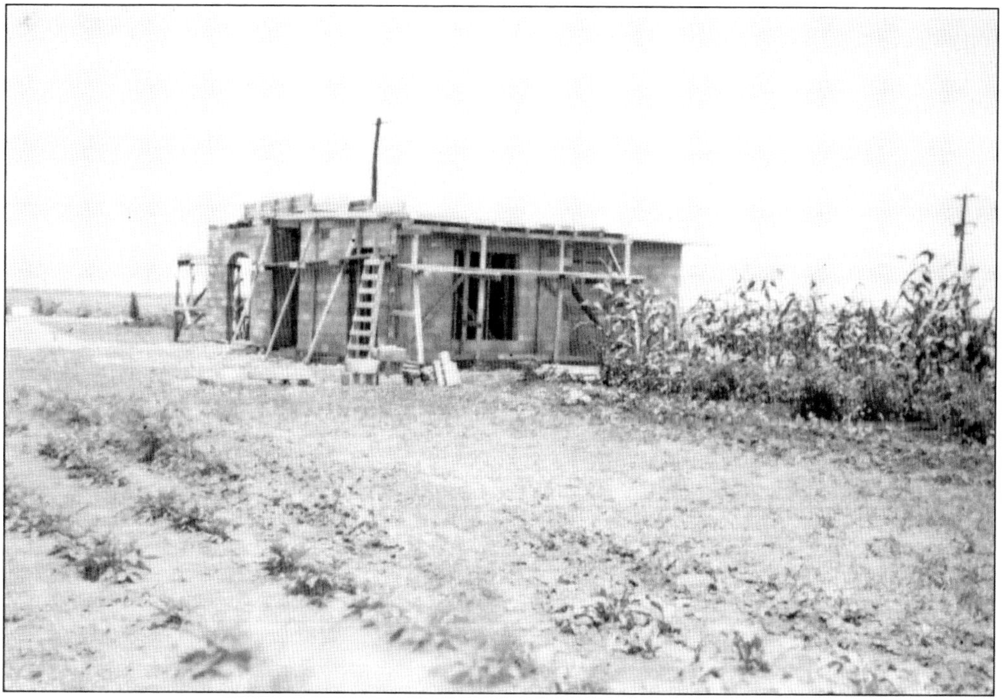

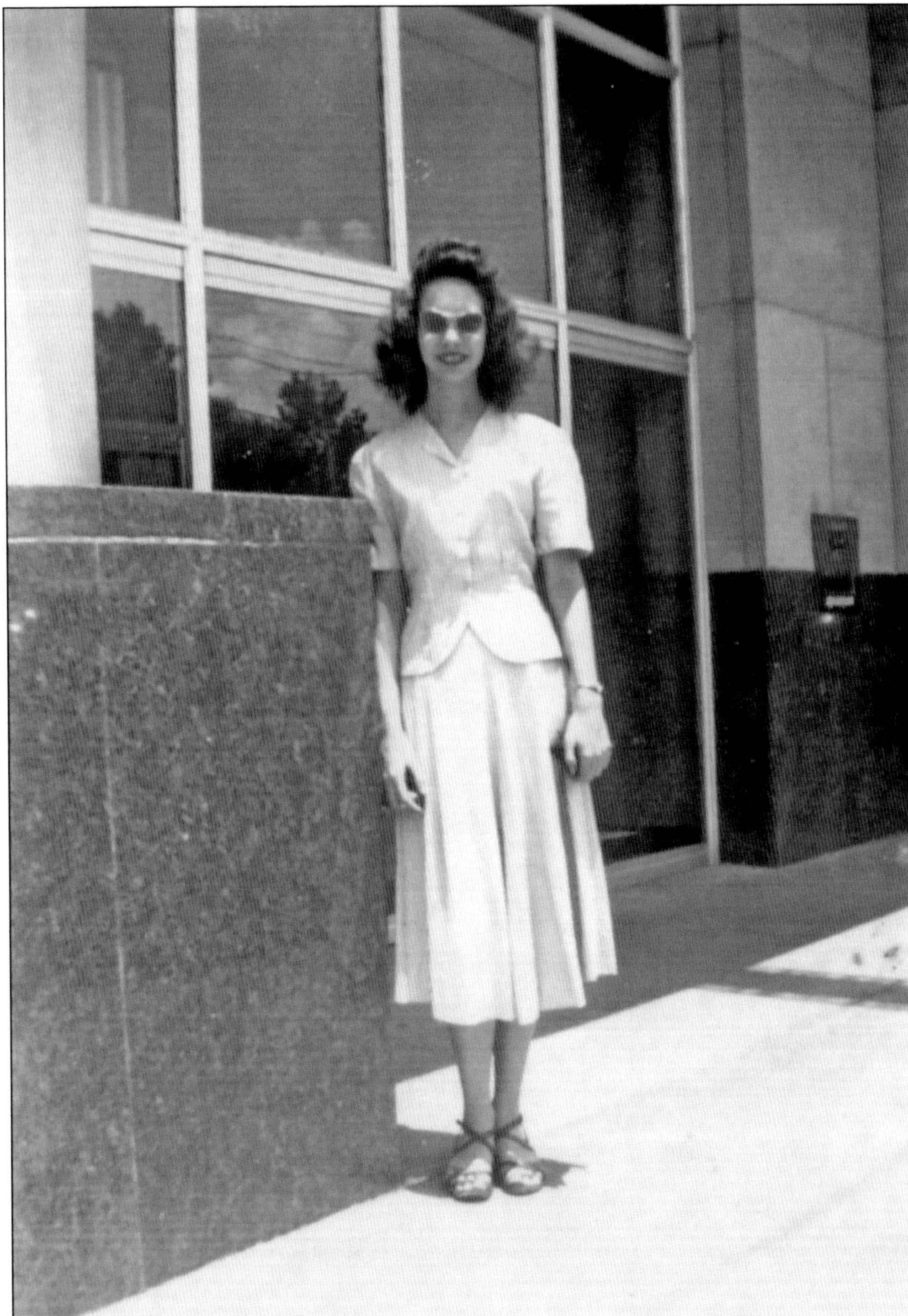

Joyce Knowles is seen here standing in front of Bossier Bank and Trust on Barksdale Boulevard in 1949. Joyce grew up on Hoyer Street and also lived on Northside Drive in the house that her father built. (Courtesy of Bossier Parish Historical Center and the Knowles-Skaggs family.)

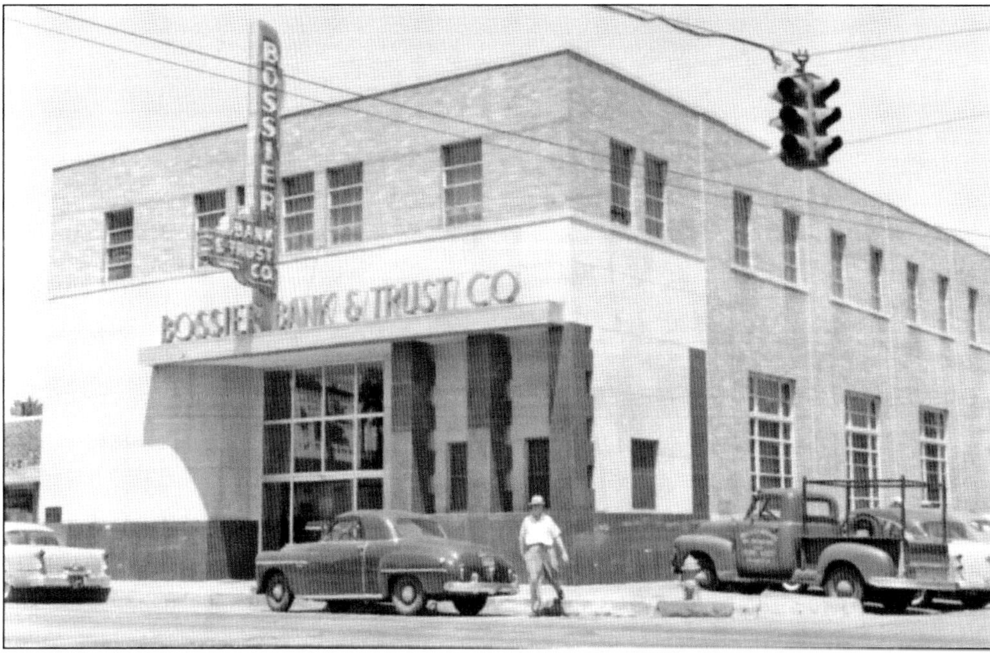

The Bossier Bank and Trust building is pictured here around 1952. The Bossier Bank and Trust started as Bossier State Bank in 1923, spearheaded by Dr. Shea Edward Prince. V.V. Whittington took over in 1941, and this structure was built in 1948 at a cost of $250,000. The architect was J. Chesire Payton, and the builder was W.A. McMichael. When the bank closed in the 1970s, it operated as a city building until the 1980s, when a new municipal complex was built. (Courtesy of Bossier Parish Library Historical Center.)

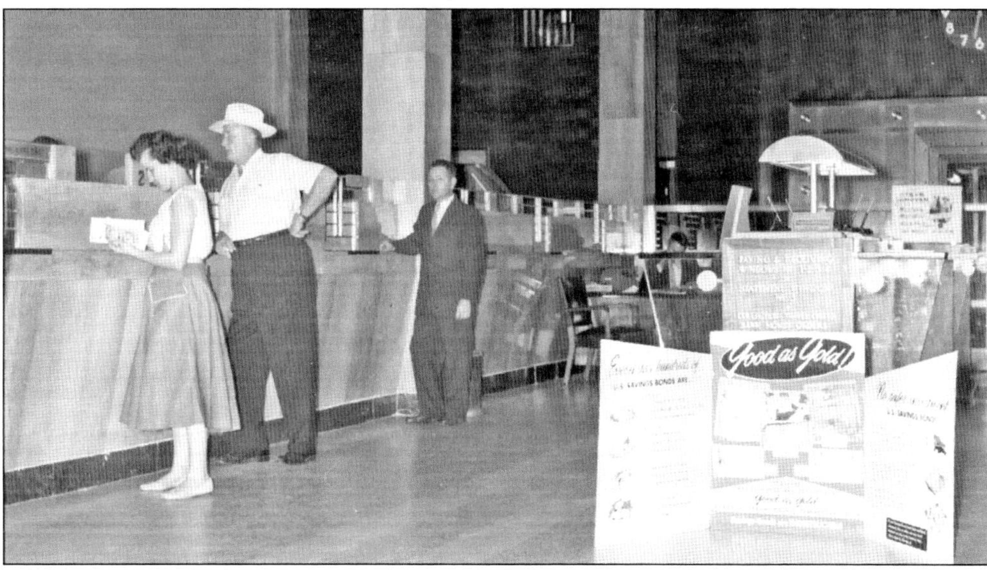

Bossier Bank and Trust had a modern and attractive lobby. The bank, pictured here in the early 1960s, had experienced a great deal of growth since moving into the new building in 1948. At the time, the bank offered separate windows for different operations; these included four paying and receiving windows, a statements window, and a window offering traveler's checks and money orders. (Courtesy of Bossier Parish Library Historical Center.)

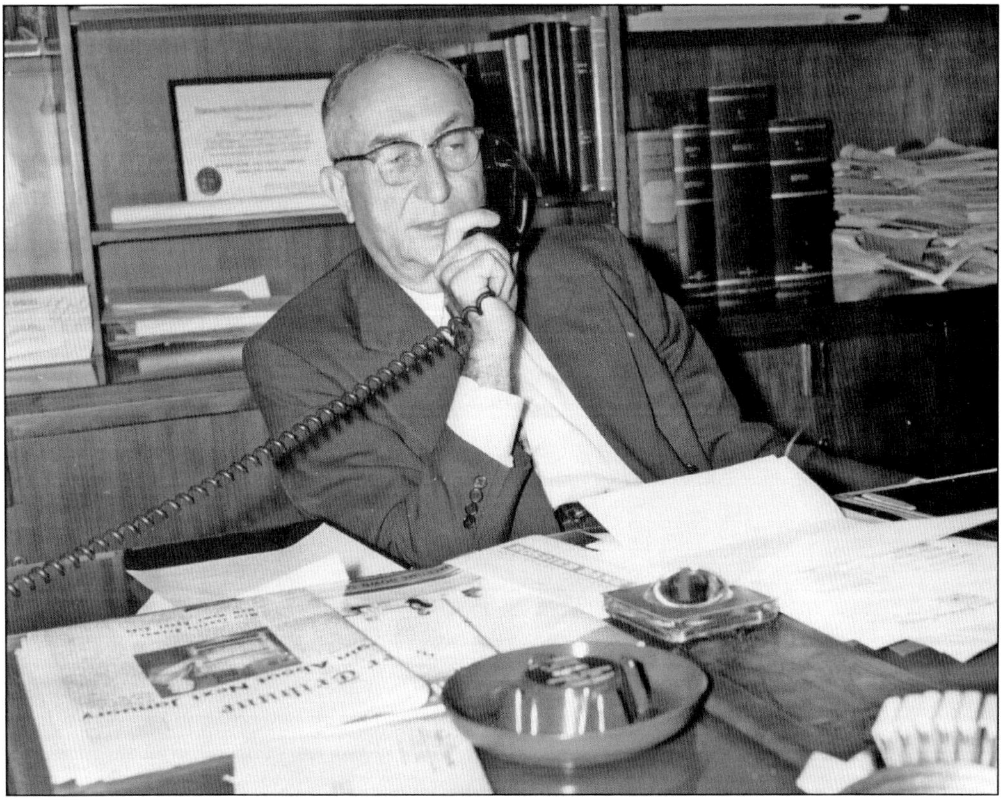

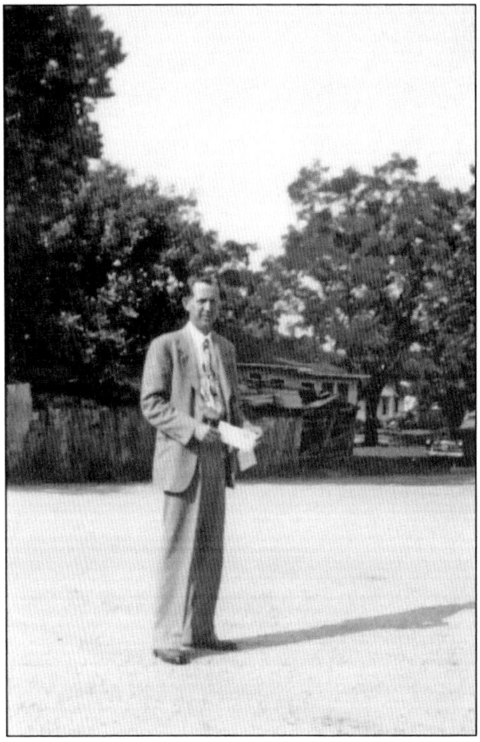

Volney Voss "V.V." Whittington was president of Bossier Bank and Trust. He also served as president of the Louisiana Bankers Association, a term as president of the State Levee Board Association, and for 34 years was treasurer of the Bossier Parish Police Jury. He also served as president of the Bank of Benton and chairman of the board of the Gibsland Bank. This image was taken around 1962. (Courtesy of Bossier Parish Library Historical Center.)

Judson Naremore, one of the Bossier Bank and Trust's vice presidents, is pictured here standing in the parking lot of the bank in 1949. (Courtesy Bossier Parish Historical Center and the Knowles-Skaggs family.)

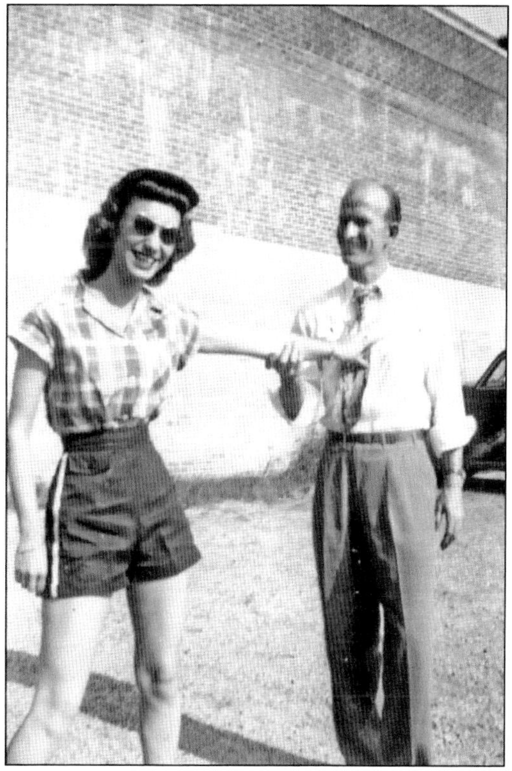

At right, two Bossier Bank and Trust employees, Bobbie Stewart (left) and Raymond Bond, were photographed beside the bank building in 1949. Below, three other bank employees, Ruby Carter (left), Morris Birdwell, another vice president, and Bobbie Stewart are seen behind the bank building. (Courtesy of Bossier Parish Library Historical Center.)

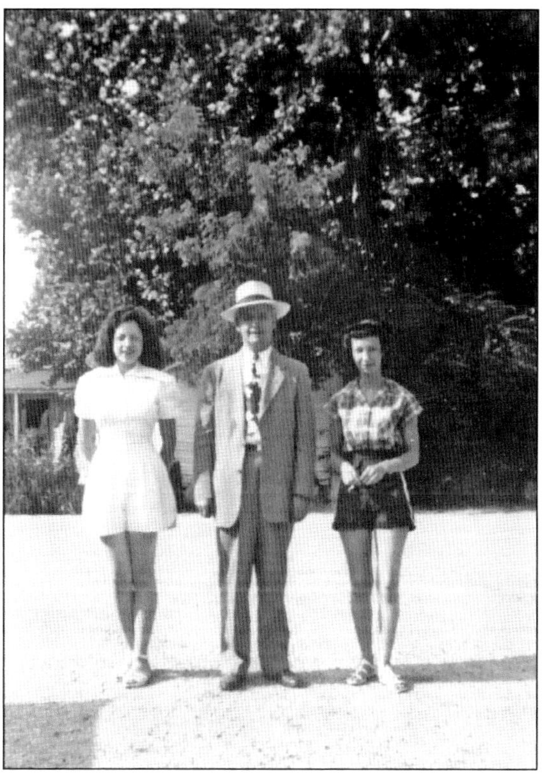

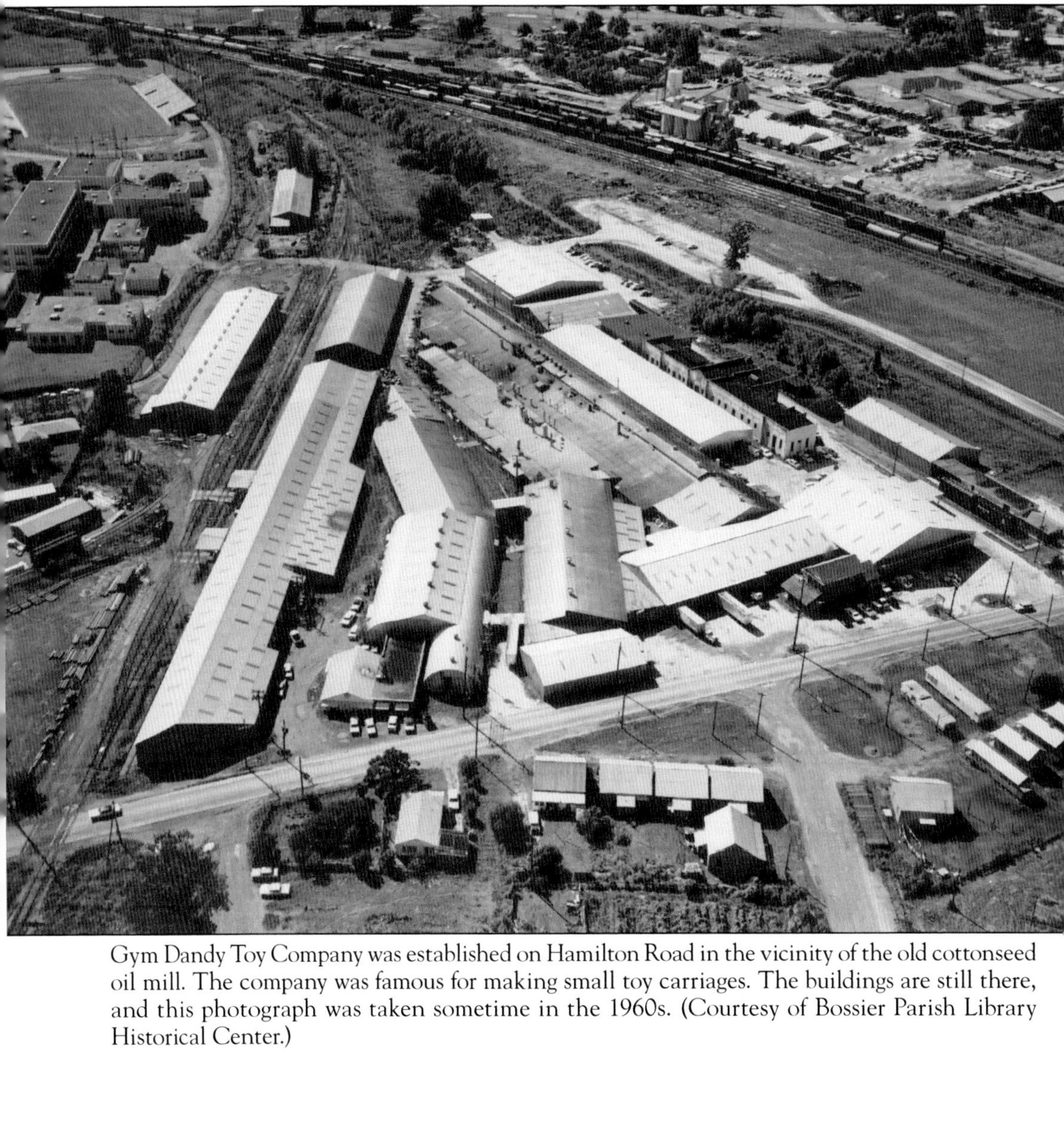

Gym Dandy Toy Company was established on Hamilton Road in the vicinity of the old cottonseed oil mill. The company was famous for making small toy carriages. The buildings are still there, and this photograph was taken sometime in the 1960s. (Courtesy of Bossier Parish Library Historical Center.)

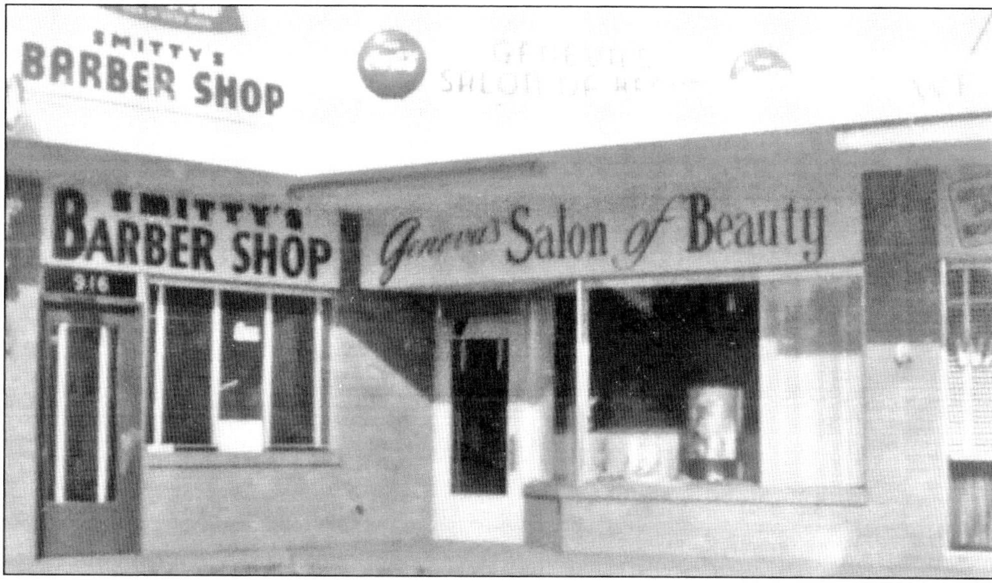

Pictured here in the 1950s, Smitty's Barber Shop and Geneva's Salon of Beauty were located next door to each other in downtown Bossier City. (Courtesy Bossier Parish Historical Center and the Wyatt family.)

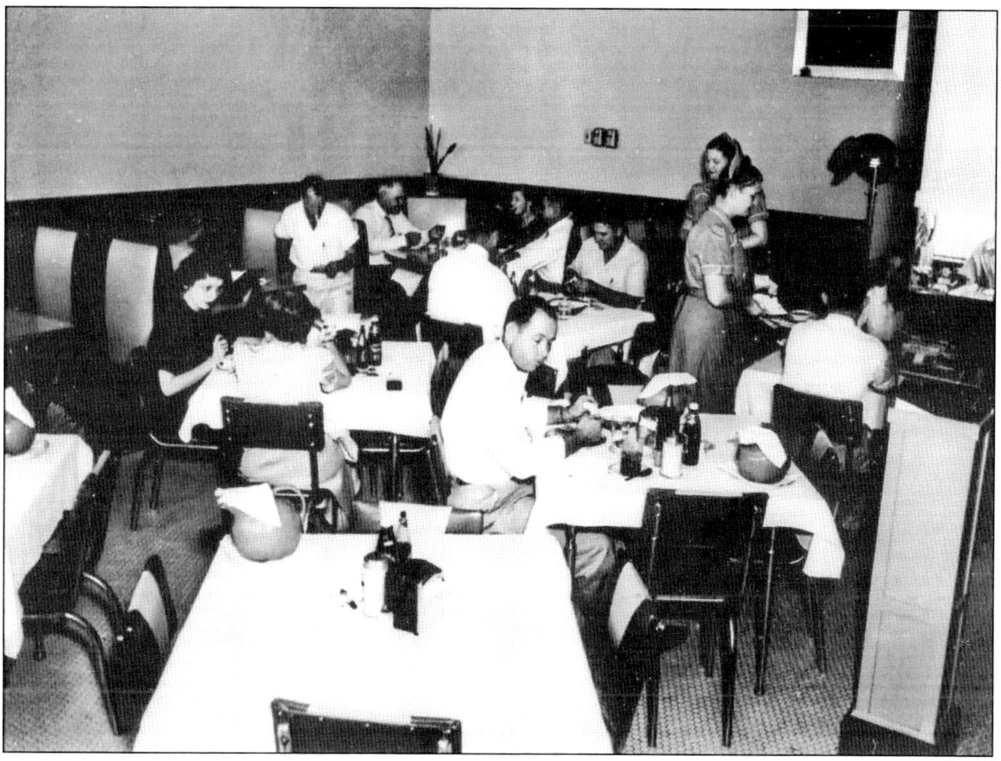

This early-1950s image captures the interior of the Amber Inn, which was run by brothers P.B. and Charley Lombardino from 1946 until 1978. The café offered plenty of seating for inside guests as well as carhops for guests who wished to stay in their cars. (Courtesy of Bossier Parish Library Historical Center.)

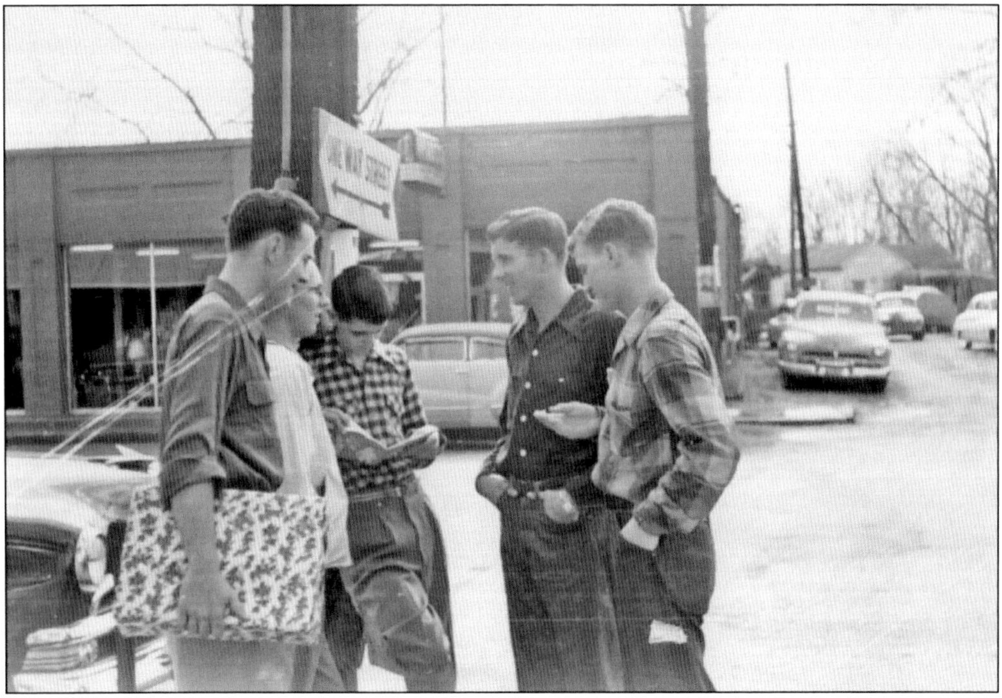

Above, from left to right, Donnie Patrick, Darcy Hutto, Dale Robinson, Bill Howell, and Sammie Green are standing on the street corner in front of Barksdale Drug Store in downtown around 1951. Below, "Wee" Willie White is pictured crossing the street toward Barksdale Drug Store in downtown Bossier City in 1952. (Courtesy of Bossier Parish Library Historical Center.)

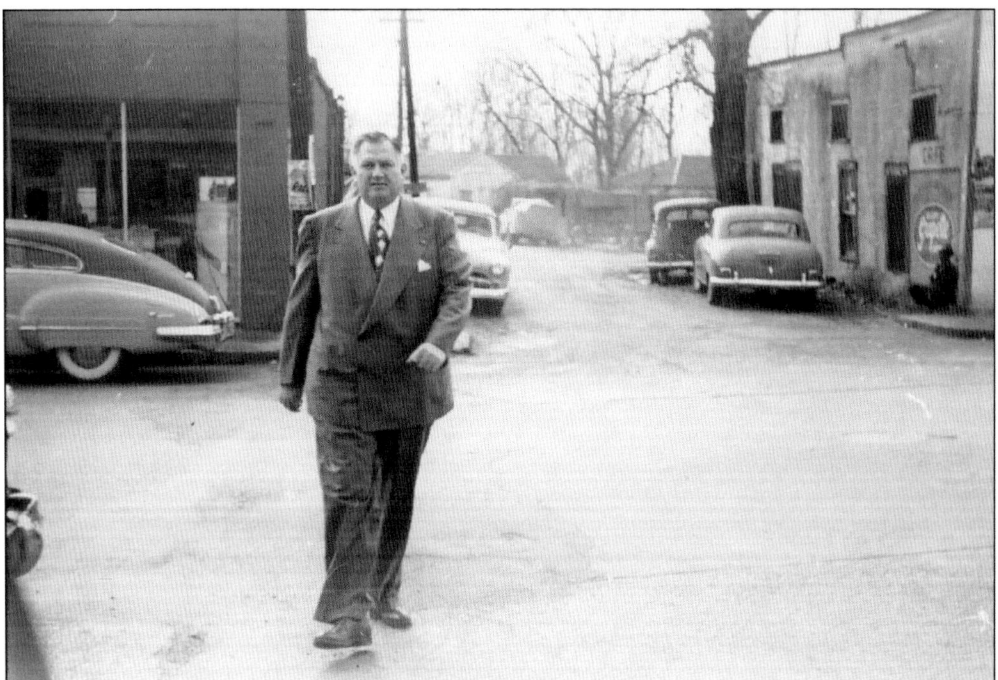

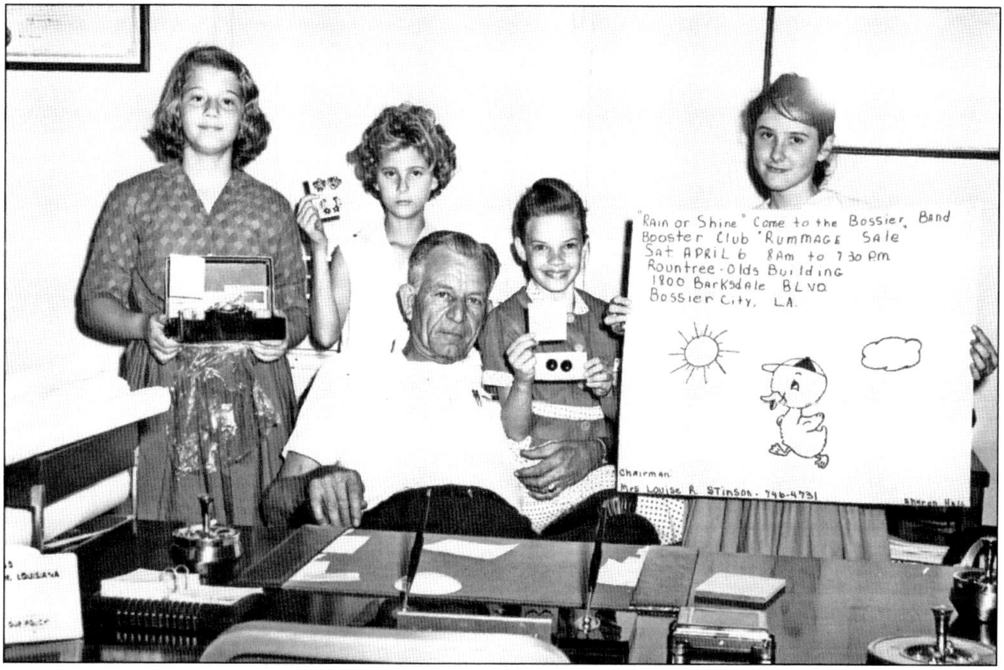

Ivy C. "Rex" Tinsley is seen here in the early 1970s surrounded by schoolchildren. Rex served as the street and parks commissioner for Bossier City beginning in 1974, serving until his death in 1981. The poster is an advertisement for the Bossier Band Booster Club's all-day rummage sale, which was held at 1800 Barksdale Boulevard. The telephone number for the booster club's chairman, Louise R. Stinson, is listed at the bottom of the poster. (Courtesy of Bossier Parish Library Historical Center.)

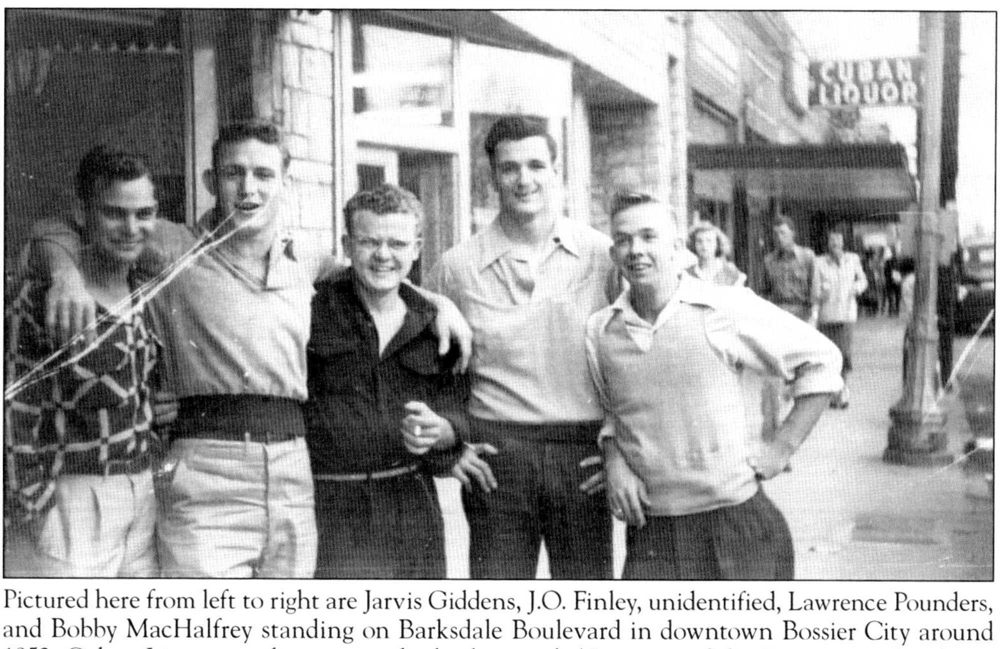

Pictured here from left to right are Jarvis Giddens, J.O. Finley, unidentified, Lawrence Pounders, and Bobby MacHalfrey standing on Barksdale Boulevard in downtown Bossier City around 1952. Cuban Liquor can be seen in the background. (Courtesy of the Bossier Parish Library Historical Center.)

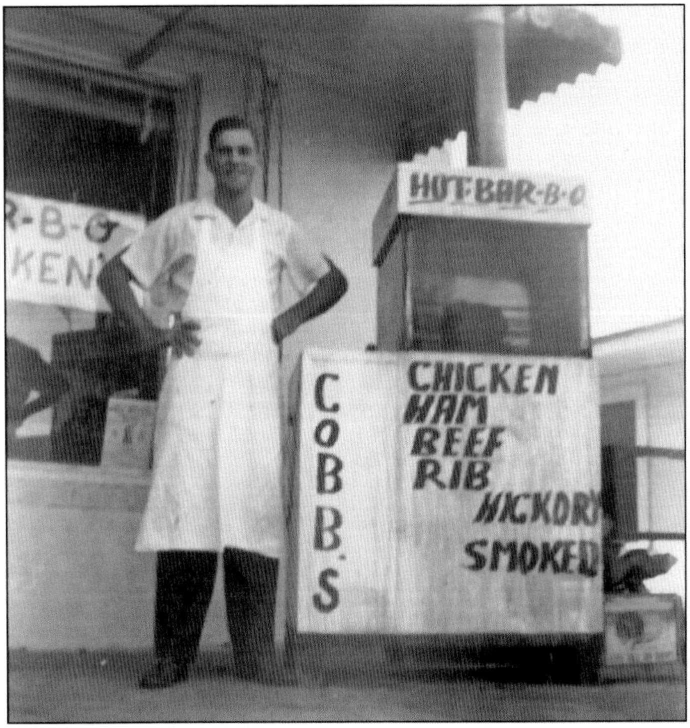

Joe Cobb, at left, specialized in barbeque, and Cobb's BBQ opened for business on Barksdale Boulevard in 1952. The family-owned restaurant is still located in its original building. Cobb's BBQ was and still is a staple of downtown Bossier City. Below, Cobb (left) and an unidentified employee are unloading the food from the smoke pit around 1965. (Courtesy of the Cobb family.)

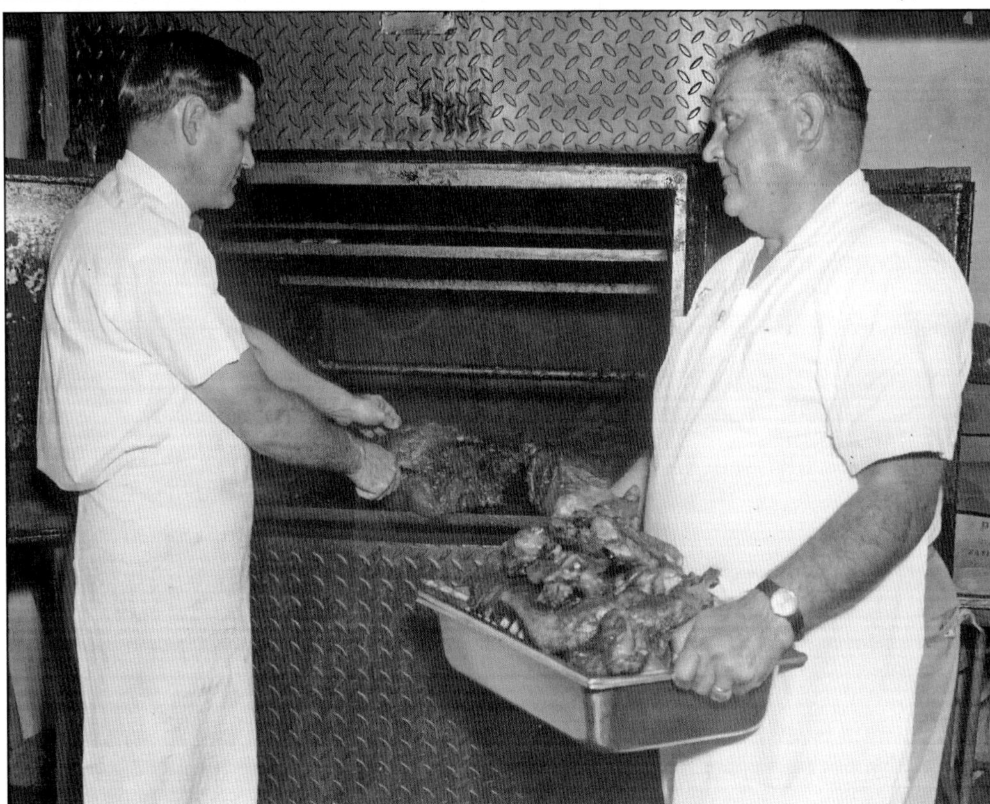

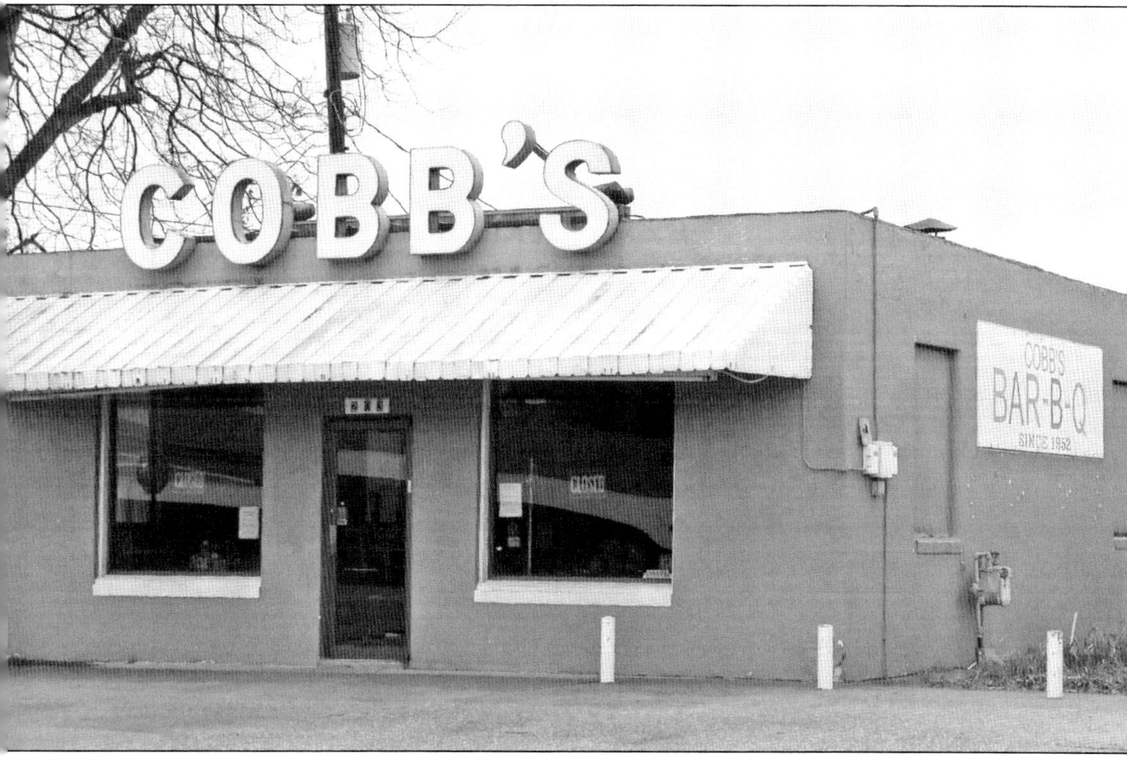

This image shows Cobb's BBQ in 2015 at its location at 203 McCormick Street. Note the painted sign on the exterior of the building reads "Bar-B-Q." (Author's collection.)

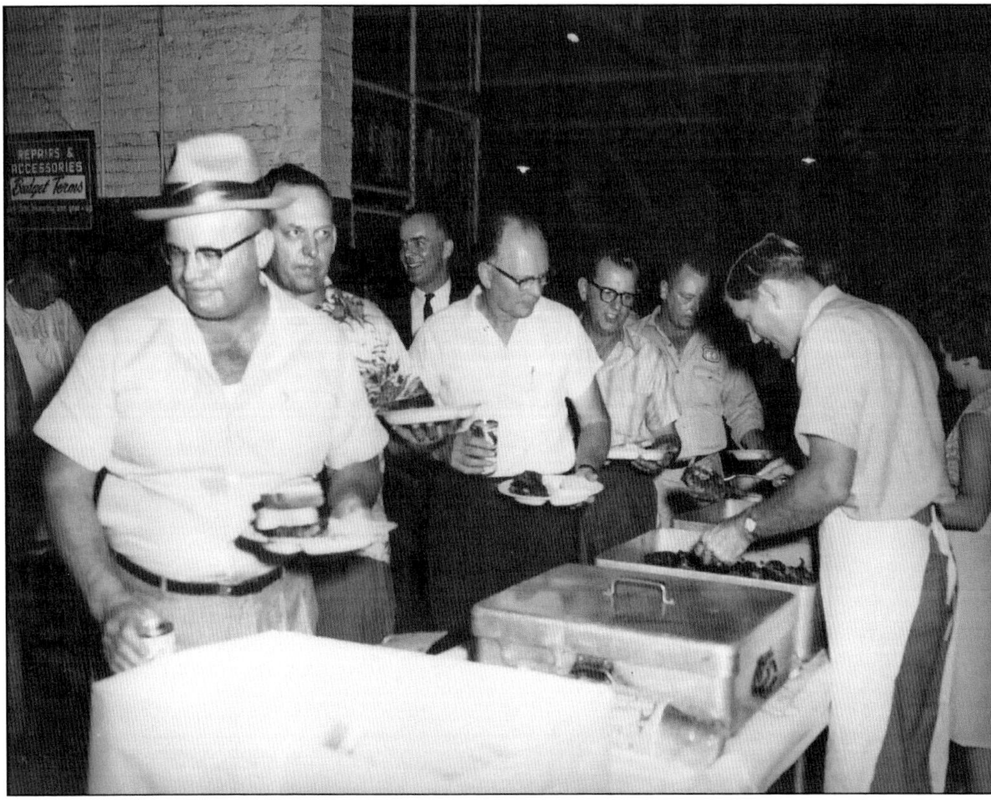

Cobb's BBQ would cater to many businesses and events in Bossier City. Above, Joe Cobb is pictured serving during an event he catered at Red River Motors in the 1960s. Cobb catered many events for Red River Motors throughout the years. Below, employees are seen gathered around a Chevrolet truck bed, which was filled with ice to double as a drink cooler. (Courtesy of the Cobb family.)

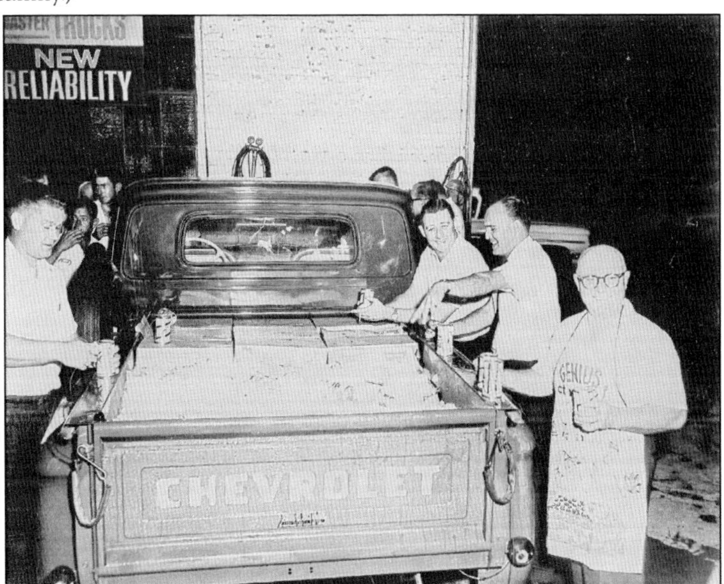

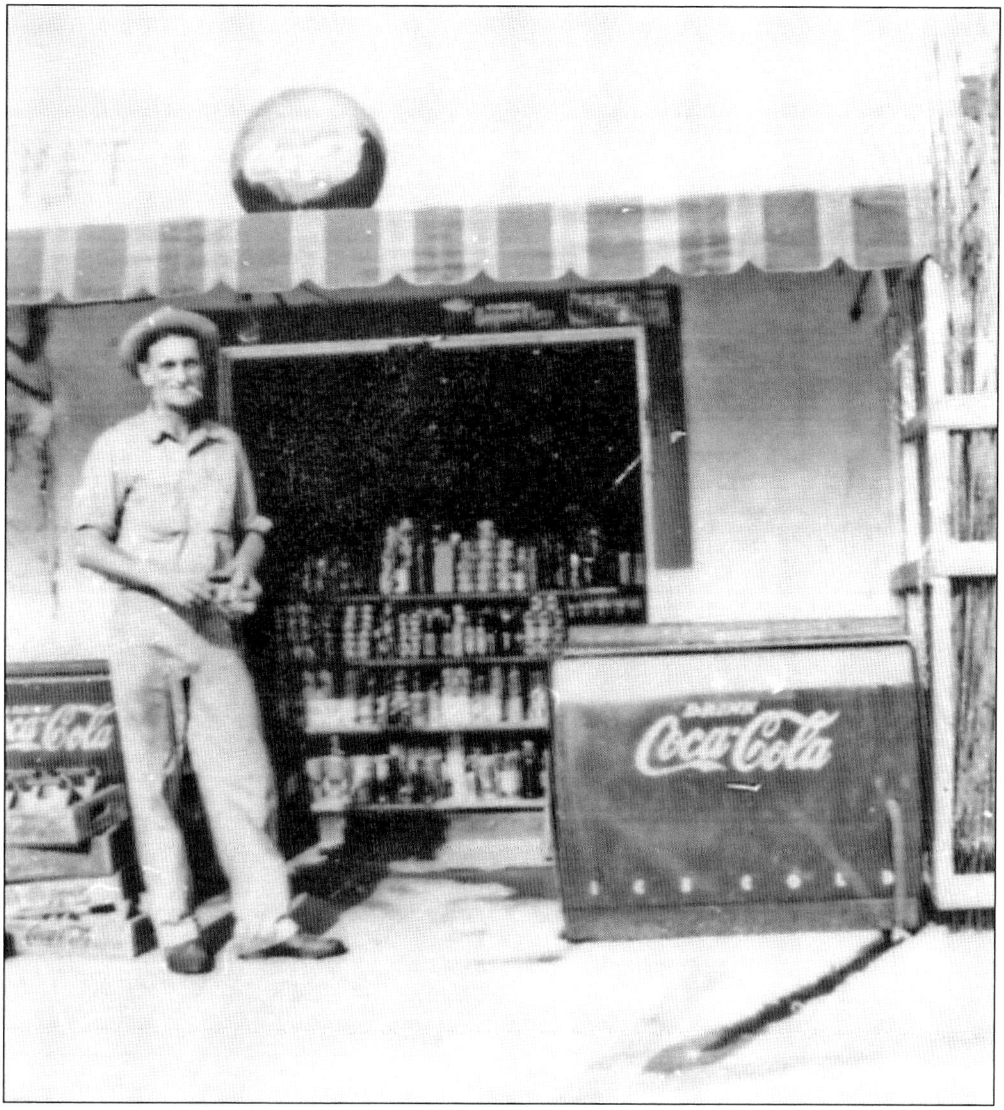

A small grocery stand, locally remembered as the Fruit Stand by longtime Bossier City residents, is featured in this undated photograph. An unidentified man stands in front of it. The Fruit Stand was located next to the Bossier Ice Company. (Courtesy of Noel Memorial Library.)

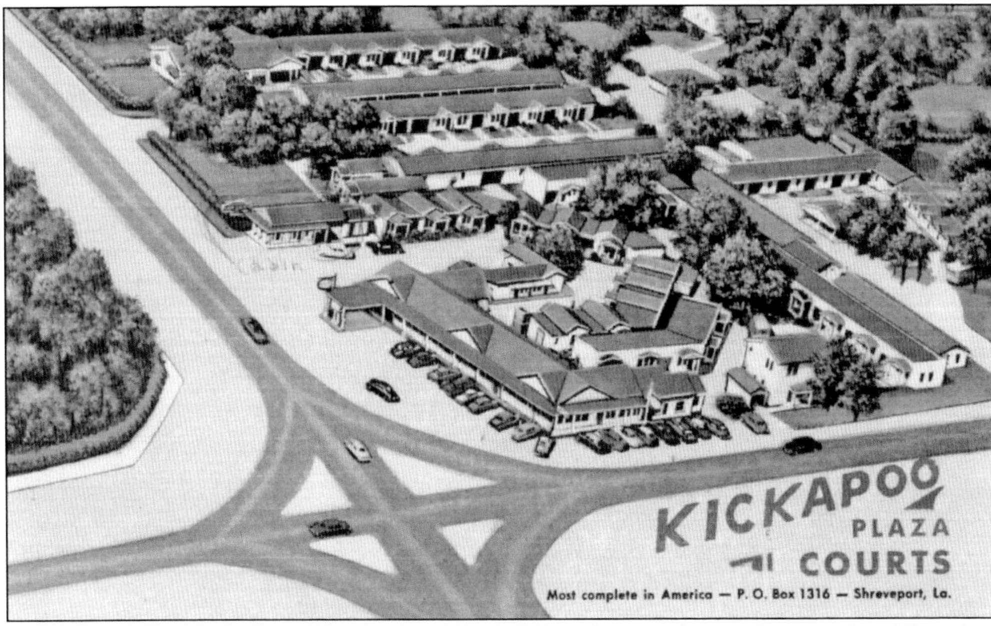

This is an original early-1950s postcard advertising Kickapoo Plaza in Bossier City. The plaza had guest cabins, trailer courts, a service station, and a café. The plaza was located on the corner of East Texas and Benton Roads, and it functioned as a rest stop for travelers along Highway 80. There is a shopping center with the same name now located in the original plaza. (Courtesy of Bossier Parish Library Historical Center.)

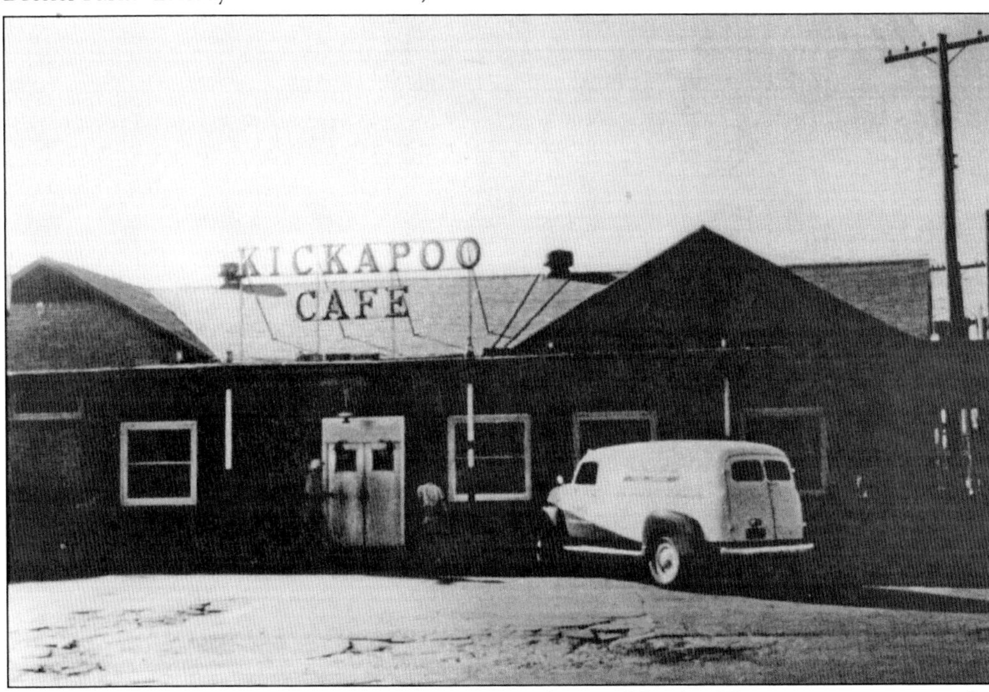

Kickapoo Cafe, pictured here in 1935, was open most hours of the day. The restaurant was popular with locals as well as guests staying at the Kickapoo Plaza. (Courtesy of Bossier Parish Library Historical Center.)

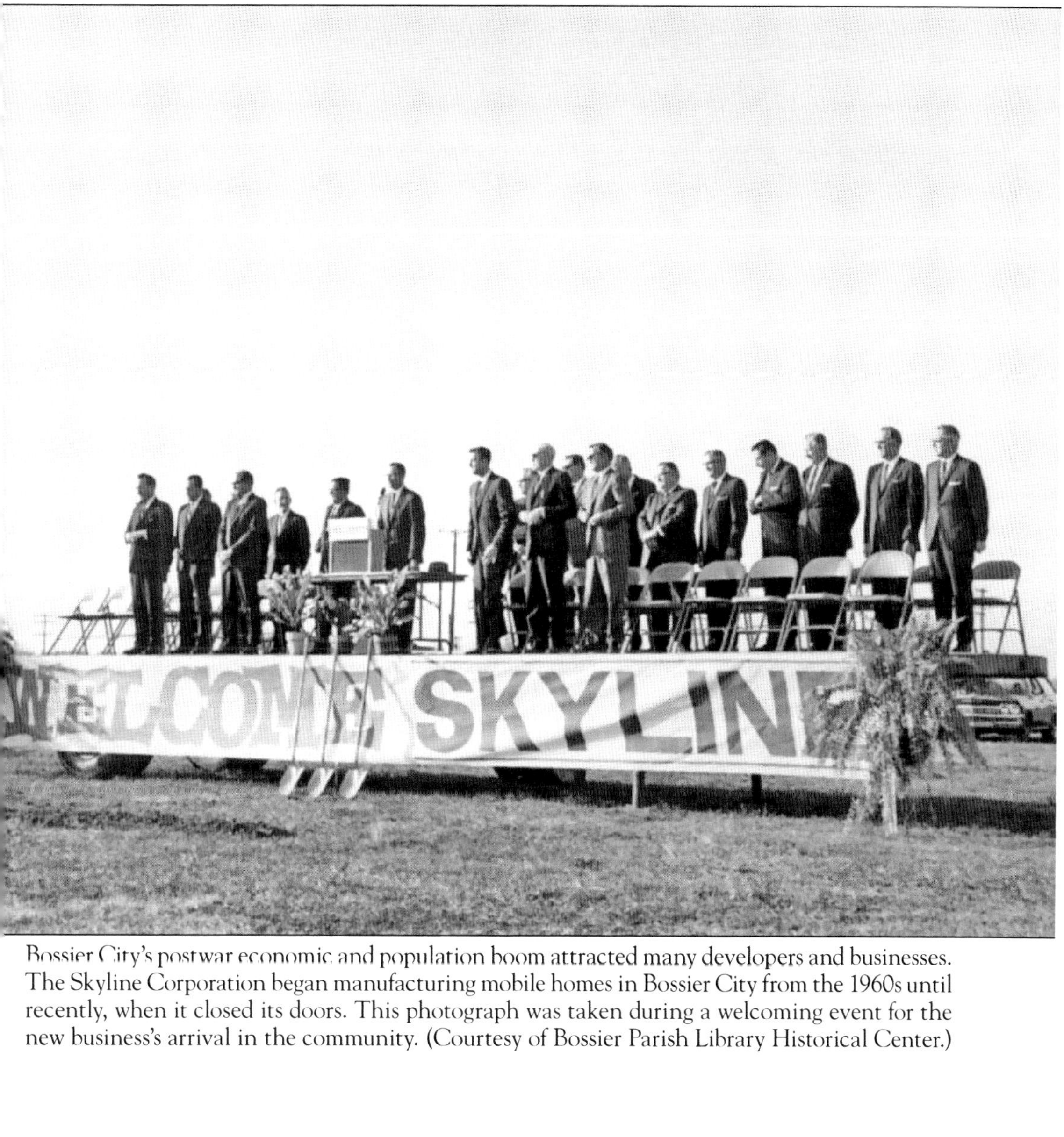

Bossier City's postwar economic and population boom attracted many developers and businesses. The Skyline Corporation began manufacturing mobile homes in Bossier City from the 1960s until recently, when it closed its doors. This photograph was taken during a welcoming event for the new business's arrival in the community. (Courtesy of Bossier Parish Library Historical Center.)

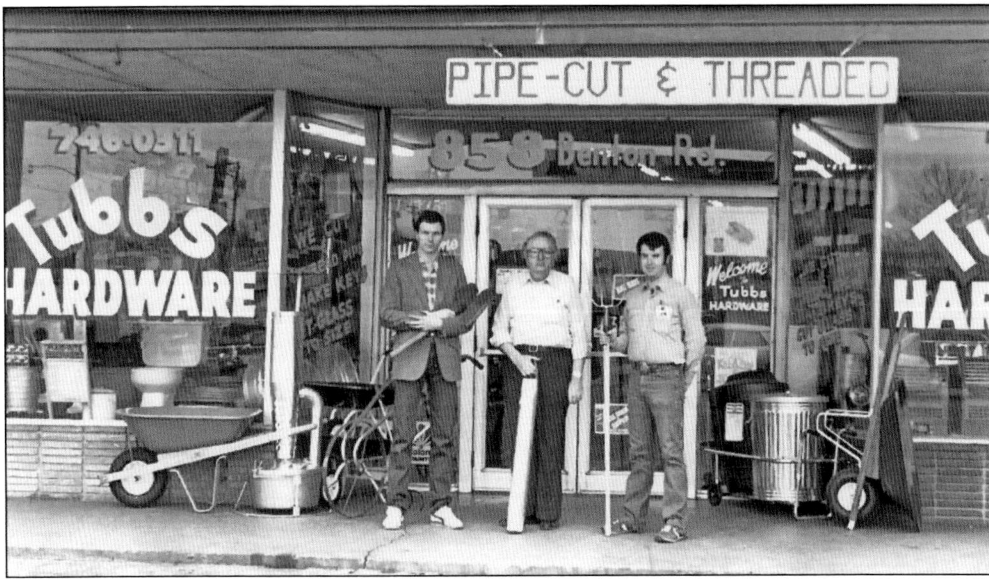

Tubbs Hardware, pictured above in the early 1980s, can trace its lineage all the way to 1922, when Holmes Hardware opened in downtown Bossier City. The owner, Don Tubbs, began working at the store when he was 12 and eventually purchased it. At the time of the photograph, Tubbs Hardware was located at 858 Benton Road. Within the store, customers could have pipe cut and threaded, get keys made, and have glass cut to size. Today, the store has two locations (one of which is pictured below), and its offerings have expanded, as is evident by its slogan, "We have it." (Courtesy of the Tubbs family.)

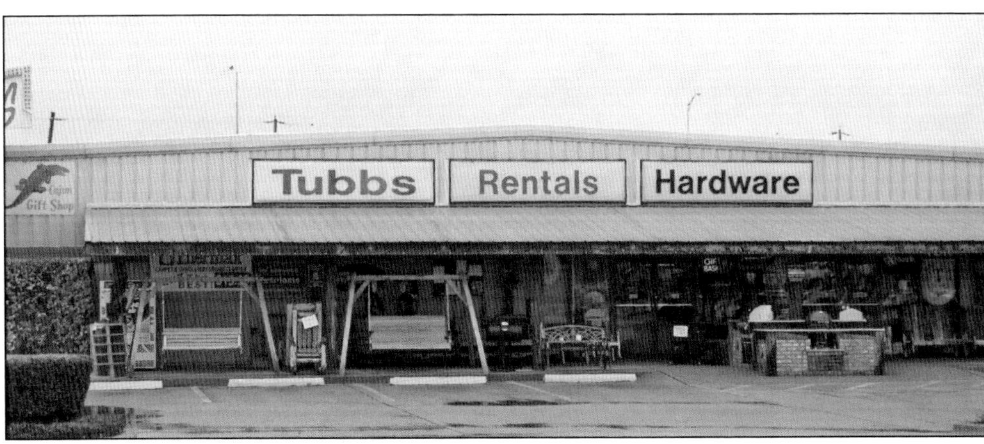

Two

Bossier City and the Military
Soldiers, Civil Servants, and Municipal Services

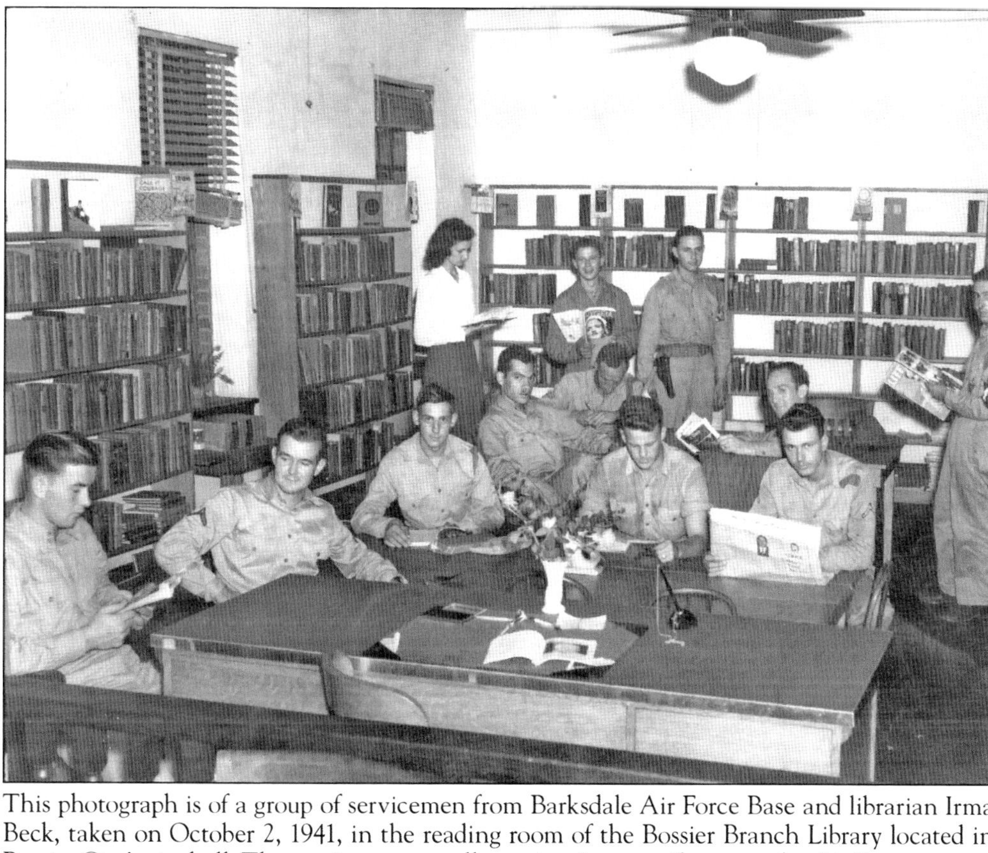

This photograph is of a group of servicemen from Barksdale Air Force Base and librarian Irma Beck, taken on October 2, 1941, in the reading room of the Bossier Branch Library located in Bossier City's city hall. The servicemen are all wearing Army uniforms, as the Air Force was not yet a separate branch. (Courtesy of Bossier Parish Library Historical Center.)

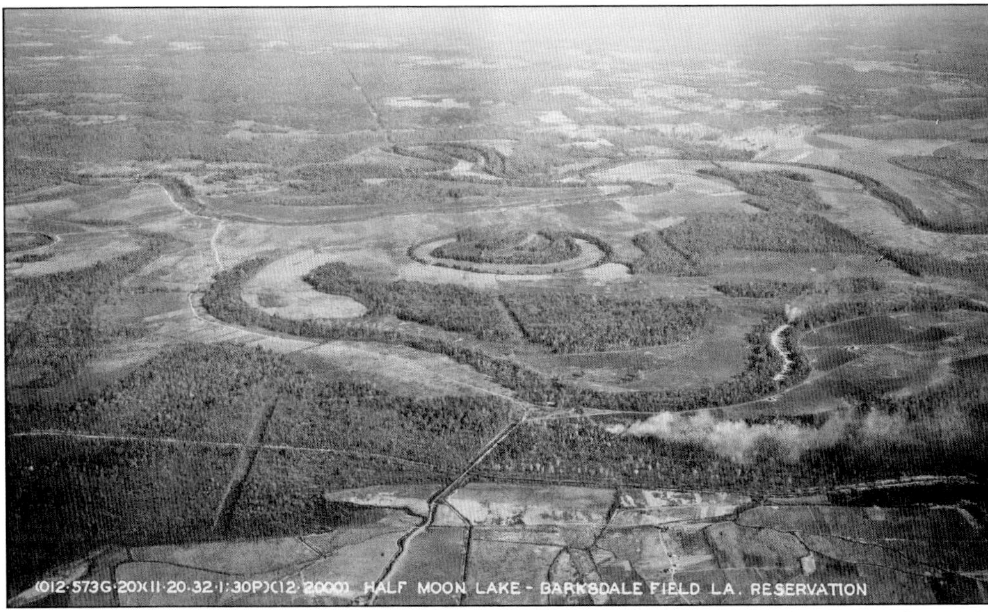

This photograph shows the eastern part of Barksdale AFB as it appeared in 1932. Over 800 landowners and farmers were moved to establish the base. Several pecan trees still stand on the base as a reminder of the old groves. In the center is Moon Lake, which dried up during the drought of 2011. (Courtesy of Bossier Parish Library Historical Center.)

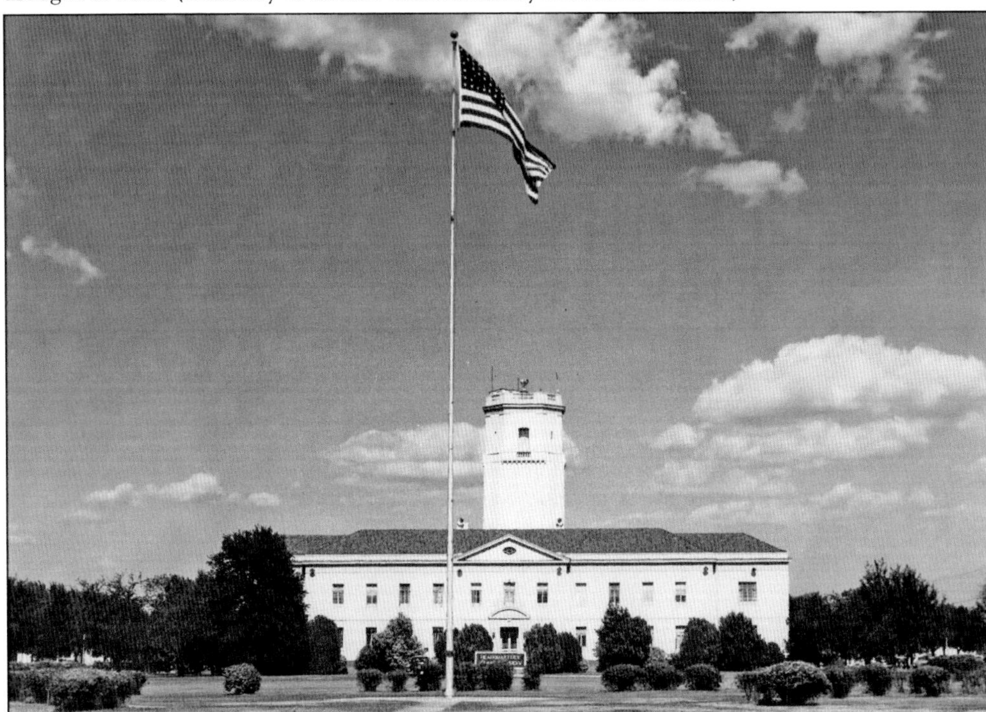

Pictured here in the 1940s are the base headquarters building and the water tower, just visible behind the building. The water tower was originally just a painted standpipe, but it was bricked over in 1934 for aesthetic purposes. (Courtesy of Noel Memorial Library.)

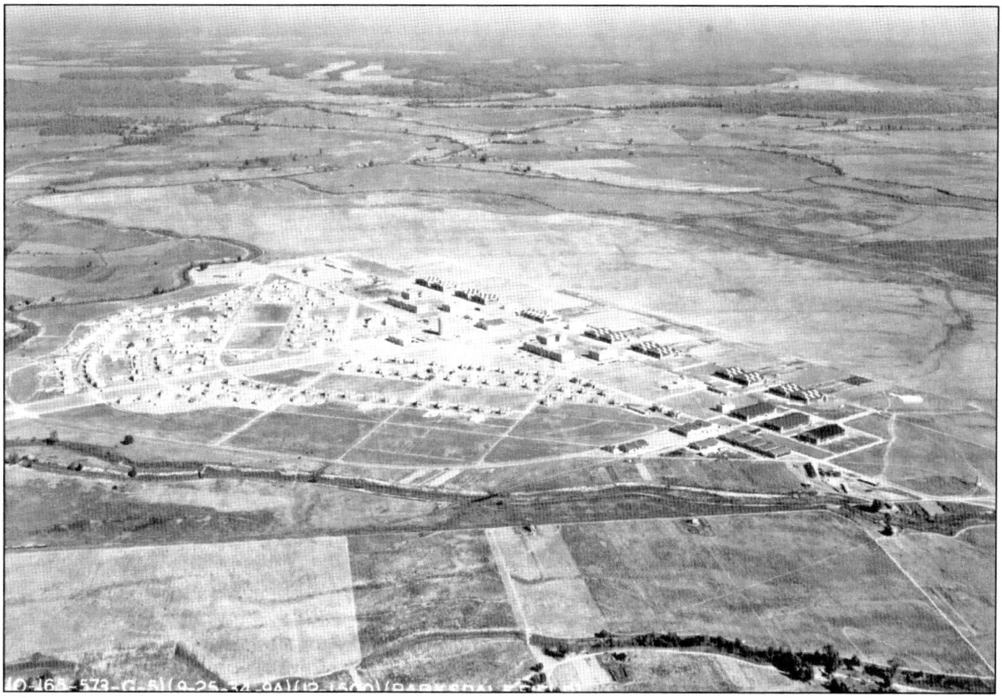

This view is of the main base as it appeared in 1934. The symmetrical layout of the base reflects the vision of its designers. (Courtesy of Noel Memorial Library.)

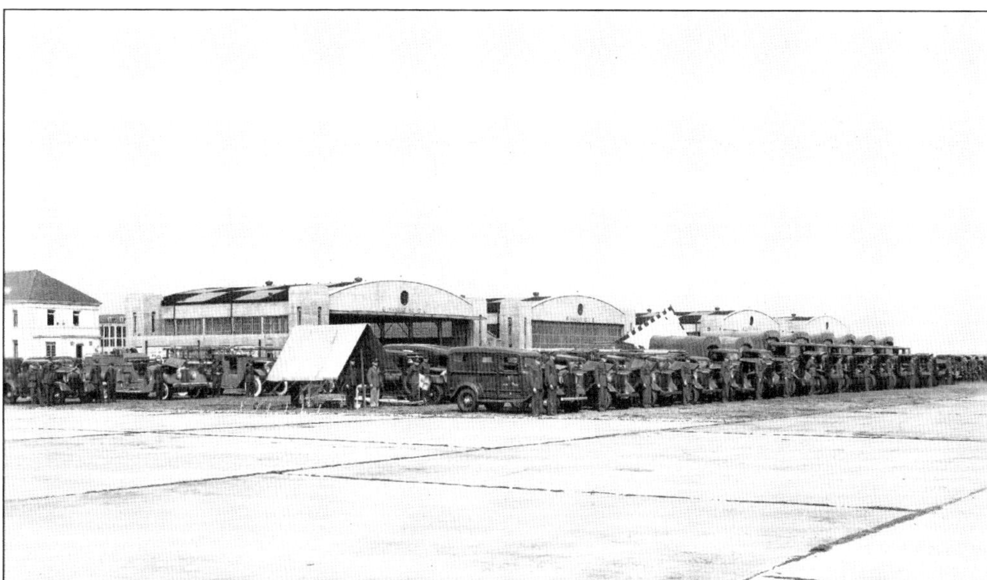

Barksdale's transportation wing is pictured during a 1937 review. (Courtesy of Bossier Parish Library Historical Center.)

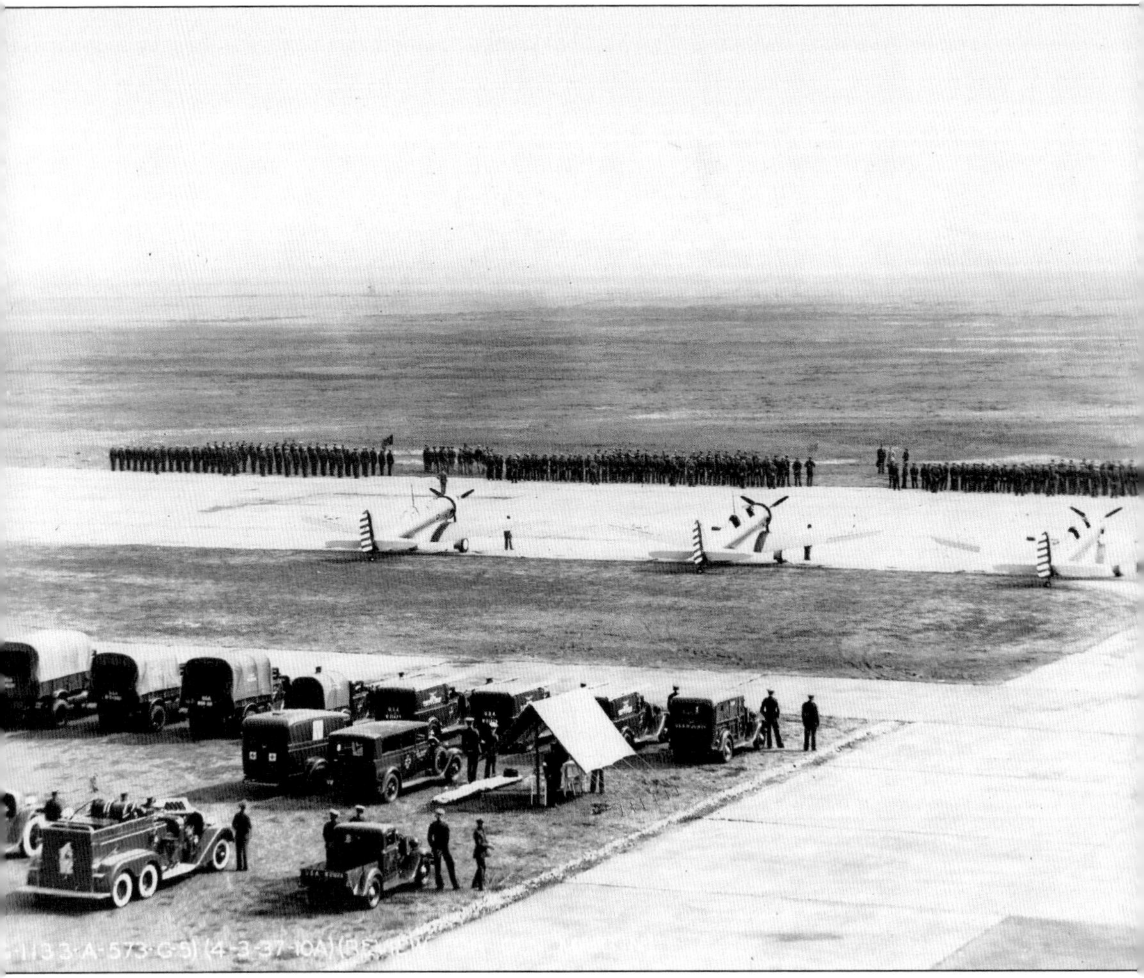

As seen in both this photograph and the image on the previous page, Barksdale had a large fleet of non-aerial vehicles under its command. (Courtesy of Bossier Parish Library Historical Center.)

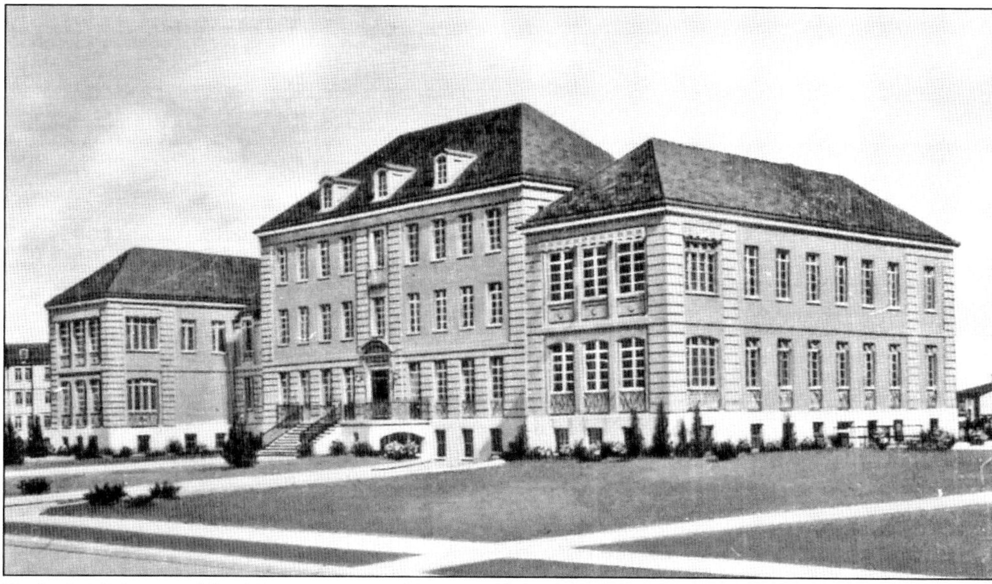

Barksdale's hospital building is pictured here in the 1930s before it was converted to offices and a new facility was constructed on the southern end of the base. The building currently houses the 2nd Civil Engineering Squadron offices. (Courtesy of Noel Memorial Library.)

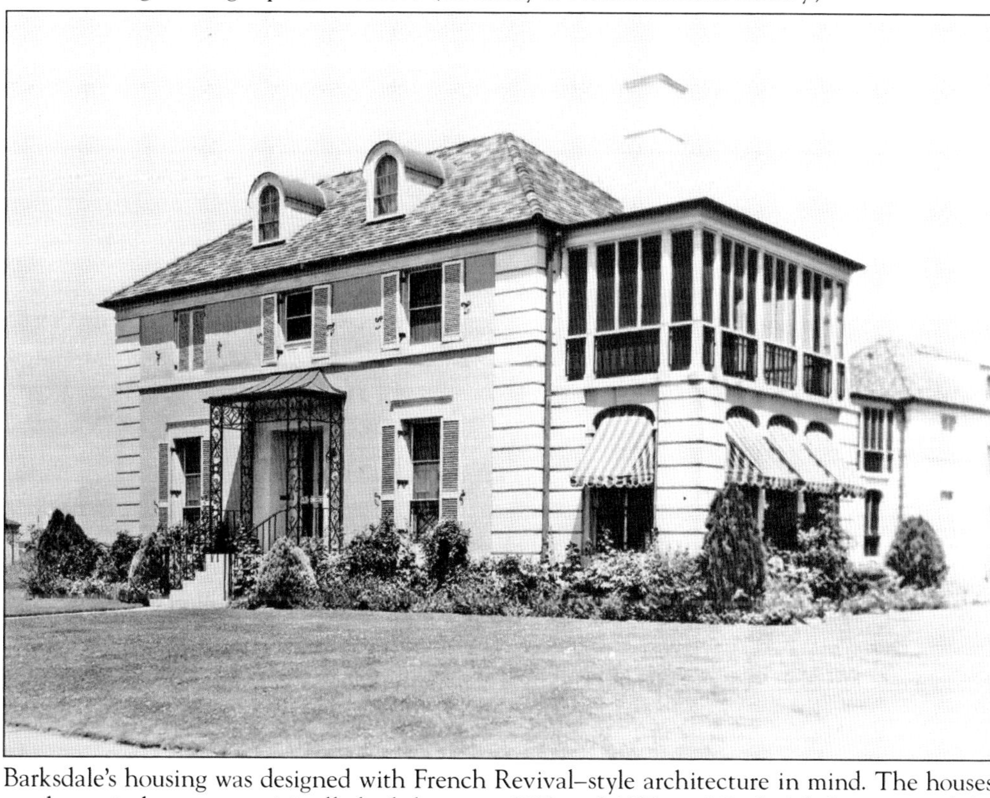

Barksdale's housing was designed with French Revival–style architecture in mind. The houses on the main base were originally built between 1932 and 1959, and Barksdale has some of the oldest continuously occupied housing in the military. These homes were placed in the National Register of Historic Places in 1992. (Courtesy of Noel Memorial Library.)

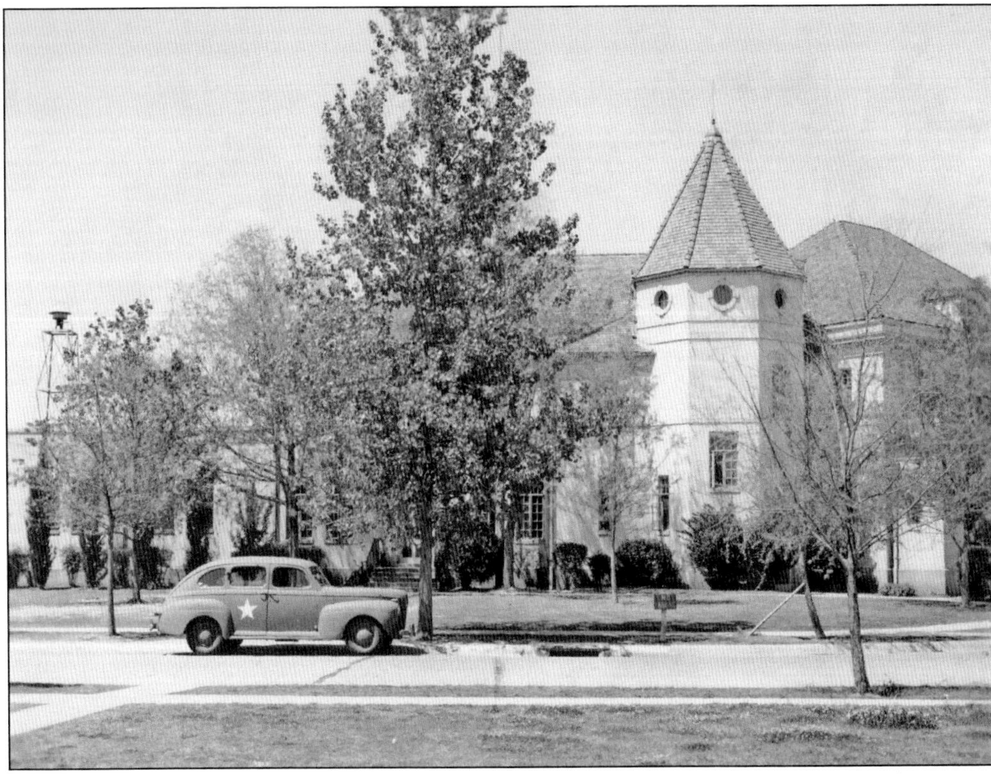

The building seen here is the guardhouse, which housed the military police. "The Palace," as it was known, was also the location of the fire station and the jail. It served as the base jail until just a few years ago. Future plans for the building include relocating the emergency management unit there. (Courtesy of Bossier Parish Library Historical Center.)

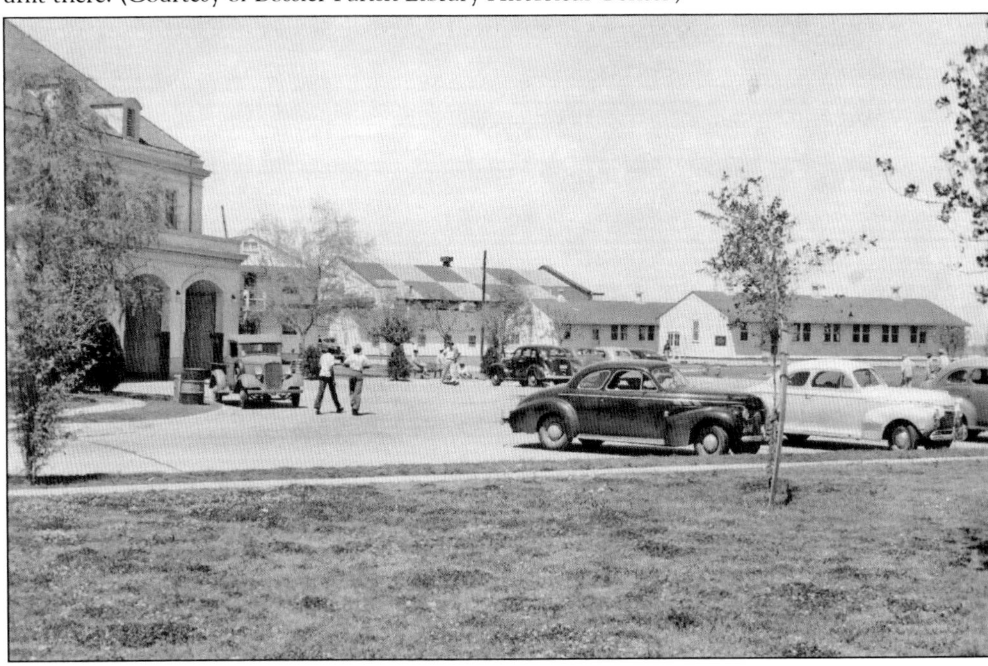

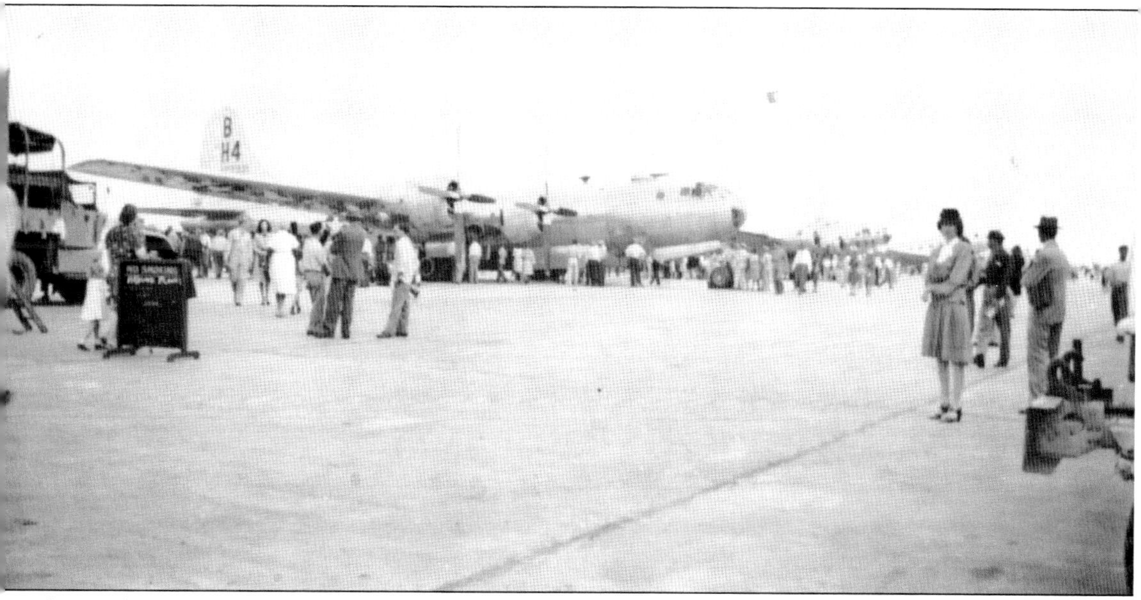

The mighty B-29 Flying Fortress is on display for the public to see on Air Force Day in 1946. (Courtesy of Bossier Parish Library Historical Center)

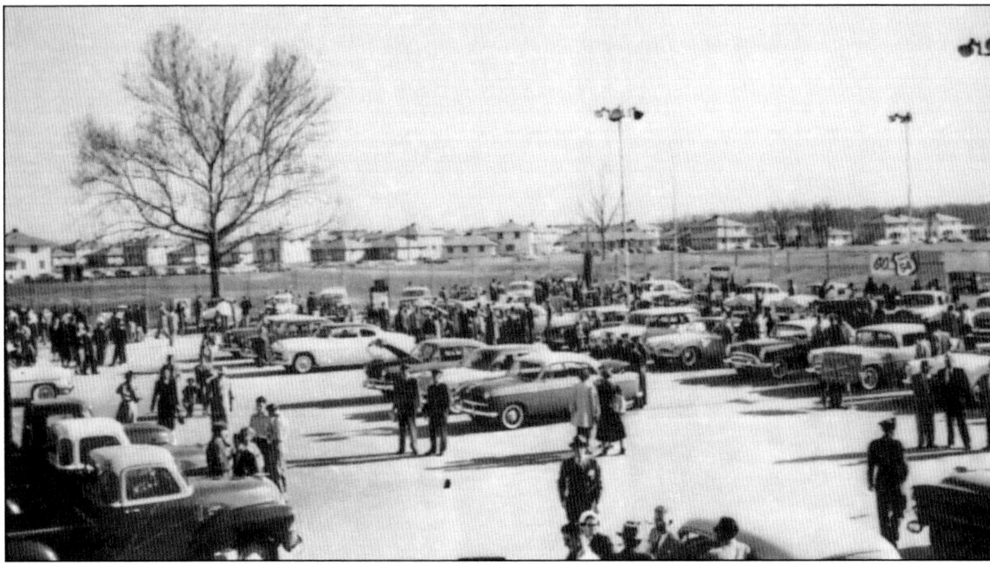

Part of living on base included MWR (morale, welfare, and recreation) events. Pictured here are car shows taking place during the 1950s. The events also allowed the larger Bossier City community to interact with base inhabitants. (Courtesy of Noel Memorial Library.)

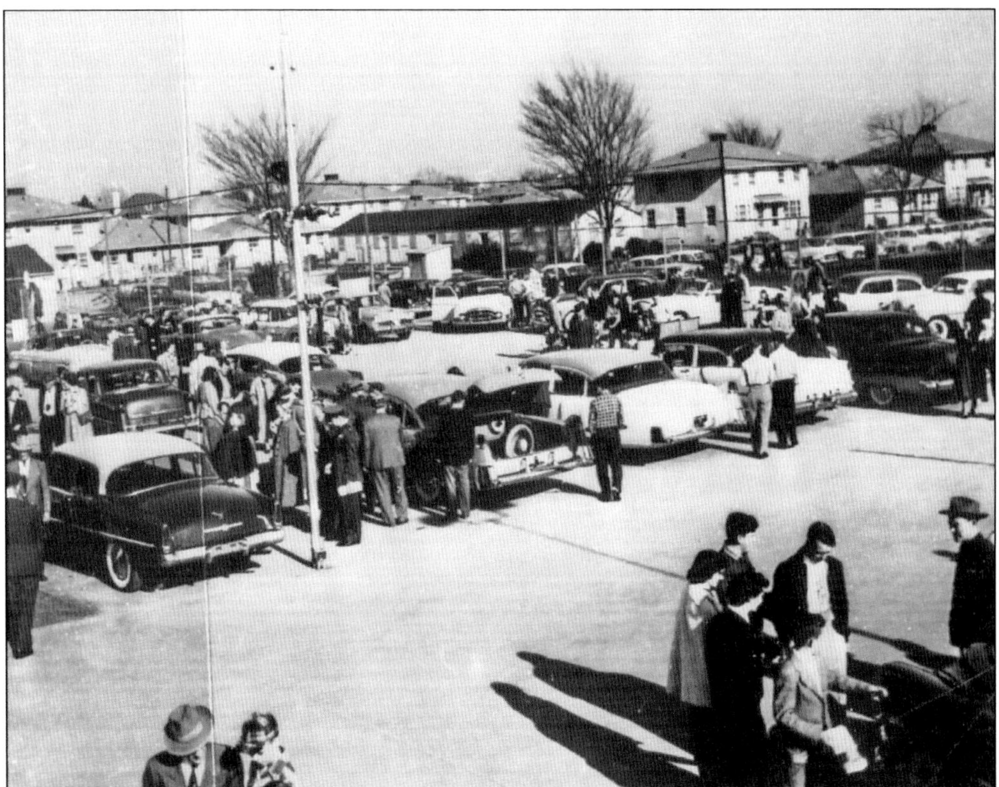

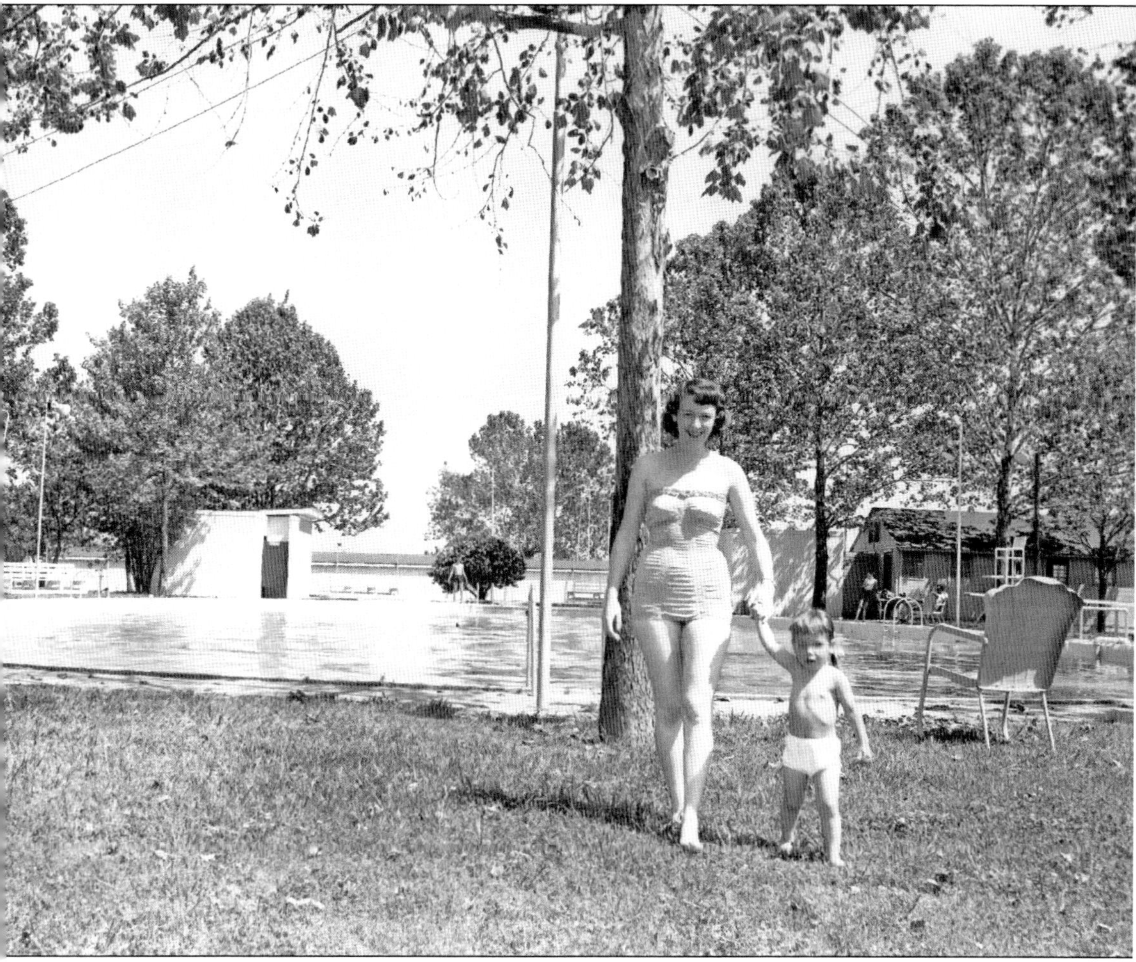

Pictured here are an unidentified woman and her child at the Barksdale Officer's Club pool in the 1940s. The pool later had a wall built around it and is still in use. (Courtesy of Noel Memorial Library.)

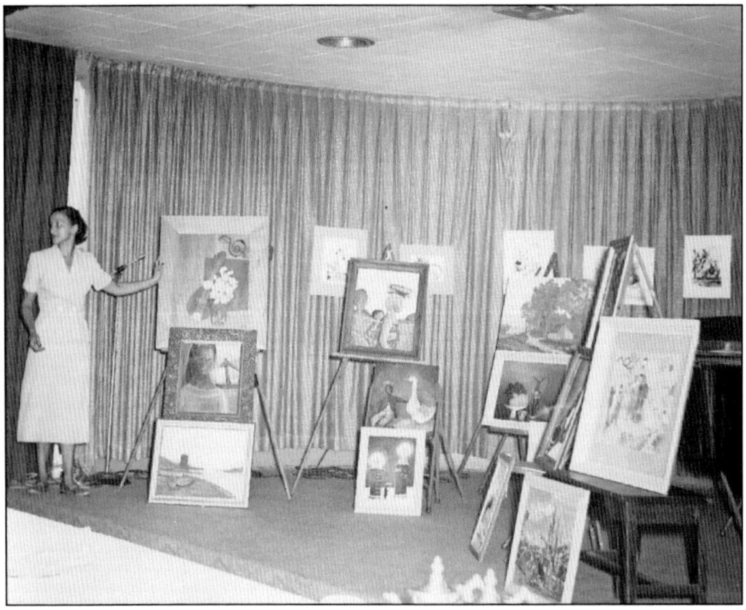

The Barksdale Officers' Wives Club hosted many events throughout the years. This photograph is of Jackie Pearl, chairwoman of the Art Club Show, during an event in 1953. (Courtesy of Bossier Parish Library Historical Center.)

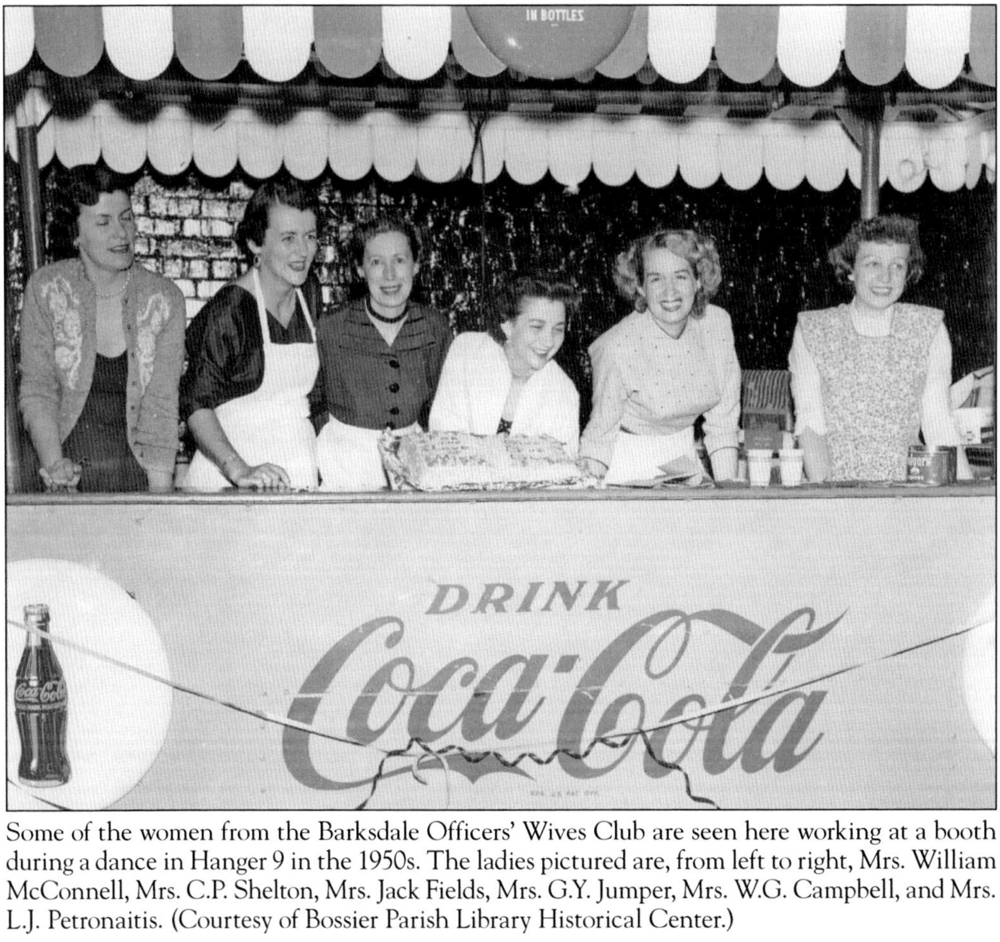

Some of the women from the Barksdale Officers' Wives Club are seen here working at a booth during a dance in Hanger 9 in the 1950s. The ladies pictured are, from left to right, Mrs. William McConnell, Mrs. C.P. Shelton, Mrs. Jack Fields, Mrs. G.Y. Jumper, Mrs. W.G. Campbell, and Mrs. L.J. Petronaitis. (Courtesy of Bossier Parish Library Historical Center.)

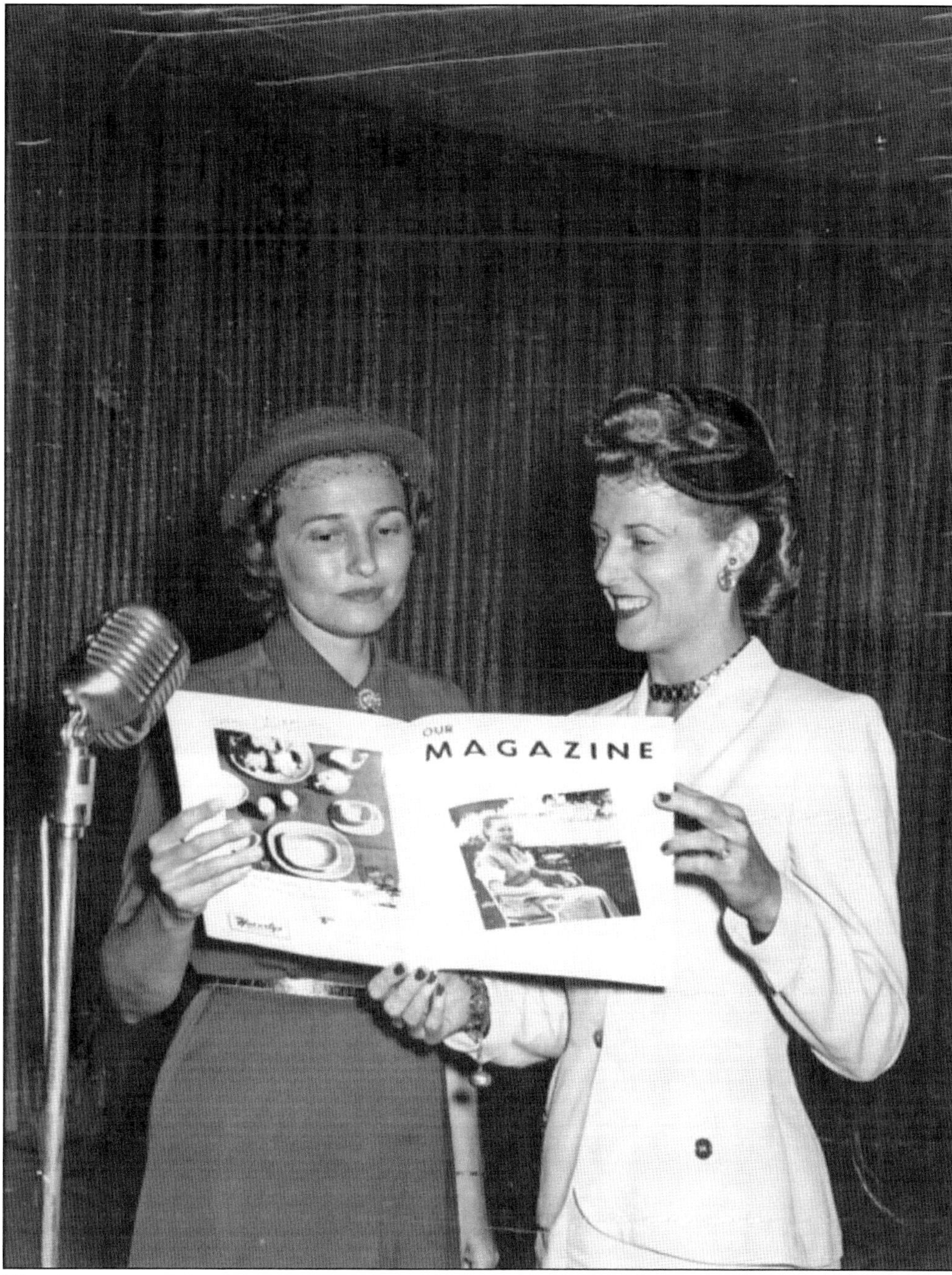

The first copy of *Our Magazine* is presented to Agnes Finlan (left), president of the Barksdale Officers' Wives Club, by the magazine's editor, Zina Worley, in October 1952. (Courtesy of Bossier Parish Library Historical Center.)

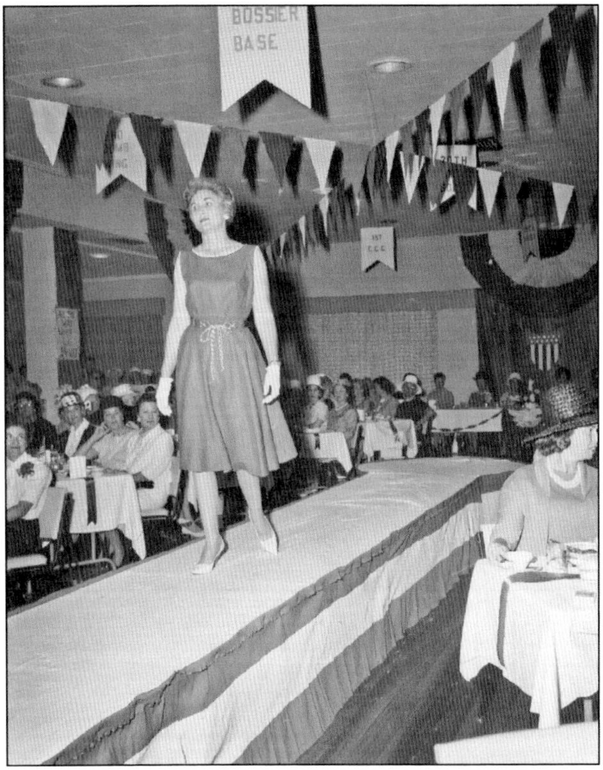

These women are taking part in a fashion show put on by the Barksdale Officers' Wives Club in the 1950s. The sign above reads, "Bossier Base," the name of the Air Reserve base that included all the buildings located on the east side of the airfield, separate from Barksdale at the time. (Courtesy of Bossier Parish Library Historical Center.)

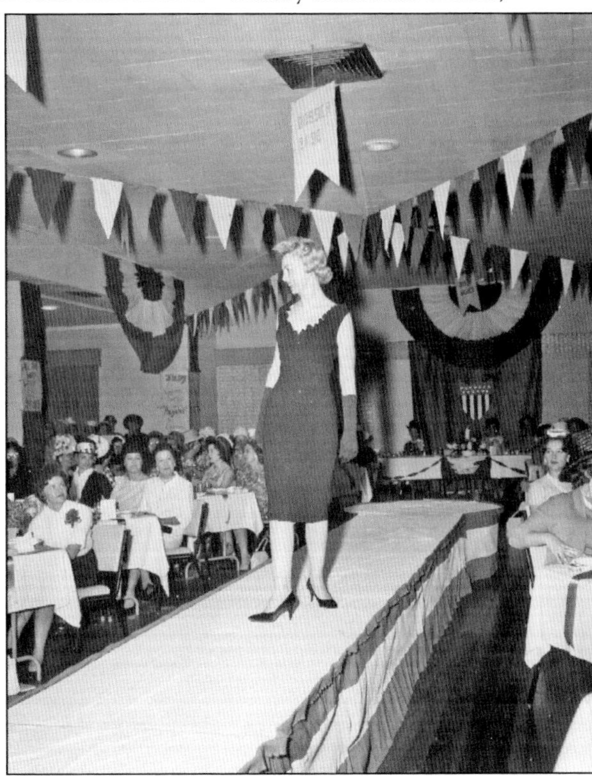

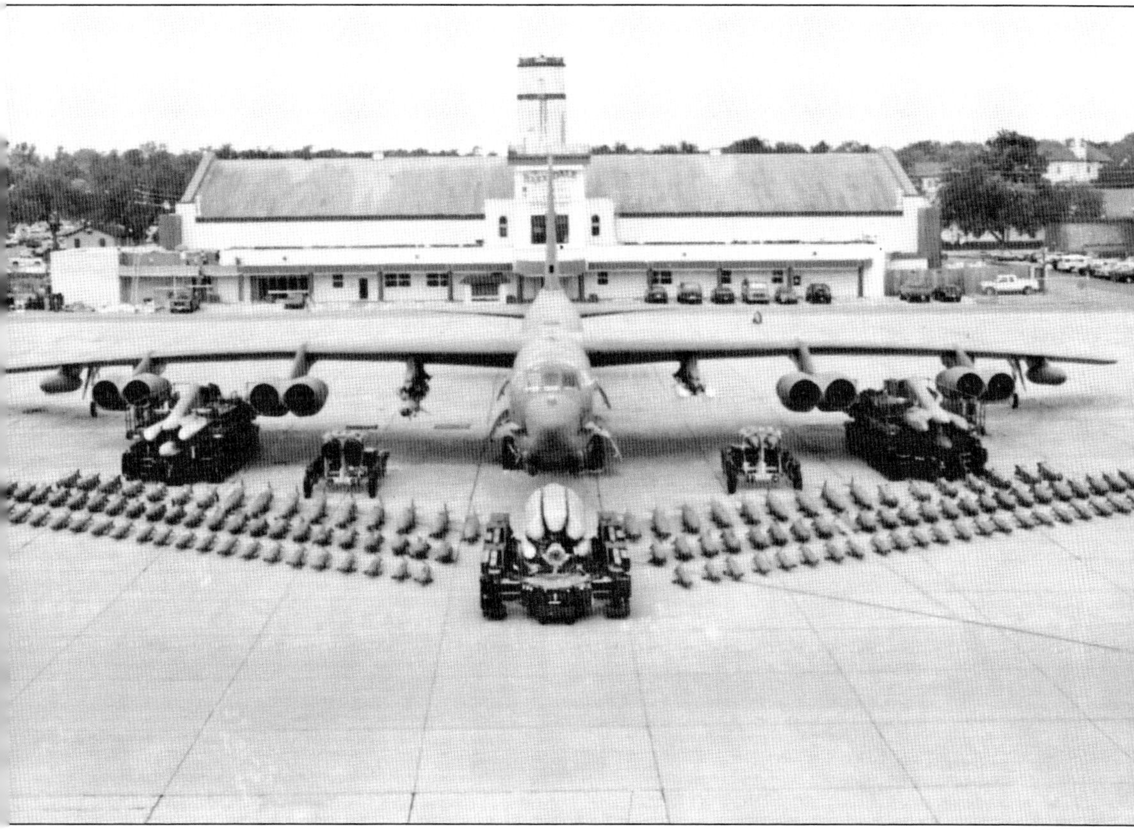

Pictured here are a B-52 Strato Fortress bomber and the many different types of ordnance it can carry. Barksdale AFB is one of two bases that have full-time, active-duty B-52 squadrons. In the background are the original control tower and the old water tower. (Courtesy of Bossier Parish Library Historical Center.)

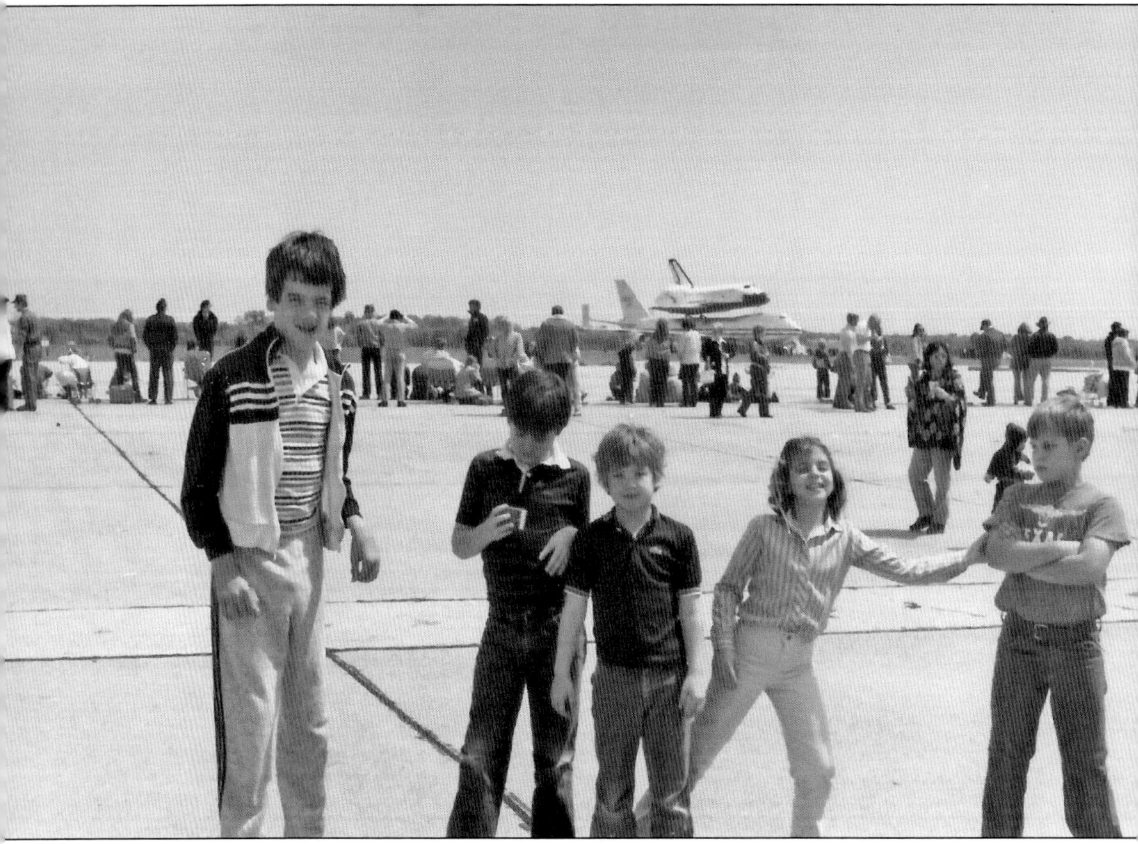

In April 1982, the space shuttle *Columbia* was ferried from the White Sands Missile Range in New Mexico to the Kennedy Space Center in Florida via Barksdale AFB. Several thousand people from around the Ark-La-Tex came to see the shuttle land while on the back of a 747. From left to right are Doug Jones, Chris Jones, Kevin Jones, Mary Beth Harrell, and Jeff Harrell. (Courtesy of the Jones family.)

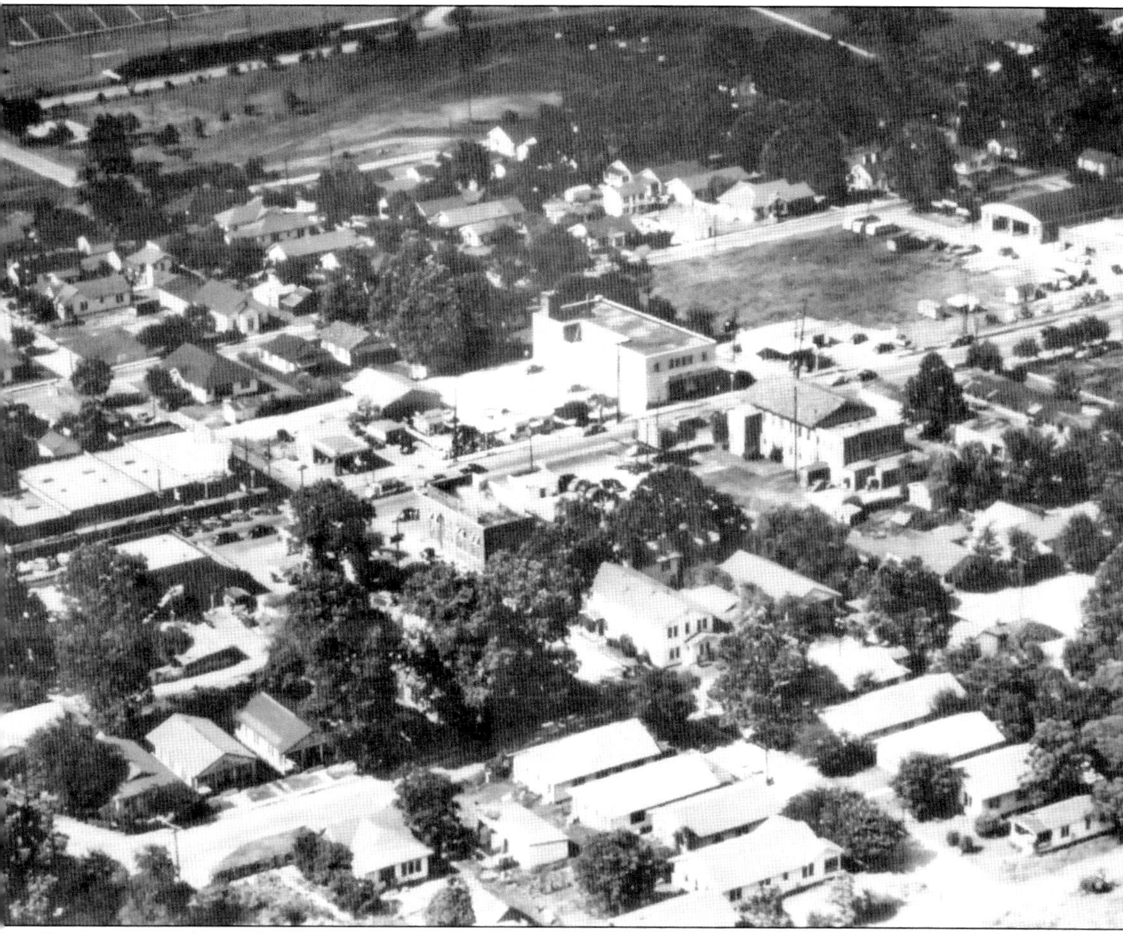

This is an aerial view looking north of downtown Bossier City in the late 1940s or early 1950s. The building almost directly in the center is the Bossier Ice Company. The large building houses the Bossier Bank and Trust, and the structure directly across the street from it is the Bossier City Municipal Building. It was used as the city hall, jail, courthouse, library, and fire station at one time. (Courtesy of the Tubbs family.)

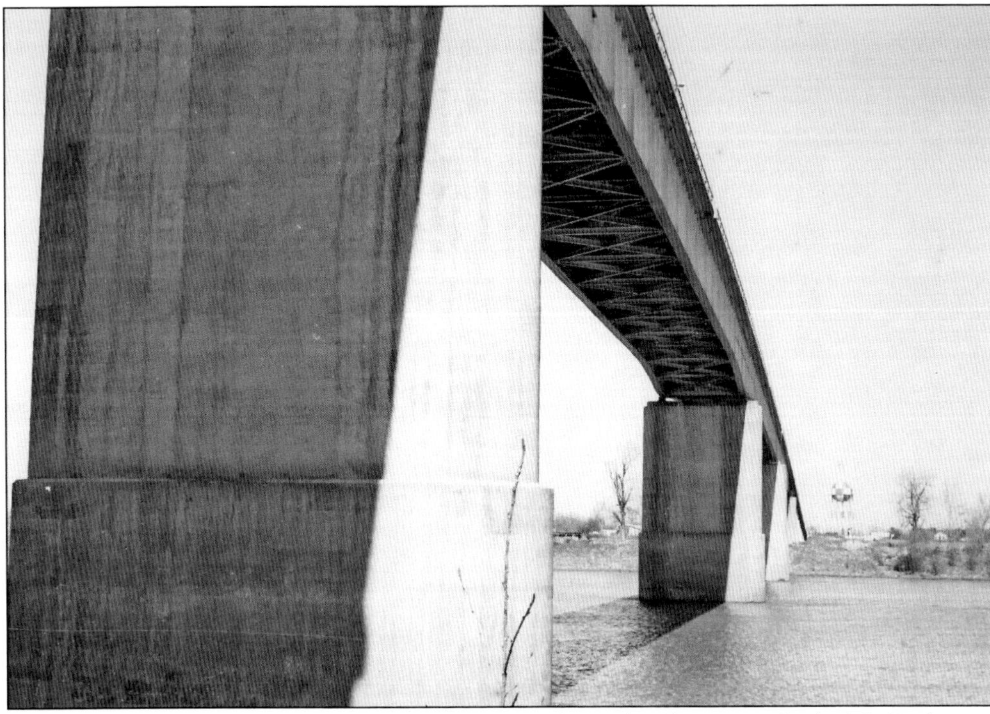

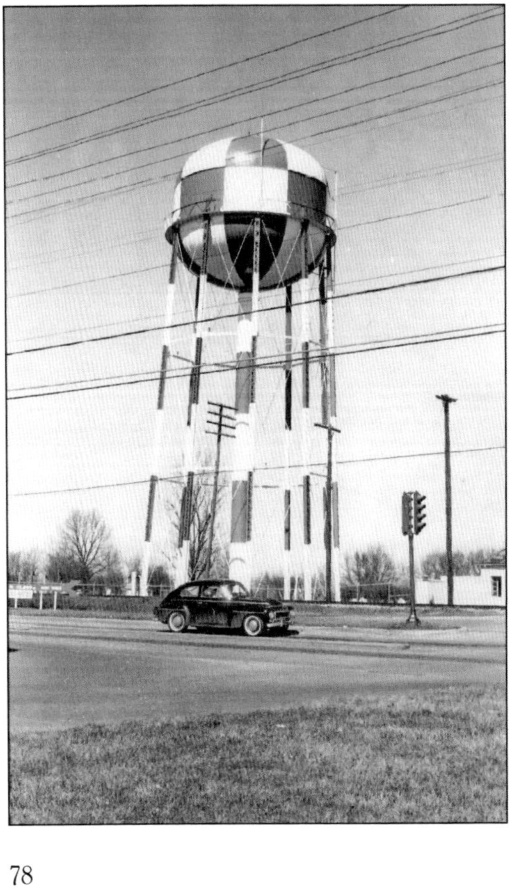

This is the Shreveport-Barksdale Bridge after its completion in the late 1950s. The bridge connected the east side of Shreveport to the main gate on the west side of the base. The water tower located near the gate can be seen in the background. (Courtesy of Bossier Parish Library Historical Center.)

The intersection of Shreveport-Barksdale and Barksdale Boulevards is pictured here in the late 1950s. The water tower still stands, although the intersection in front of it has grown considerably. (Courtesy of Bossier Parish Library Historical Center.)

Barefooted firemen and schoolchildren pose in the courtroom of the Bossier Municipal Building in the 1930s during a "community exercise." Chief Tipton is seated second from the right. (Courtesy of Bossier Parish Library Historical Center.)

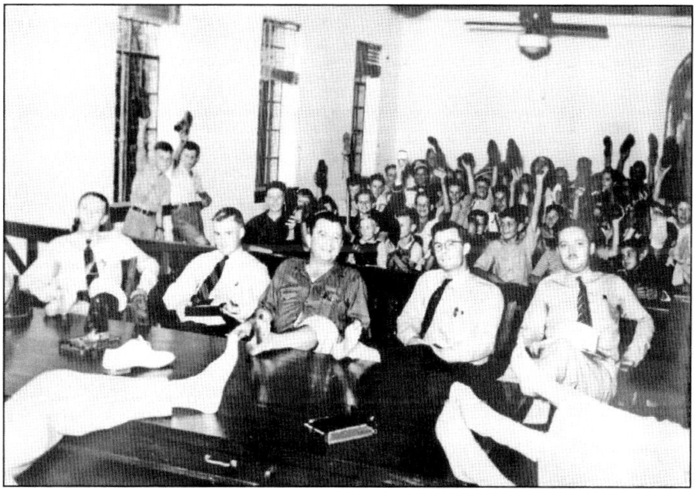

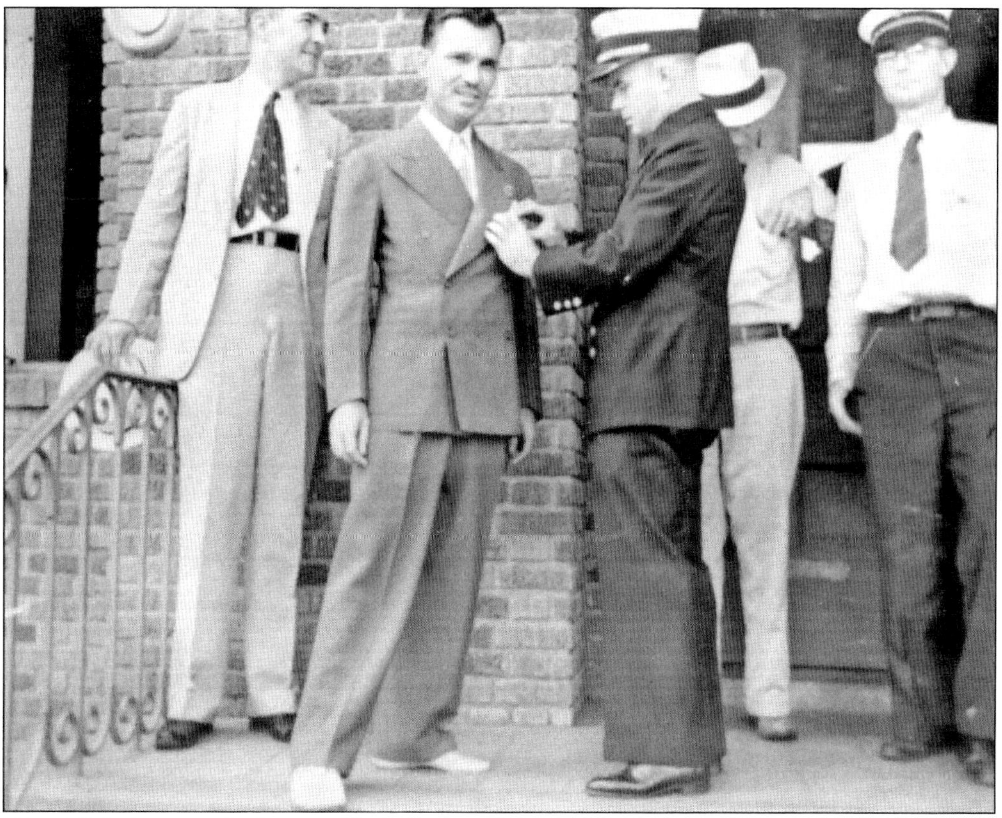

This 1928 photograph shows prominent local businessman Arthur Ray Teague (far left) and Capt. Ennis Mayfield Tipton (far right) looking on as Chief Huff congratulates a new fireman. In response to the fire of 1925, Bossier City established its own fire department, with Nathan G. Huff as the first chief. Huff and some volunteers maintained the department until 1932, when Bossier City bought its first truck and hired two full-time firemen. It was not until 1952 that Bossier City had a sizeable professional firefighting force; 18 recruits were placed on full-time status, and a new fire station was constructed next to the city building. (Courtesy of Bossier Parish Library Historical Center.)

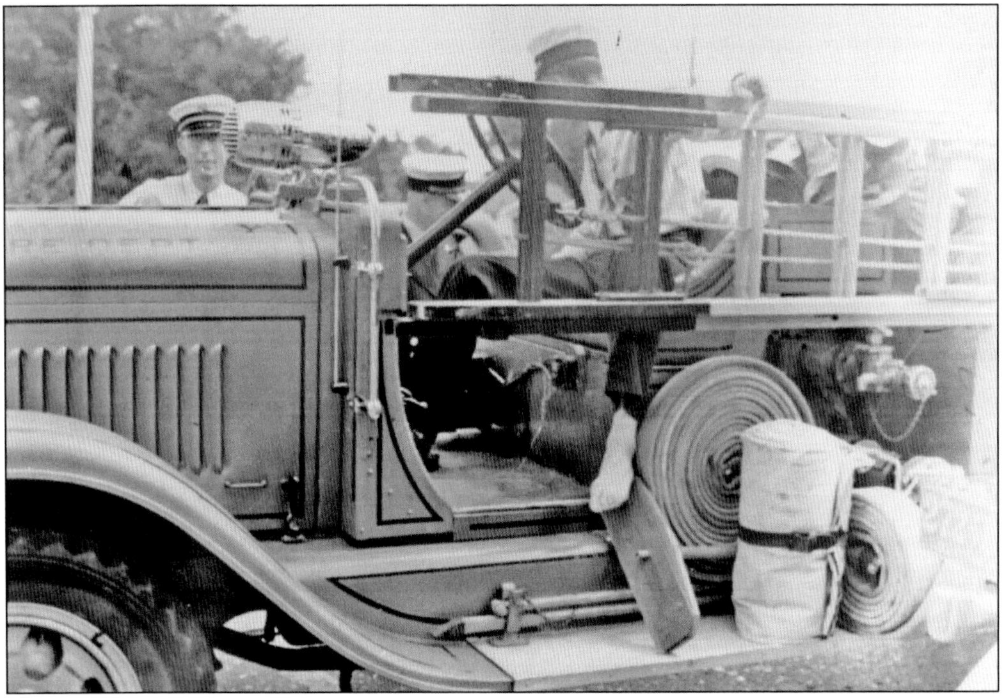

This pumper truck was the first equipment bought by Bossier City for its fire department. Pictured with the truck in 1931 are Capt. Ennis M. Tipton (far left), Chief Nathan S. Huff (standing behind the vehicle in full fire department dress uniform), and Harold Roy (in the driver's seat). (Courtesy of Bossier Parish Library Historical Center.)

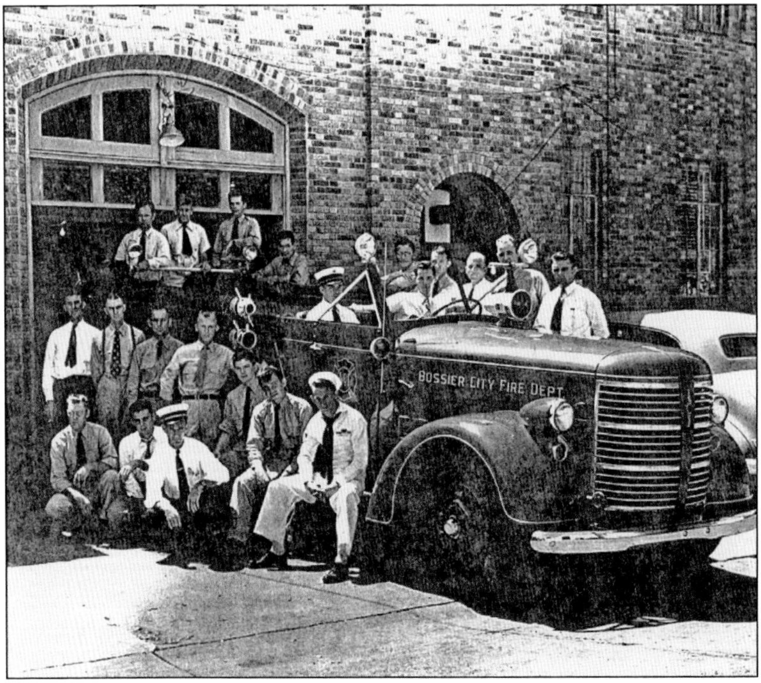

Volunteer and regular firefighters are pictured around 1942 on top of a new truck outside the Bossier City Fire Station at 630 Cane Avenue. This one bay was in the back of the Bossier City Municipal Building. This first fire department station would be utilized from 1928 until 1952, when a new station was built next door. (Courtesy of Bossier Parish Library Historical Center.)

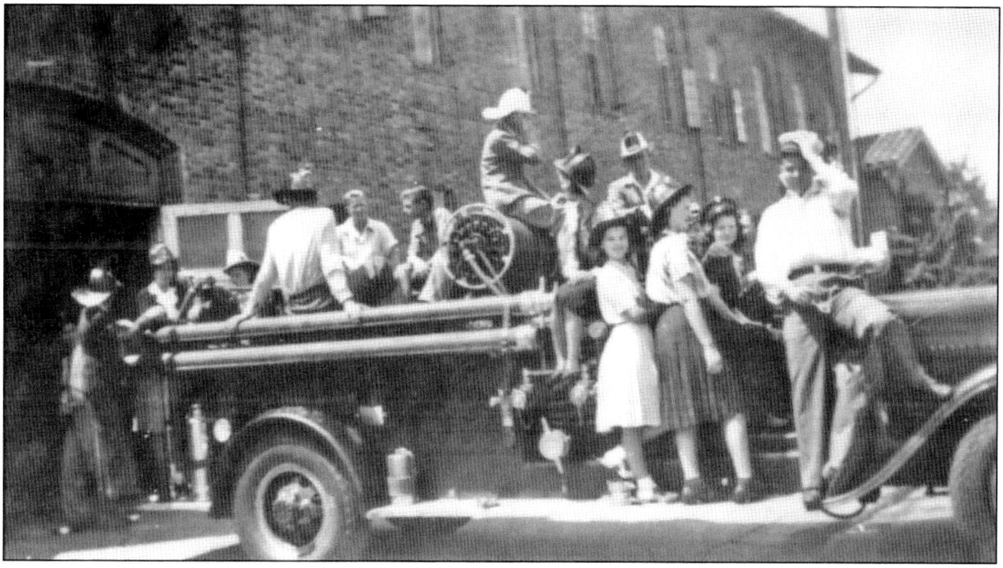

Above, a group of people is pictured standing on one of the fire department's trucks around 1950. At the time of this photograph, the fire department was still connected to the back of what is now the Bossier Arts Council building; the fire department's original doors are still there and intact today. In 1952, the fire department moved to a brand-new building next door. The image below shows the firefighters, both volunteer and regular, in front of one of the trucks. (Courtesy of Noel Memorial Library.)

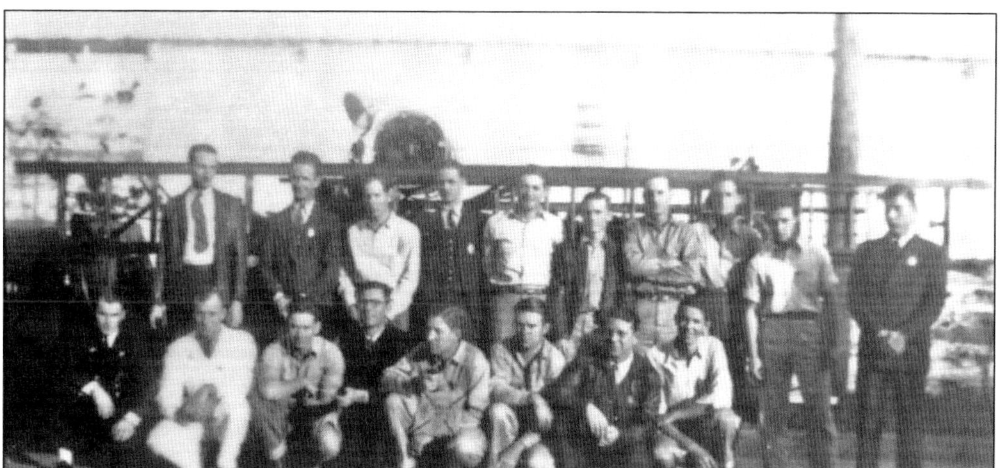

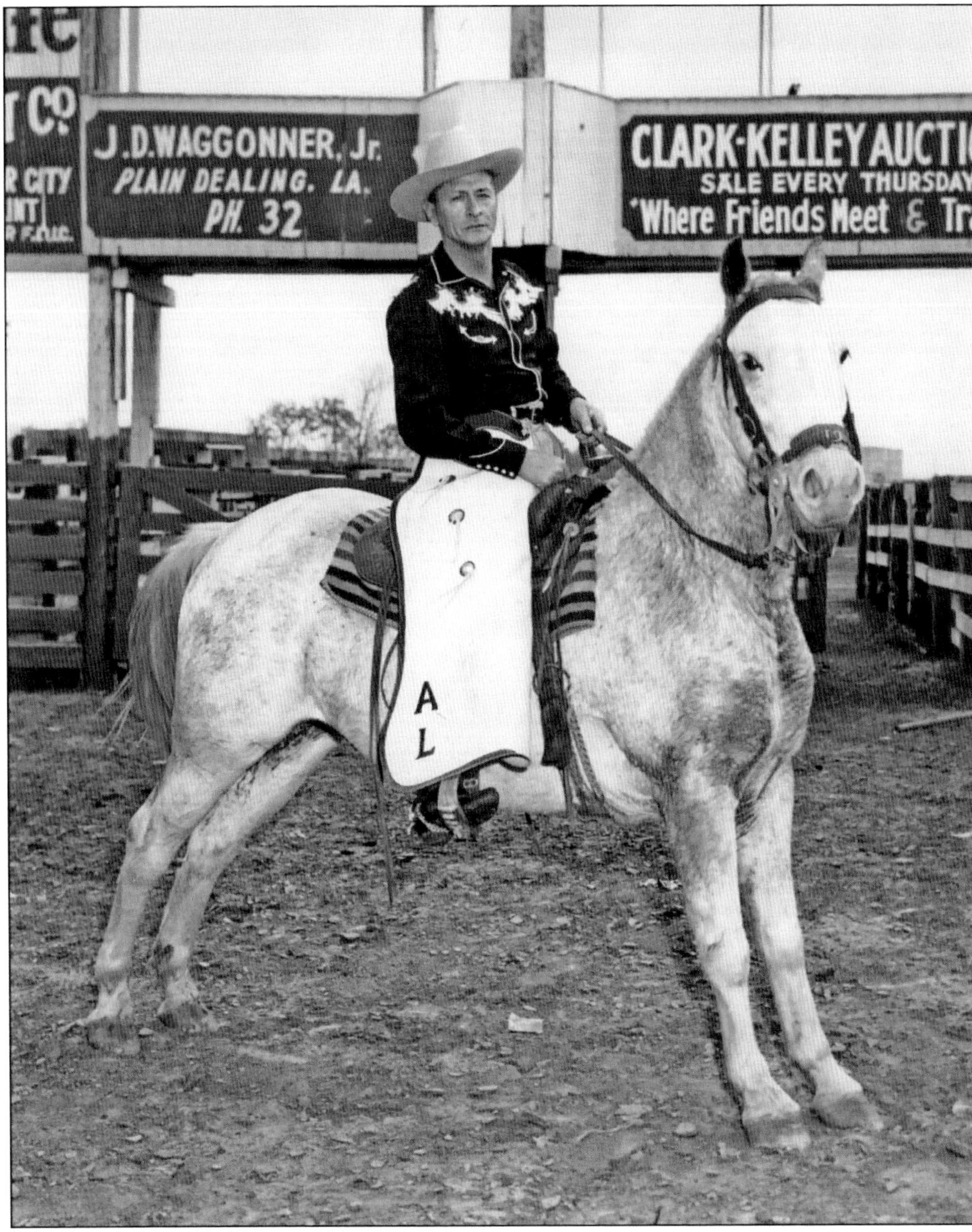

This 1953 photograph shows Bossier City Police captain Johnny Almer Jones Sr. posing on a Tennessee Walking horse that was owned by country music icon Hank Williams. His daughter Billie Jean married Williams the year before he died. (Courtesy of Bossier Parish Library Historical Center.)

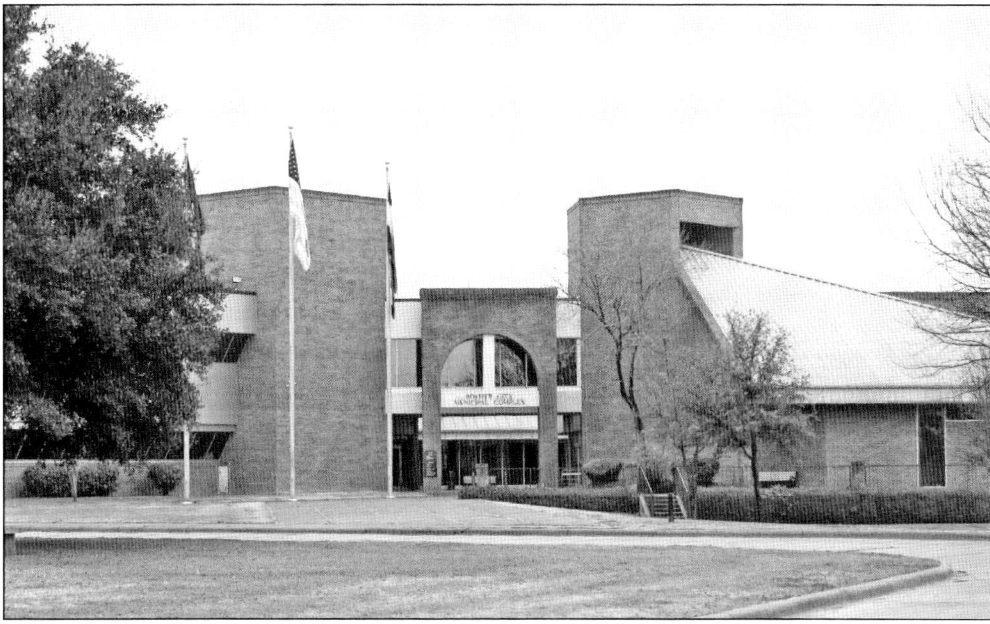

In 1986, Bossier City completed a grand municipal complex off of Benton Road that would replace the older buildings in downtown Bossier City. The image above shows the building that houses the civic center, courthouse, and municipal offices. The photograph below shows the front of the police and fire department buildings. (Courtesy of Robin Jones.)

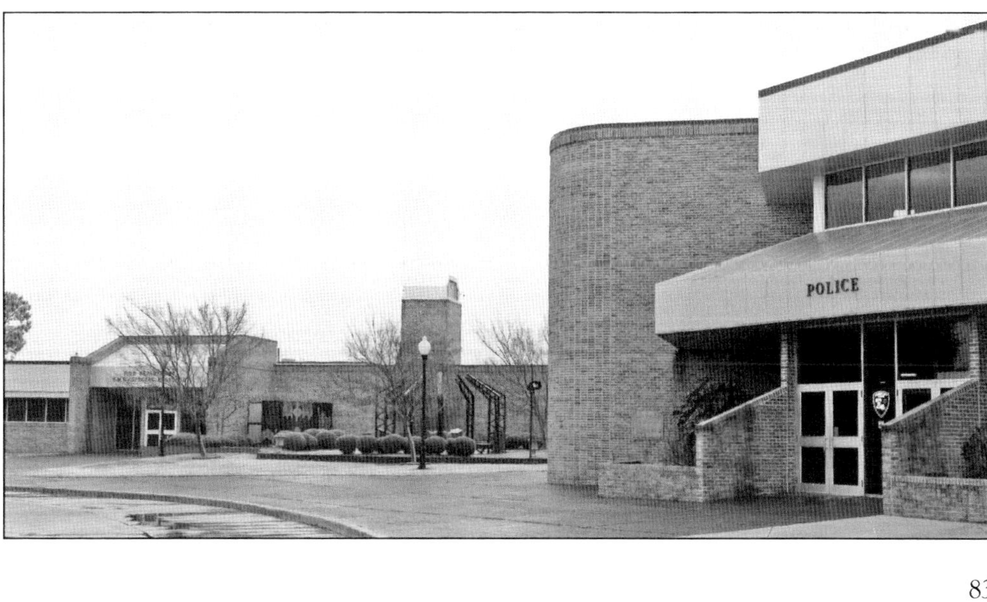

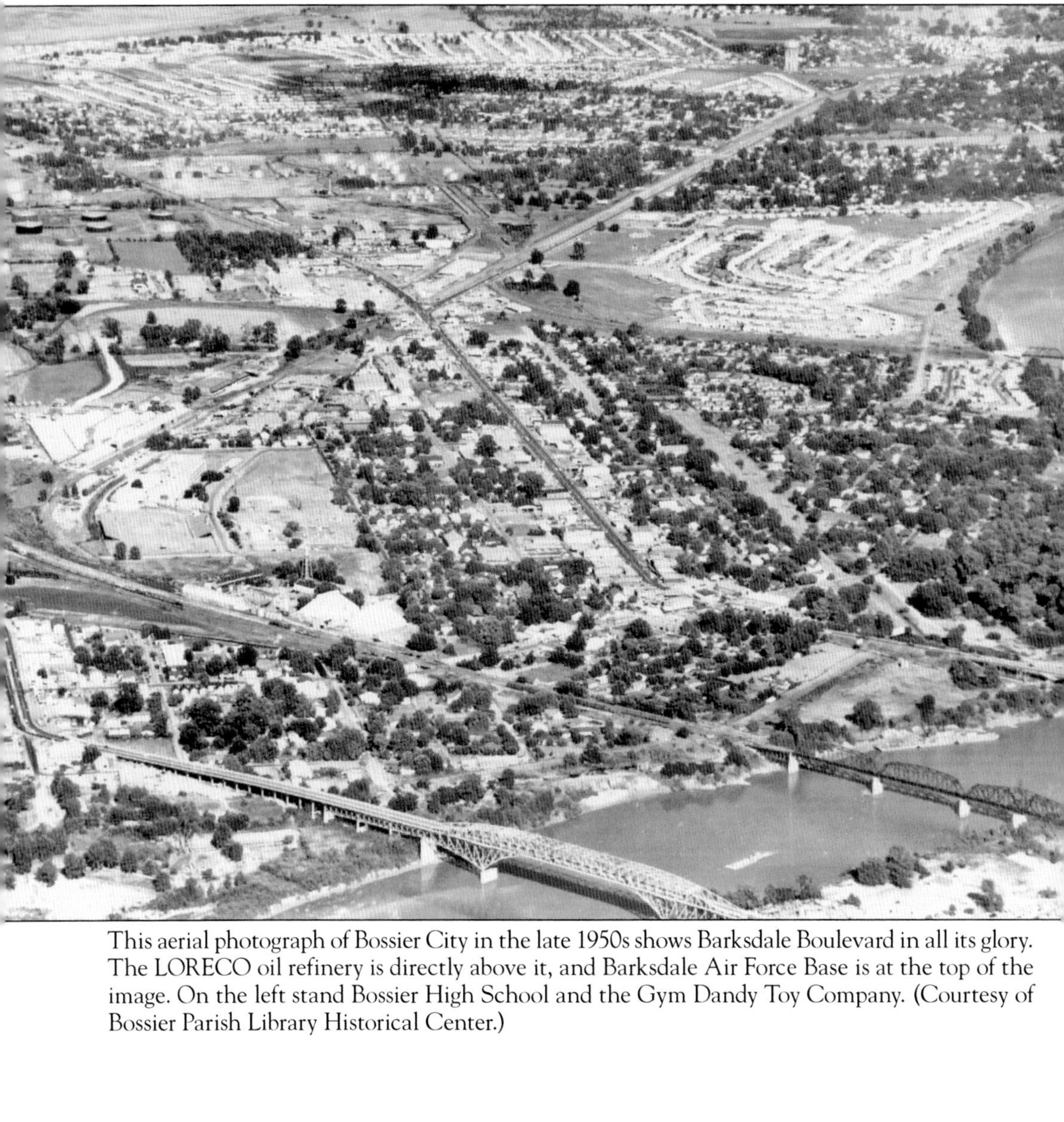

This aerial photograph of Bossier City in the late 1950s shows Barksdale Boulevard in all its glory. The LORECO oil refinery is directly above it, and Barksdale Air Force Base is at the top of the image. On the left stand Bossier High School and the Gym Dandy Toy Company. (Courtesy of Bossier Parish Library Historical Center.)

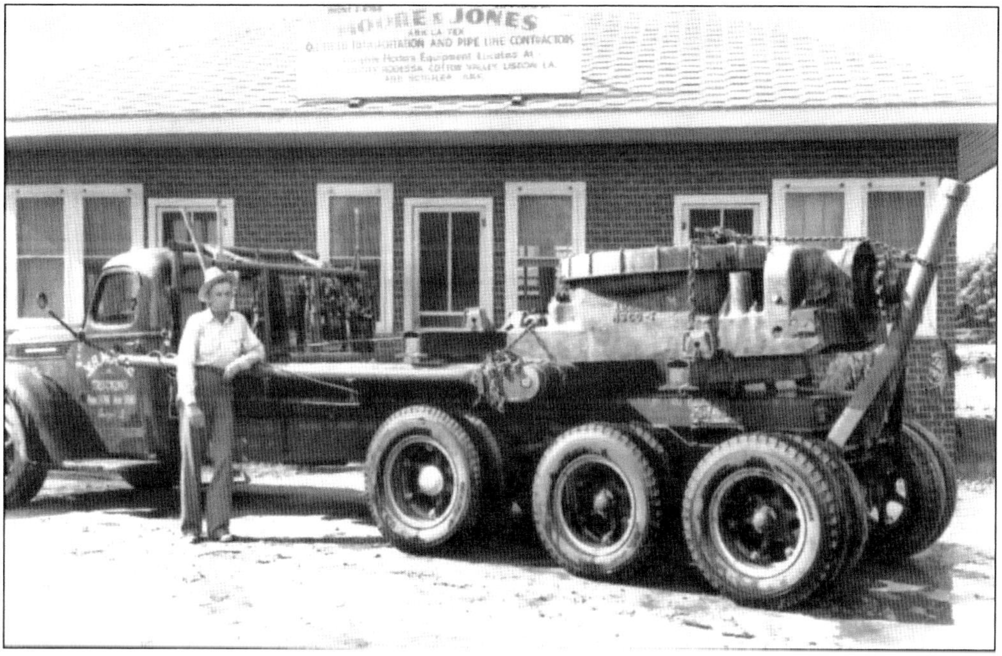

Pictured here around 1932 are a large equipment truck and J. Bonnie Moore in front of his Moore and Jones trucking company office at the foot of the Texas St. Bridge. The company provided services to the oil industry of the Ark-La-Tex. The sign on the building reads, "Moore & Jones, Ark-La-Tex, Oil Field Transportation and Pipe Line Contractors." (Courtesy of Bossier Parish Library Historical Center.)

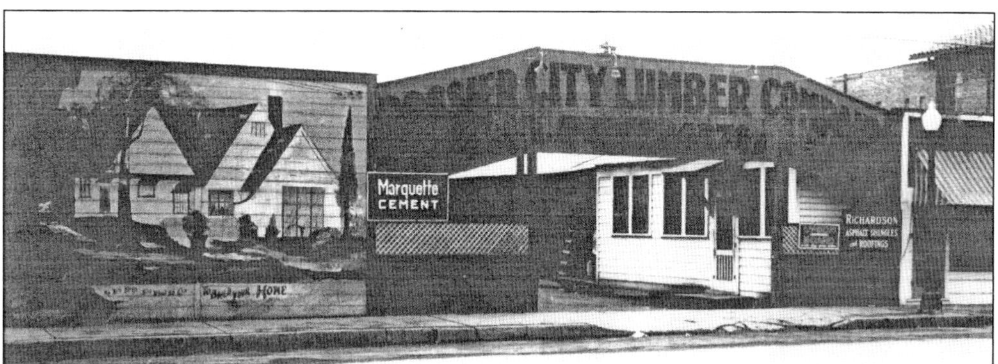

Bossier Lumber Company stood next to the Bossier City Municipal Building for about 30 years, from the late 1920s until it was torn down to make room for the new fire station in the early 1950s. (Courtesy of Bossier Parish Library Historical Center.)

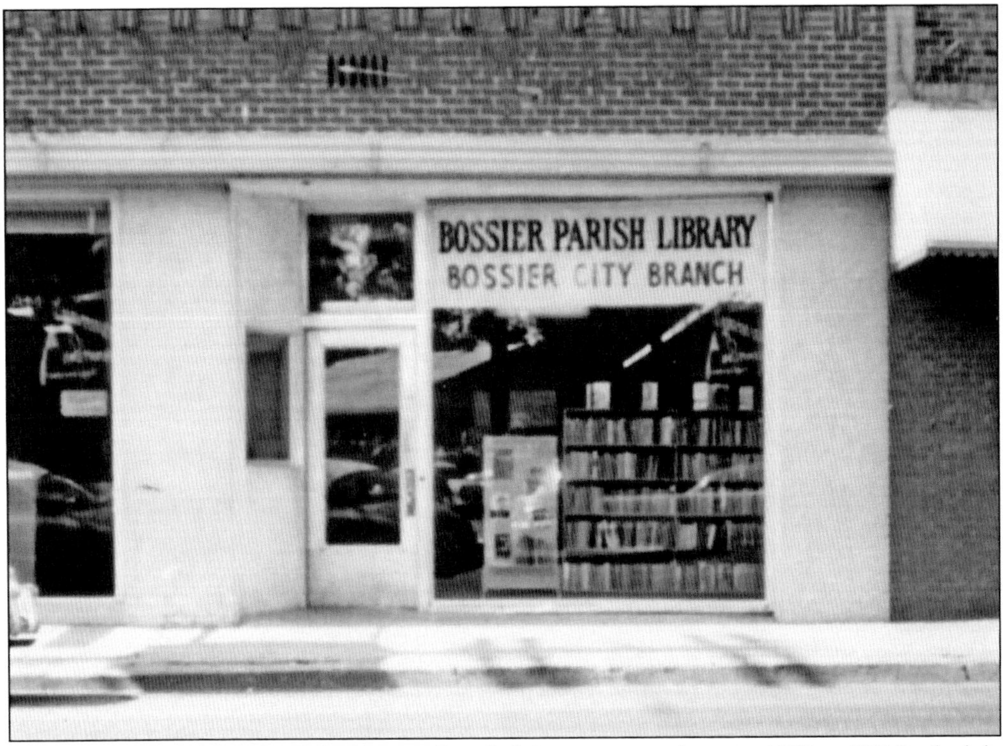

The Bossier City branch of the Bossier Parish Library is seen here in 1957 at 503 Barksdale Boulevard. This location is on the corner of Minden Street and Barksdale Boulevard. (Courtesy of Bossier Parish Library Historical Center.)

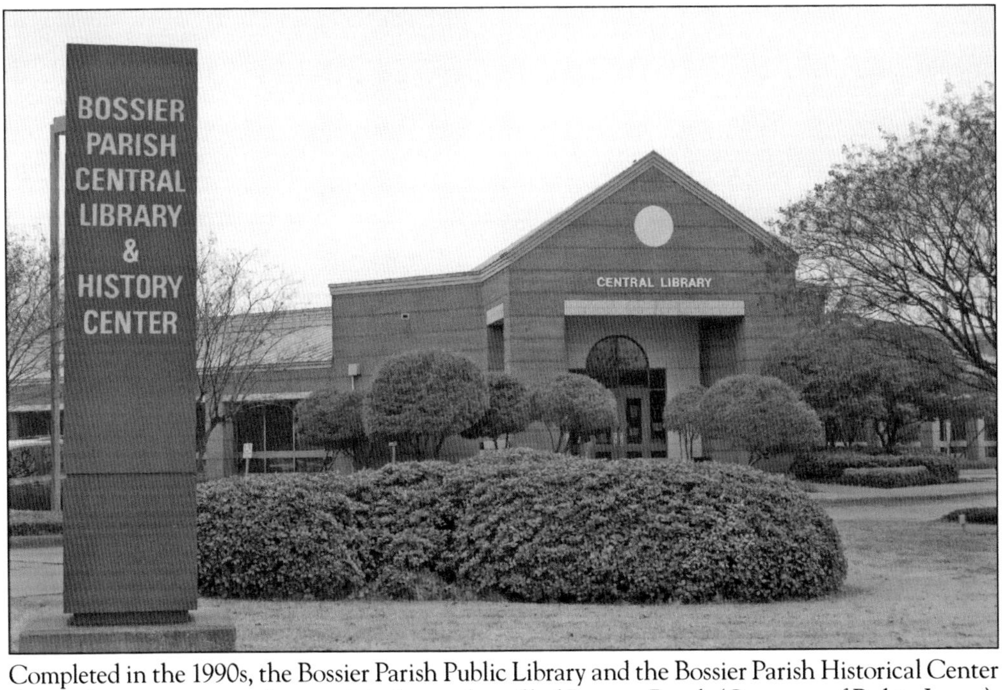

Completed in the 1990s, the Bossier Parish Public Library and the Bossier Parish Historical Center share a location next to the municipal complex off of Benton Road. (Courtesy of Robin Jones.)

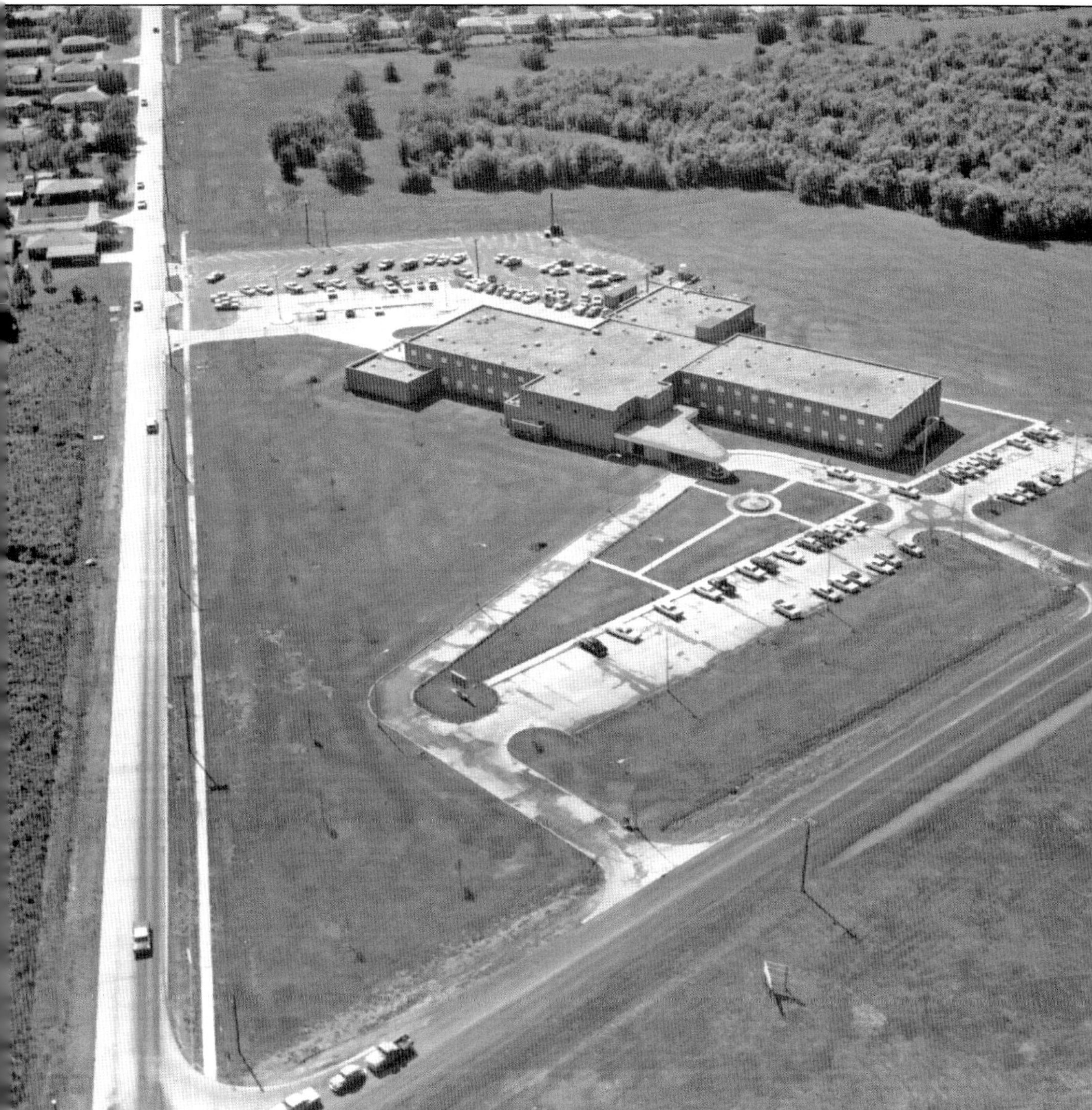

Bossier General Hospital, pictured here in 1963, is on the corner of Shed Road and Airline Drive. (Courtesy of Bossier Parish Library Historical Center.)

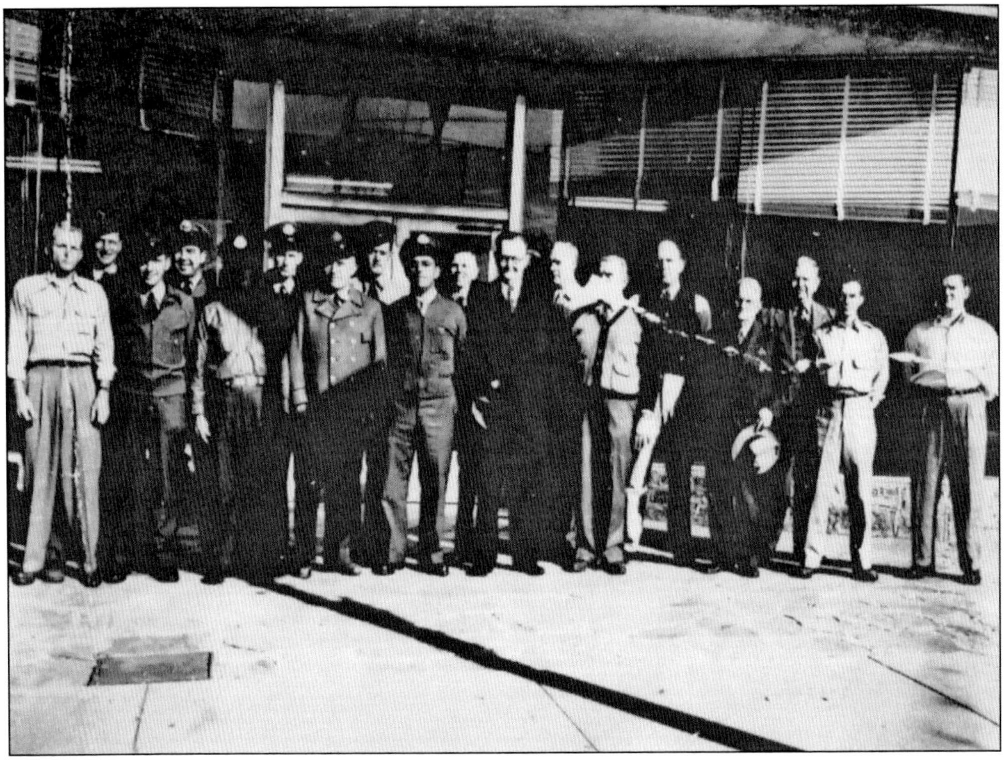

Above, Bossier City mail carriers are shown in this 1930 dedication of the Bossier City Post Office on Traffic Street. This was the location of the city post office until it was moved to its current spot on Benton Road in the 1950s. Below, the new building, which is still in use, is pictured. (Courtesy of Bossier Parish Library Historical Center.)

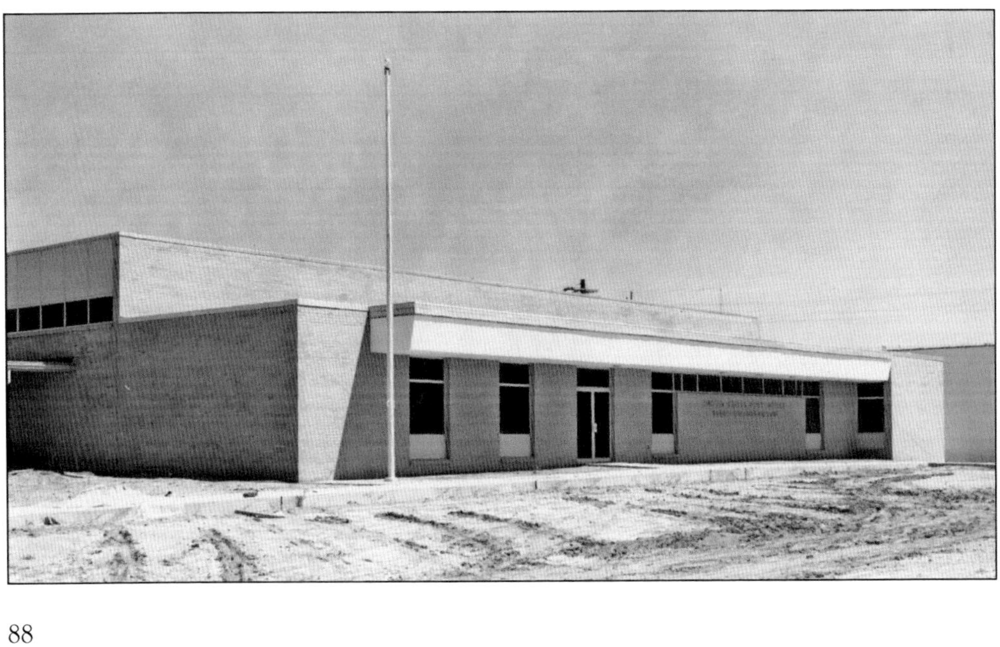

Three

CULTURAL LIFE

SCHOOLS, LODGES, CHURCHES, AND EVENTS

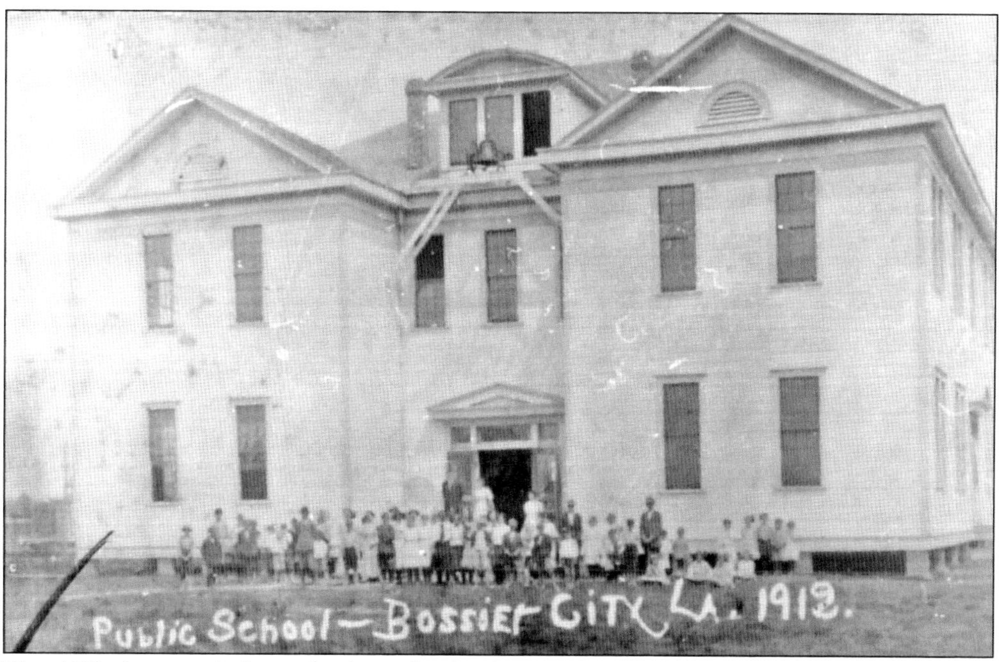

This 1918 photograph shows the first school in Bossier City and all of its pupils. This one public school housed all grades and was in use until the 1920s, when the school now known as Bossier Elementary was built as its replacement. (Courtesy of Noel Memorial Library.)

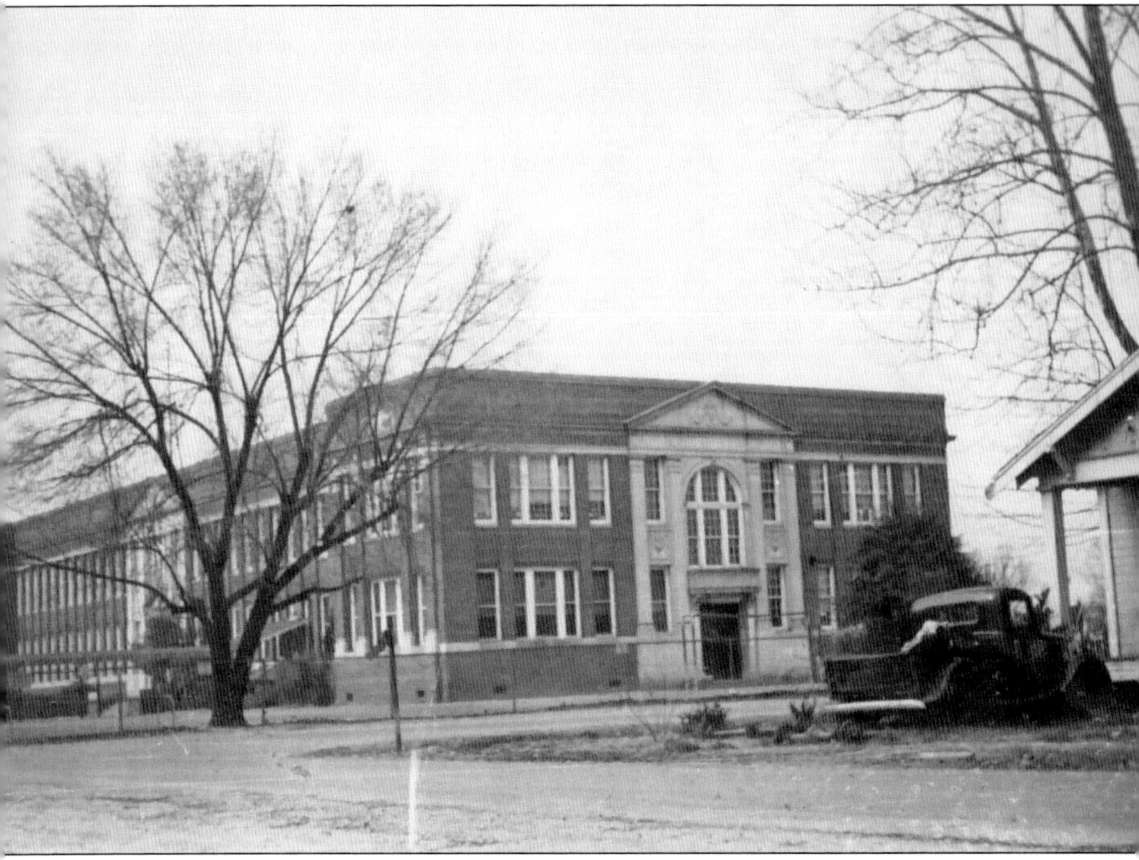

Bossier Elementary School, pictured here in 1951, was the second school built for Bossier City students. In 1928, this brick building replaced the wood structure that had been used since 1914. (Courtesy of Bossier Parish Library Historical Center.)

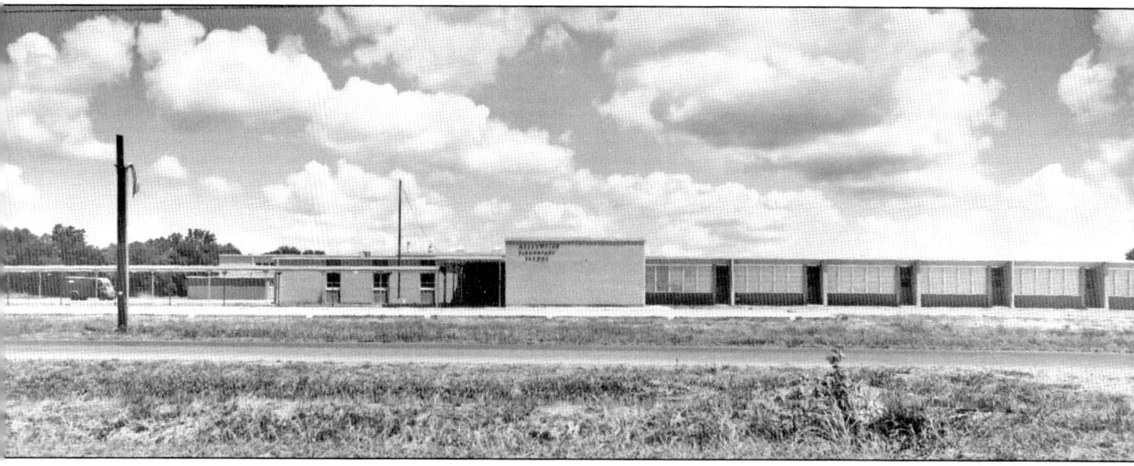

After World War II, Bossier City experienced a building boom just like much of the country. The city began rapidly spreading south on Barksdale Boulevard and to the northwest along Shed Road and the Swan Lake area. Many schools were built in this era, and they all resembled each other. A local Bossier City architect, Thomas Meredith, designed the schools. This is Meadowview Elementary School after completion in 1950. (Courtesy of Bossier Parish Library Historical Center.)

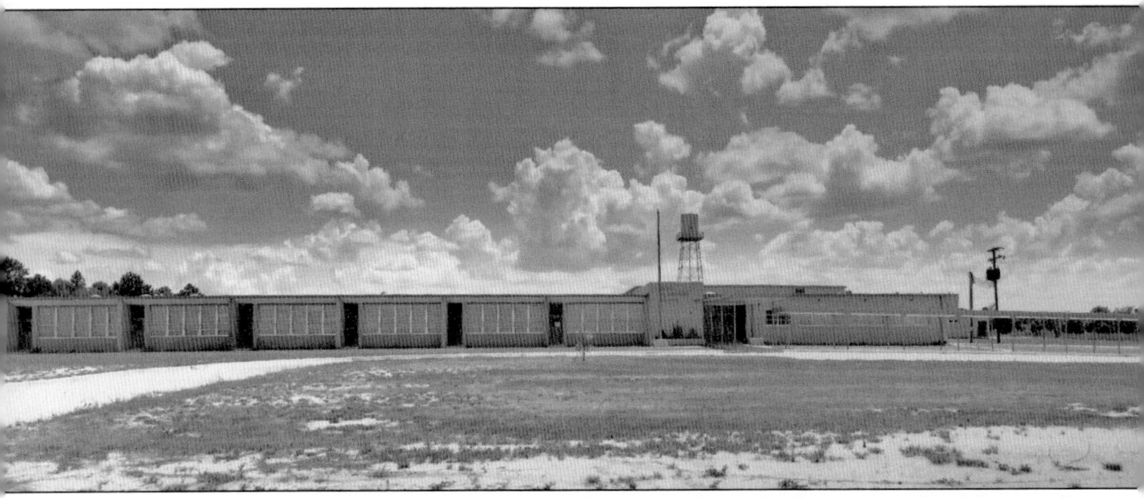

Pictured here in 1950 is Platt Elementary School, which was built just outside of Bossier City. (Courtesy of Bossier Parish Library Historical Center.)

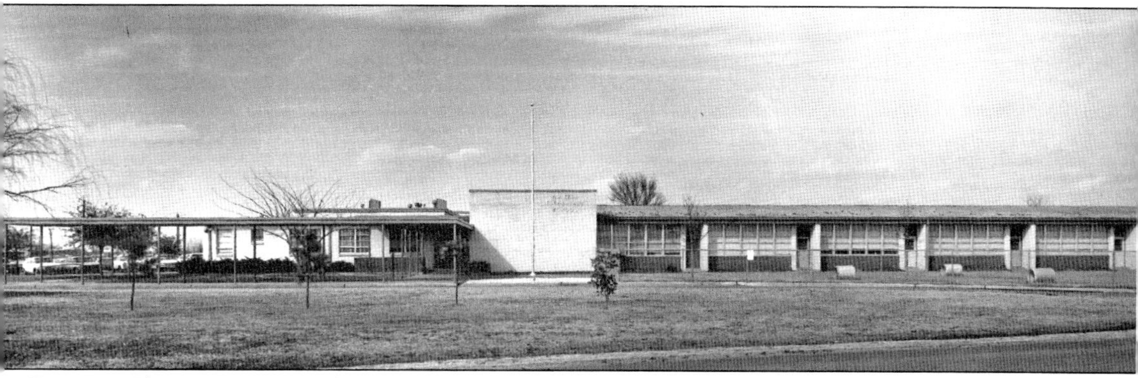

R.V. Kerr Elementary, on Airline Drive just north of Barksdale AFB, is seen here in an undated photograph. (Courtesy of Bossier Parish Library Historical Center.)

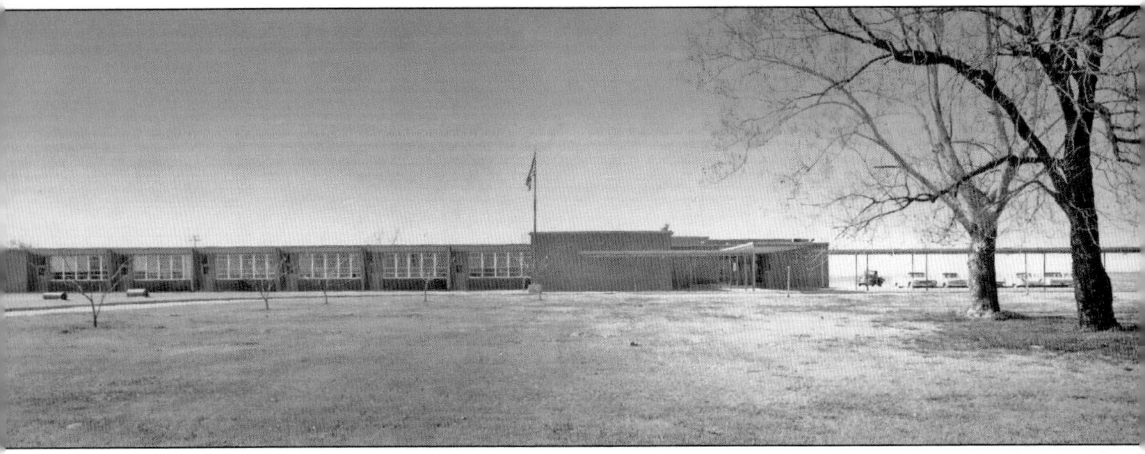

Curtis Elementary School, captured in this undated photograph, was built at the southern end of Bossier City's limits. (Courtesy of Bossier Parish Library Historical Center.)

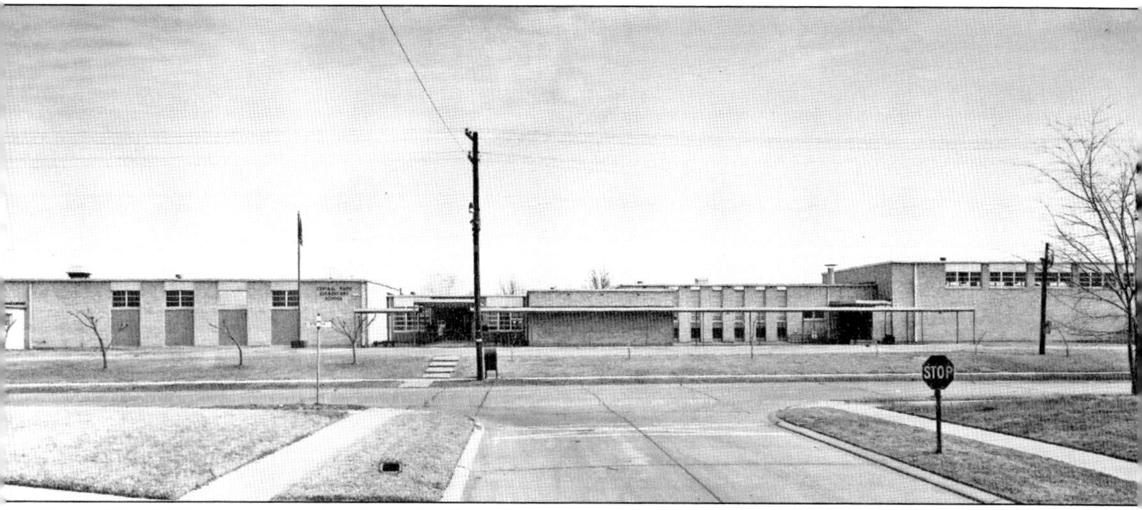

Central Park Elementary School was built in the Central Park neighborhood, which was located just south of downtown Bossier City. This image was taken in the 1950s. (Courtesy of Bossier Parish Library Historical Center.)

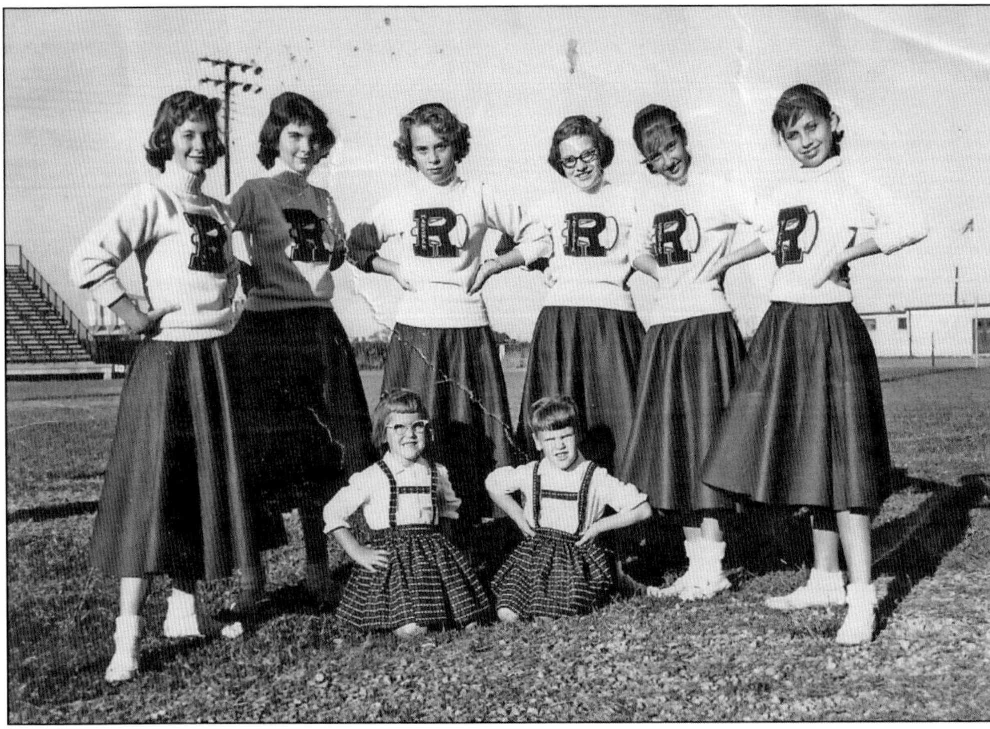

Pictured here are cheerleaders and mascots at Rusheon Junior High School in 1957. From left to right are (first row) Ginger Hardaway and Sissy Hardaway; (second row) Susie Hawkins, Julia Ann Hoyer, Marshan Kelly, Vickie Sanders, Tish McCranie, and Sue Parkerson. (Courtesy of Bossier Parish Library Historical Center.)

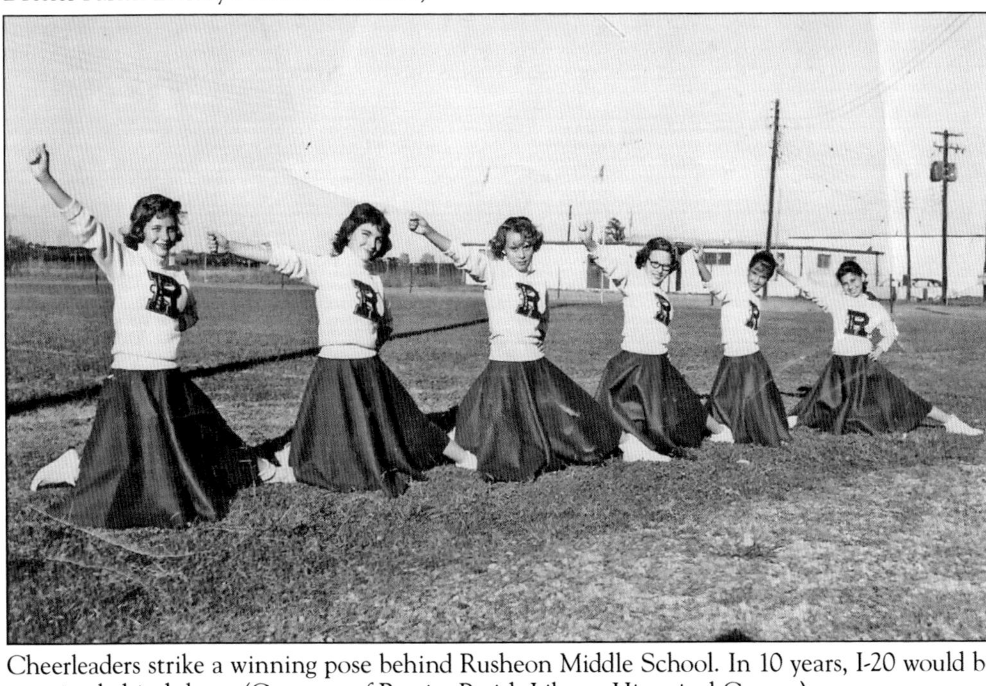

Cheerleaders strike a winning pose behind Rusheon Middle School. In 10 years, I-20 would be running behind them. (Courtesy of Bossier Parish Library Historical Center.)

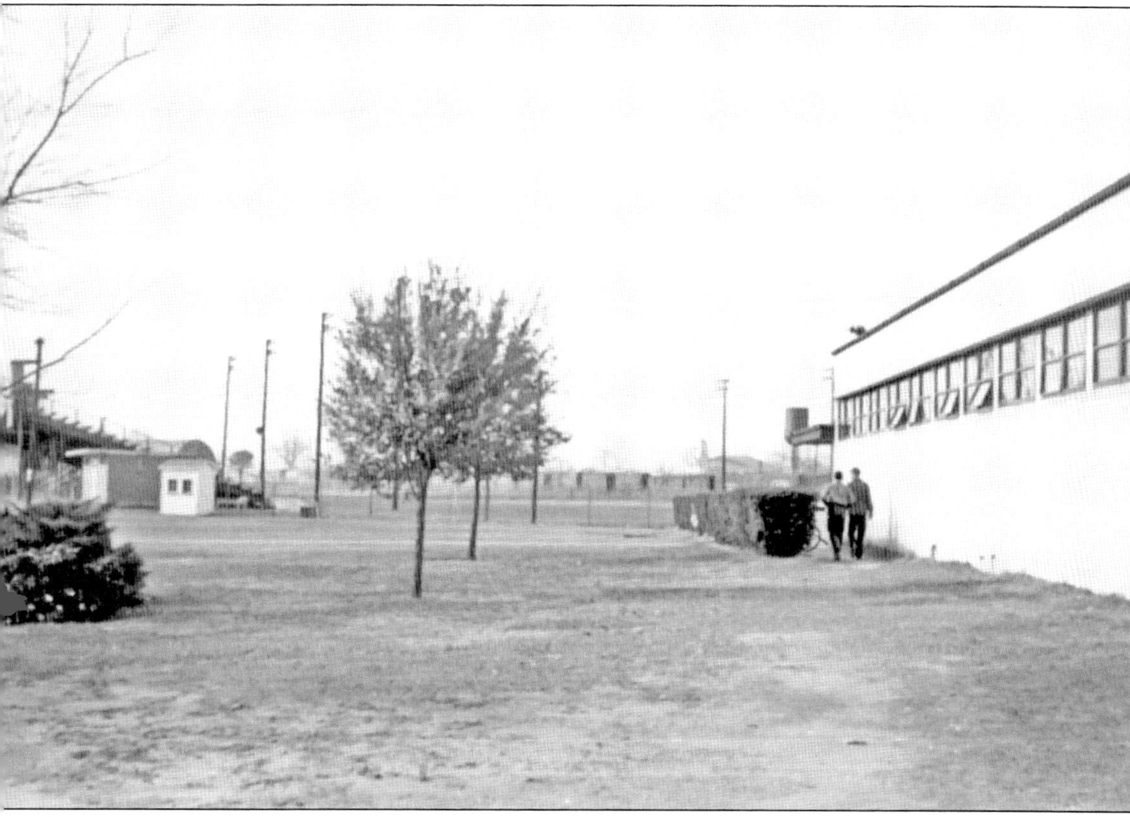

The Bossier High School football stadium can be seen in the background of this photograph, captured from the west in the early 1950s. (Courtesy of Bossier Parish Library Historical Center.)

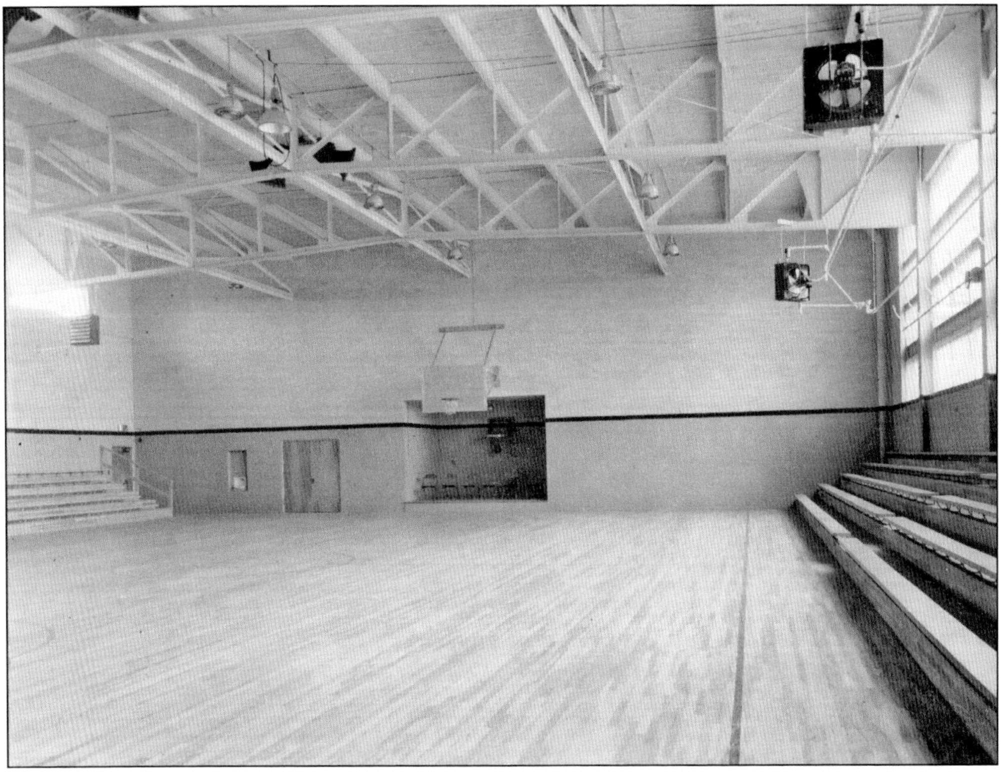

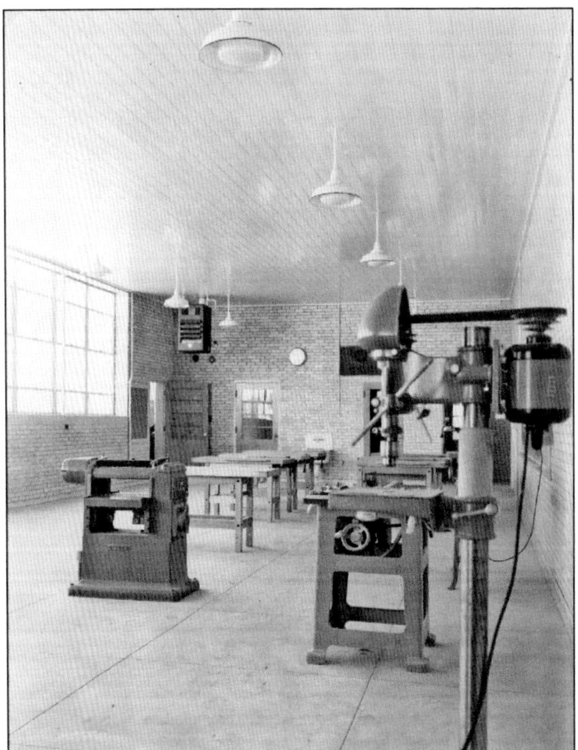

The gymnasium and the carpentry shop of Bossier High School are displayed in these two photographs, which were taken shortly after construction finished in 1941. (Courtesy of Noel Memorial Library.)

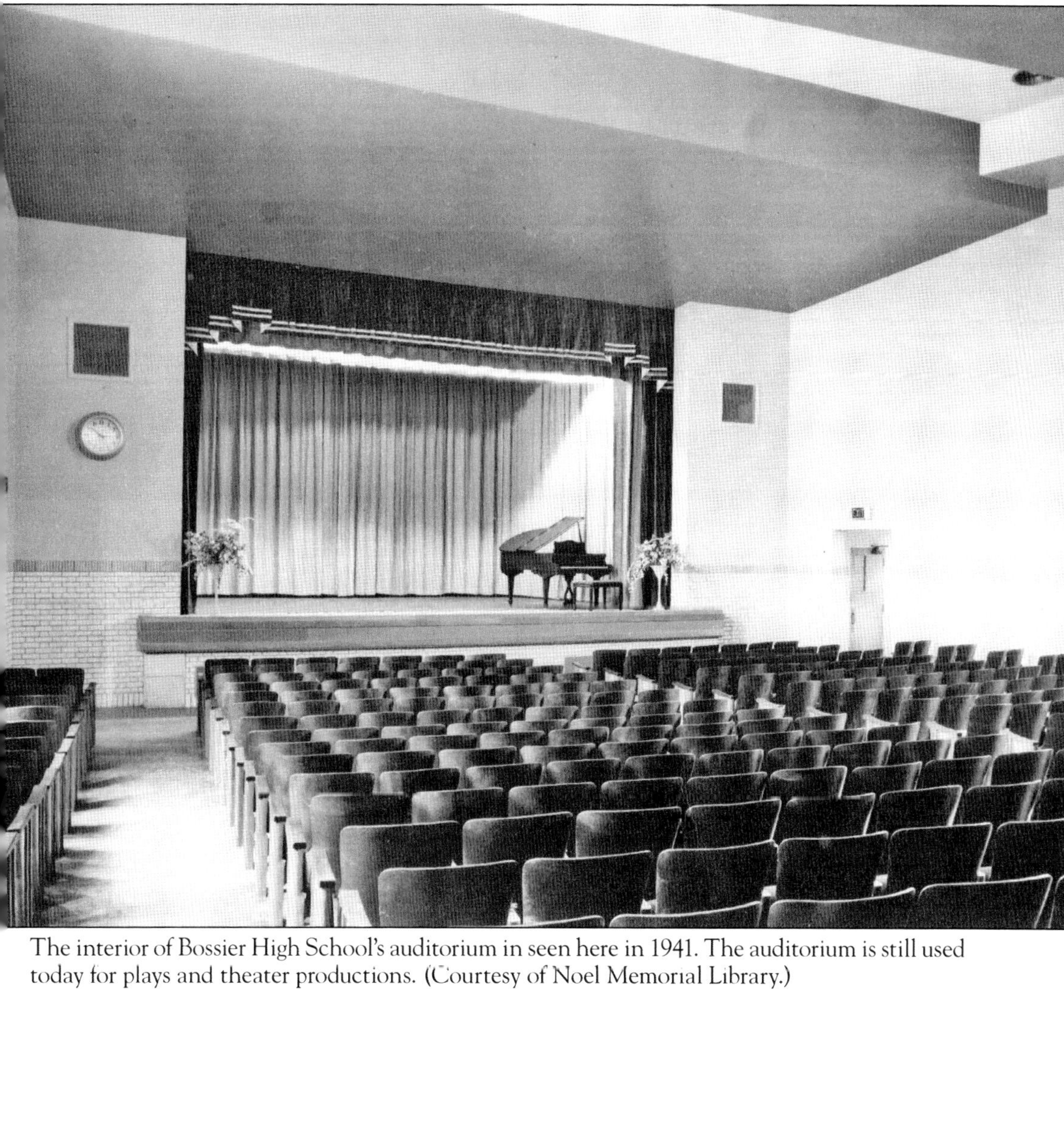

The interior of Bossier High School's auditorium in seen here in 1941. The auditorium is still used today for plays and theater productions. (Courtesy of Noel Memorial Library.)

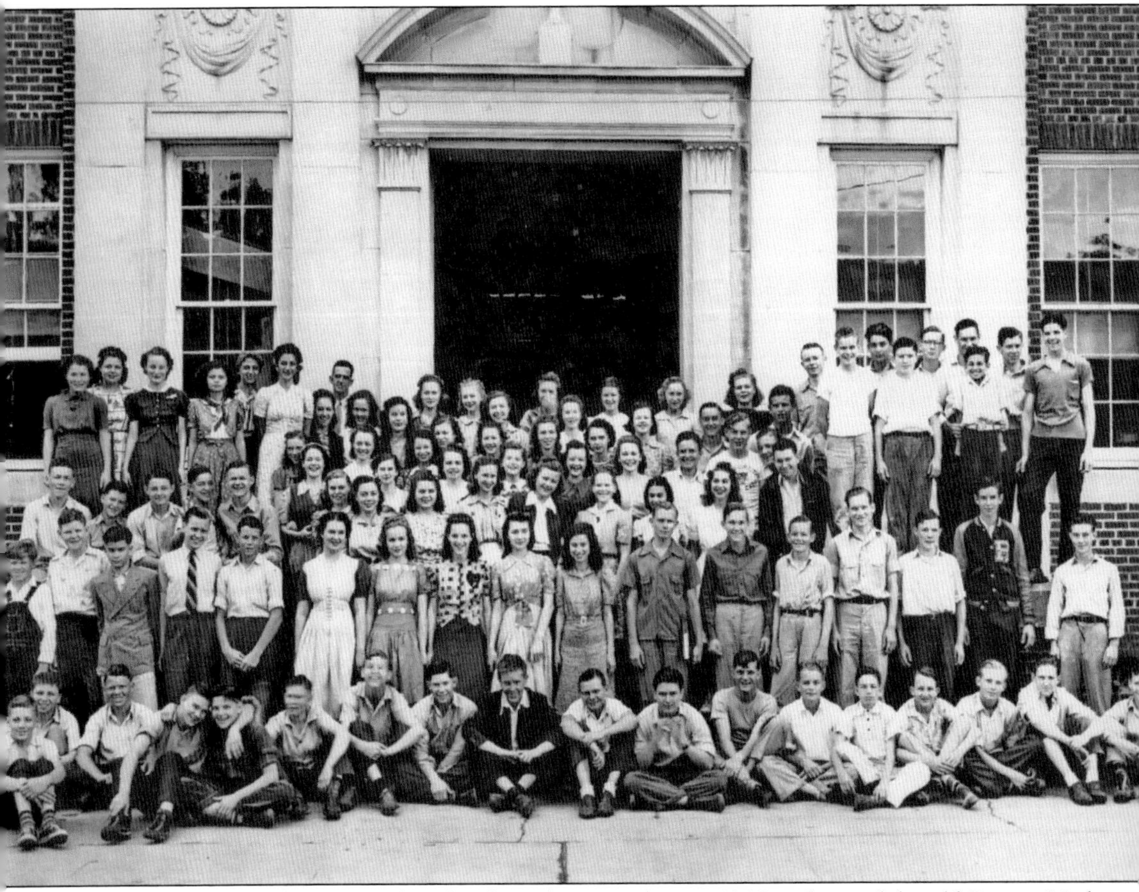

Pictured here is Bossier High School's sophomore class in 1940 in front of the old Bossier High. (Courtesy of Bossier Parish Library Historical Center.)

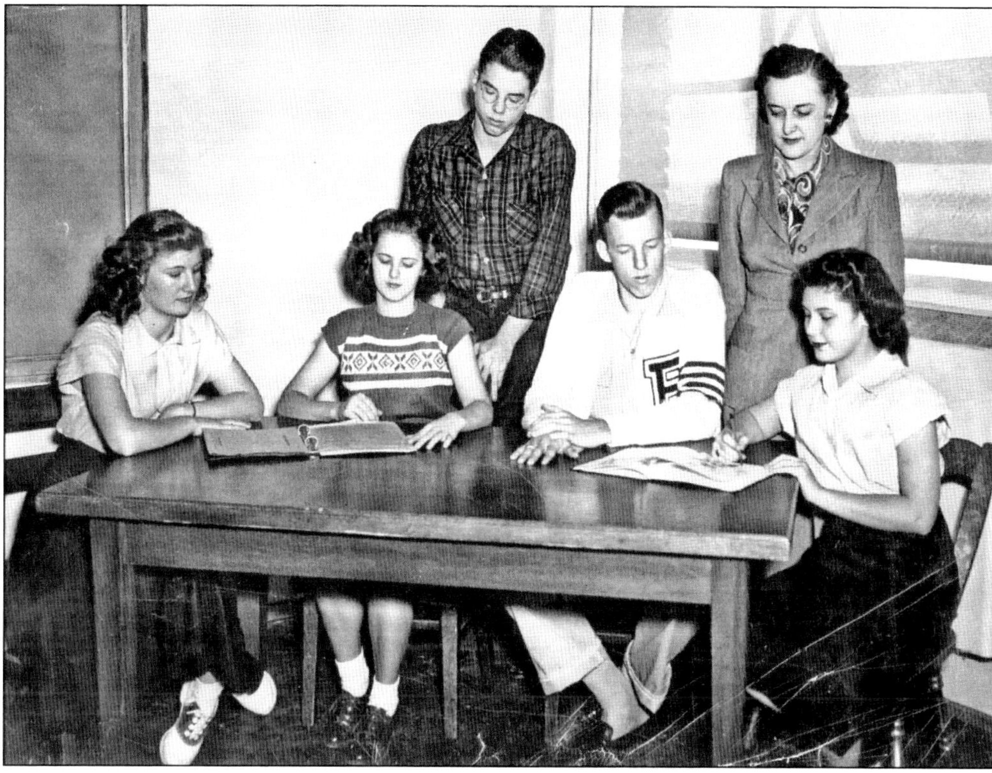

This is the 1948–1949 Bossier High Student Council. Pictured from left to right are Martel Beard, Barbara Jean Bookter, Guy Moore, Tommy Woodall, Mary McKnight, and Jackie Bomar. (Courtesy of Bossier Parish Library Historical Center.)

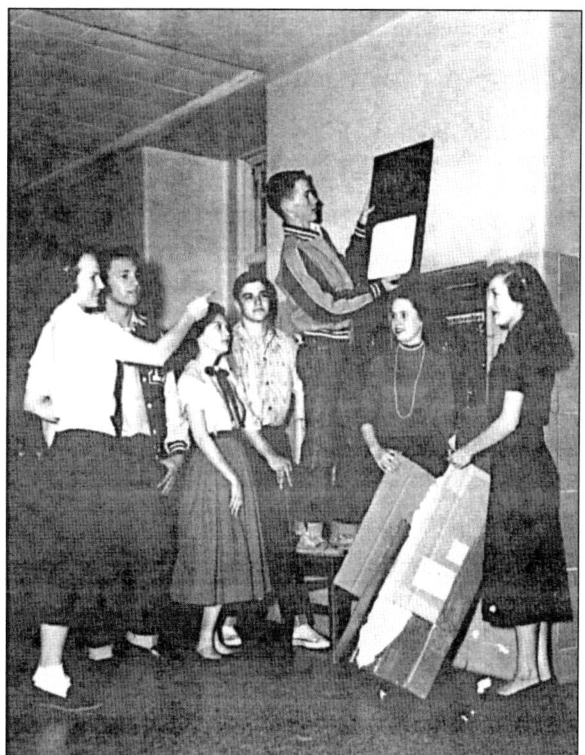

Bossier High students pose in the hallway in 1955. From left to right are Mary McDowell, Jimmie Owens Cooper, Mary McKnight, Pete Moore, Bobby Nelson, Ruth Nix, and Mitchel Quida. (Courtesy of Bossier Parish Library Historical Center.)

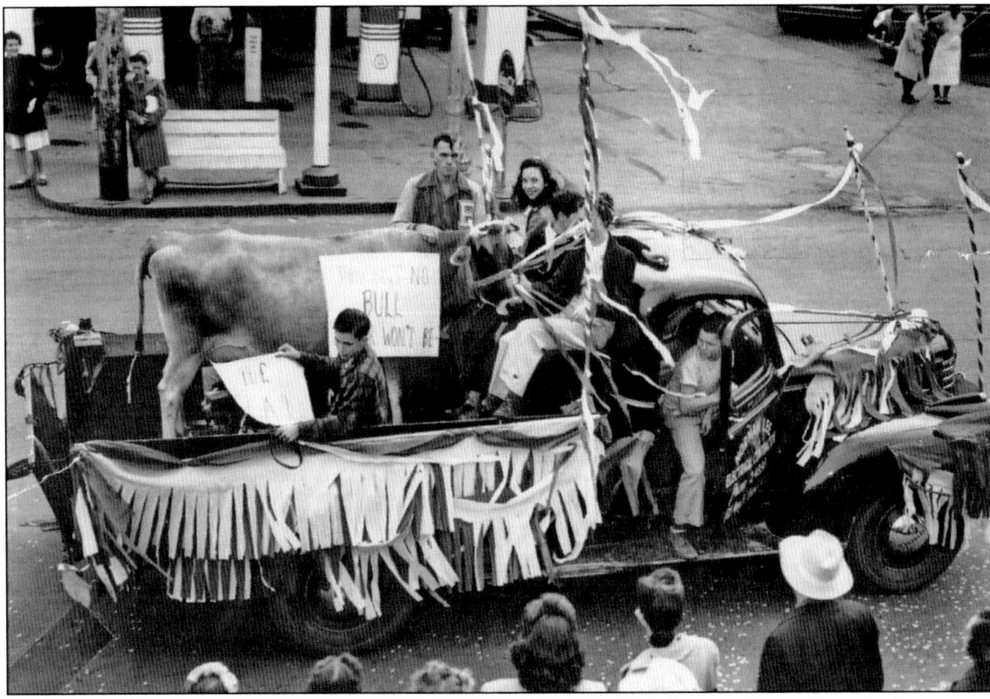

This photograph was taken in downtown Bossier during a 1947 homecoming parade for Bossier High School. Joyce Knowles is the girl looking at the camera, and Gene Hassell is the boy with his hand on the cow. The truck advertises "Norman Lee Electrical Contractor" on the passenger-side door. (Courtesy of Joyce Knowles Skaggs and the Bossier Parish Library Historical Center.)

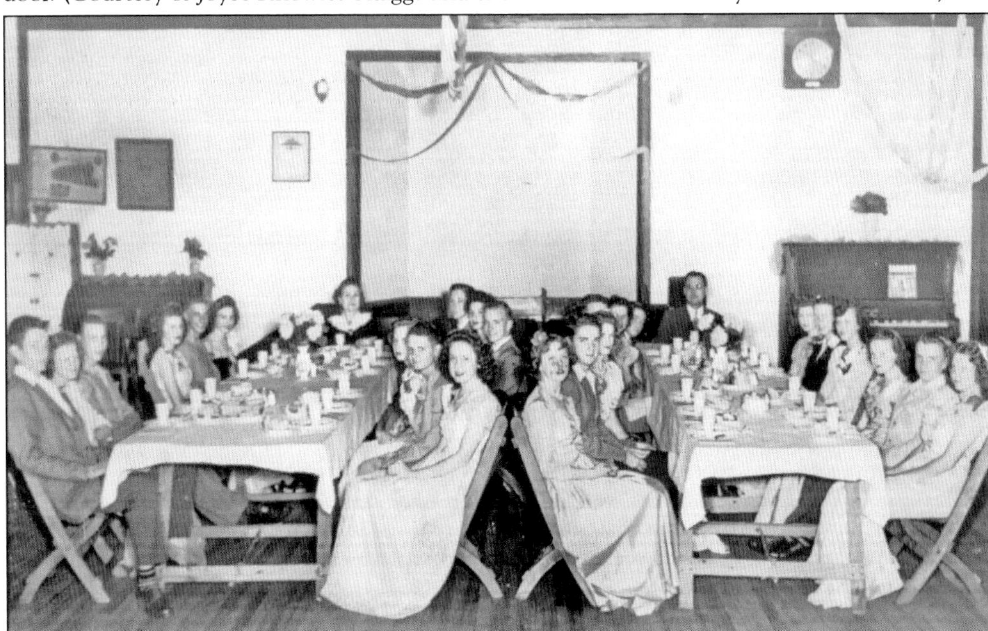

Seated at the heads of each table, Nina Sutton (left) and Quincy Lincecum treat the 1945 sophomore class of Bossier High School to a chicken dinner. (Courtesy of Bossier Parish Library Historical Center.)

This 1948 Bossier High School senior class outing took place at Caney Lake. Seen here from left to right are Olivette Montgomery (teacher), Joyce Knowles, and JoAnn Drake during the event. (Courtesy of Bossier Parish Library Historical Center.)

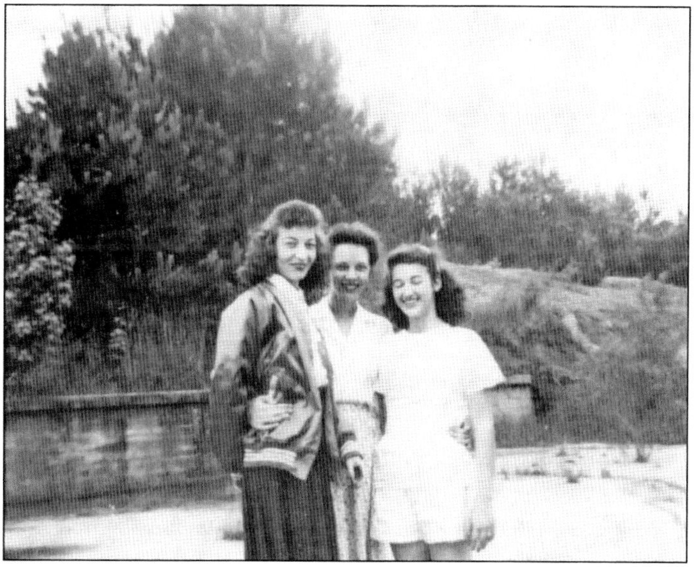

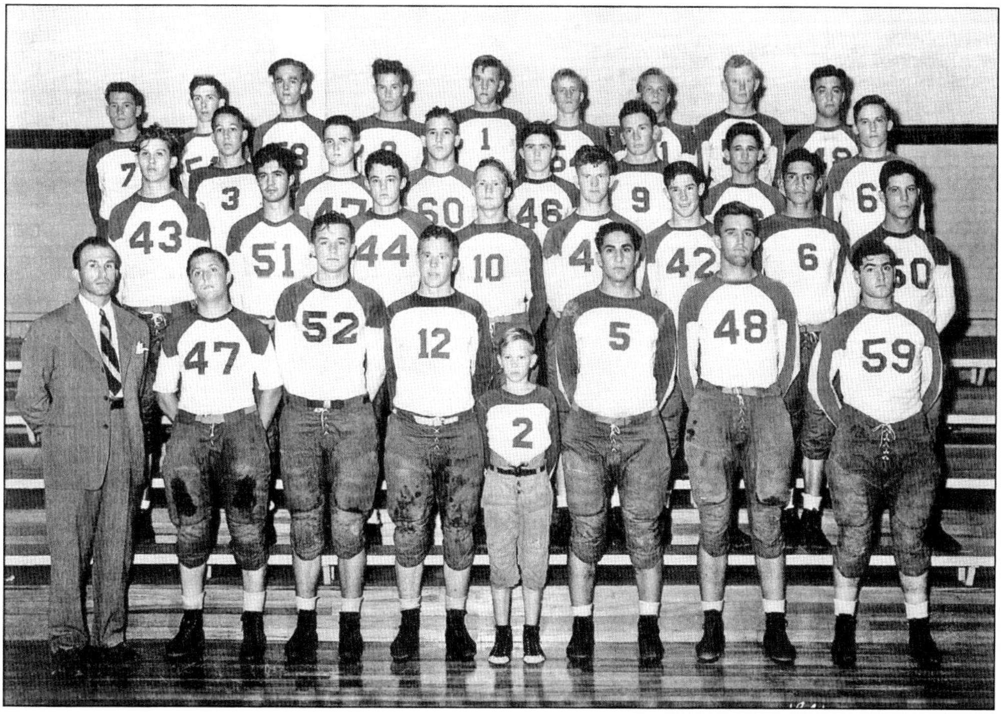

The Bossier Bearkats were the state champions in 1942. The champs pictured here are, from left to right, (first row) Norman Buckner (coach), C.L. Madden, Jack Lewis, Eugene "Red" Knight, Ottis Allen (manager), Joe Peters, Fred Roseman, and Comeal Spataro; (second row) Dennis Tibbits, Vincent Maggio, Billy Davidson, John Rowland Birdwell, Cooksey Humphreys, Bill Walker, Leo Visbol, and Vincent Montalbano; (third row) George Gray (manager), Douglas "Bubber" Green, Byram O'Donnell, Bobby Murray, Johnny Robinson, Joe Maggio, and Joe Beard; (fourth row) Arthur Shockley, Lonnie Colwell, D.W. Barnes, Charles Shockley, Fred Bell, Harold Bond, Albert Johnson, James Plummer, and Buster Vergo. (Courtesy of Bossier Parish Library Historical Center.)

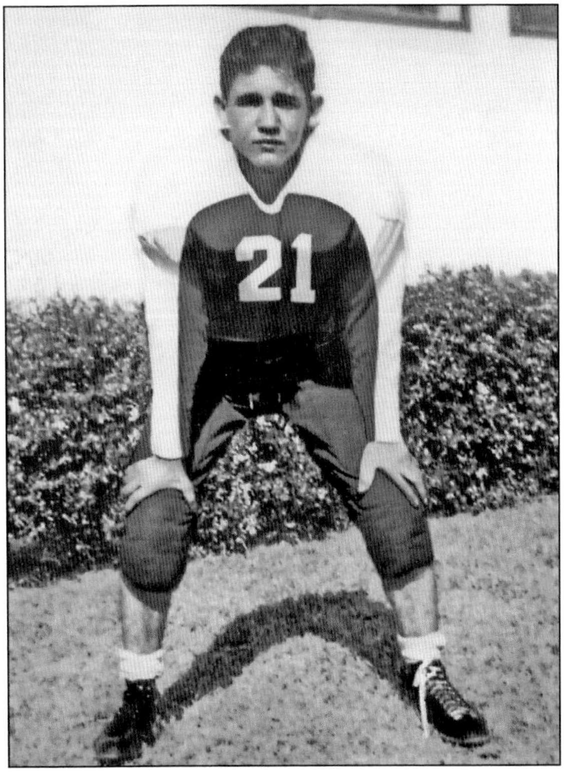

Joe Maggio, pictured at left in his no. 21 uniform, was a much-heralded "scat back" on the 1941 Bossier City High School state champion football team. Only 130 pounds and scarcely over five feet tall, he claims, "Once I got in front of you there was no catching me." Below is Maggio's grammar school football photograph from the 1940s. Maggio is famous for once responding to the question "what play do you want to run?" with "just don't get in my way" and then going on to score on a 40-yard quarterback sneak. (Courtesy of Joe Maggio and family.)

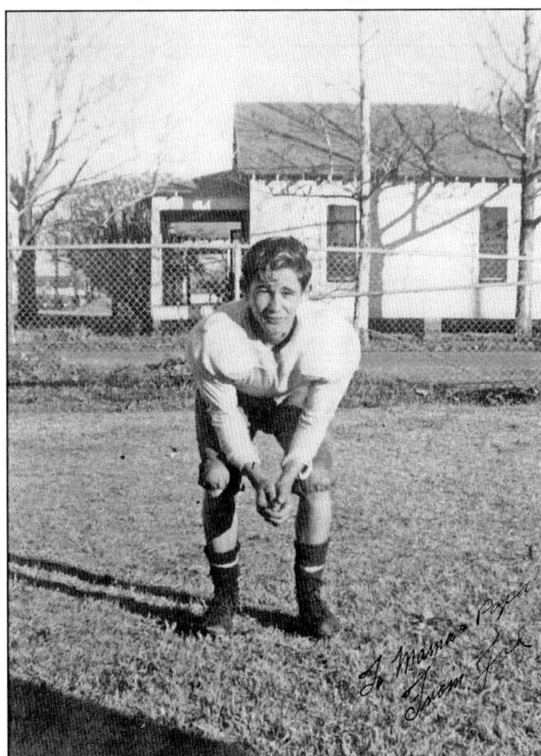

Vincent Maggio is pictured in his no. 60 football jersey. He was an all-state guard and played on the 1941 Bossier City High School state championship team. The note on the photograph, which is dated 1940 and signed from Vince to his parents, states he received "honorable mention," got All State," and was North Louisiana "Guard." (Courtesy of Joe Maggio and family.)

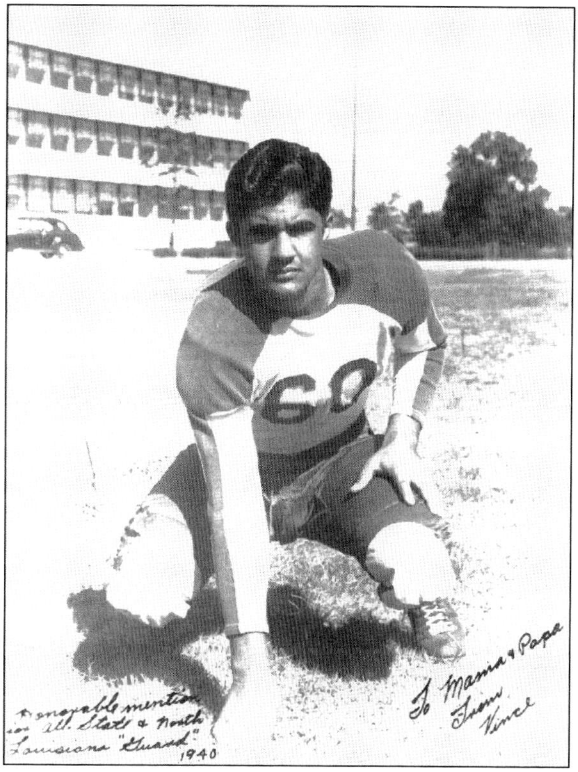

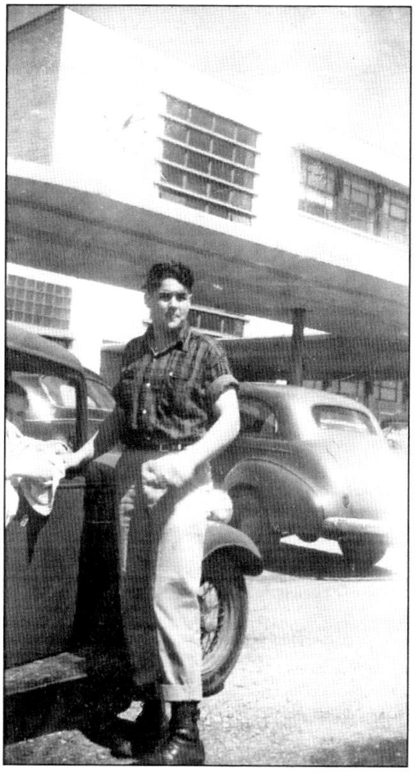

Roy Adley, the young man seen here in the plaid shirt and light-colored pants, stands near a car outside of Bossier High School in the 1940s. (Courtesy of Bossier Parish Library Historical Center.)

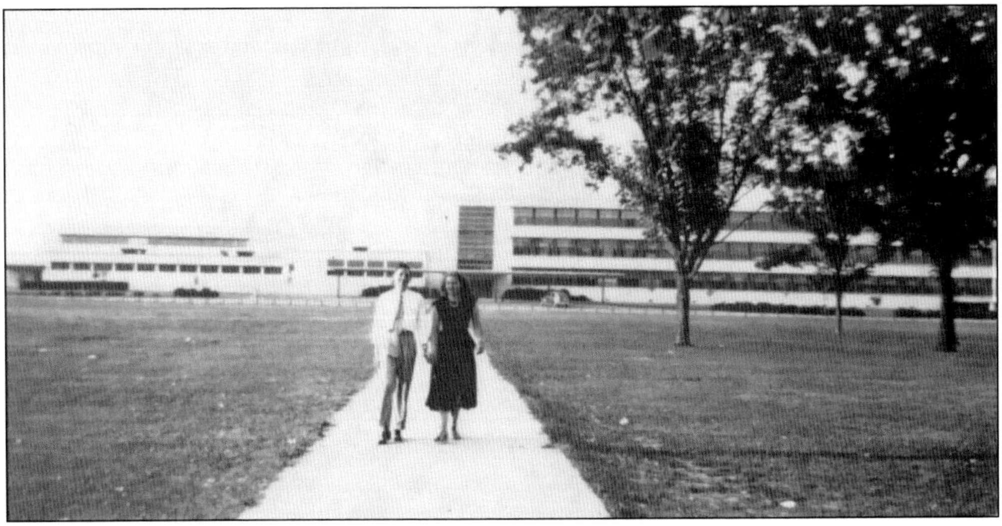

Above, Billy Taylor and Laverne McHalffey are pictured in 1948 walking away from the front entrance of Bossier High School. Below, Taylor and McHalffey are again outside the front of Bossier High School as part of a group. From left to right are Joyce Knowles, Margie Burt, Taylor, Larry Owens, and McHalffey. Note that the female students are in dresses or skirts and blouses, while the males are wearing ties and button-down shirts. (Courtesy of Bossier Parish Library Historical Center.)

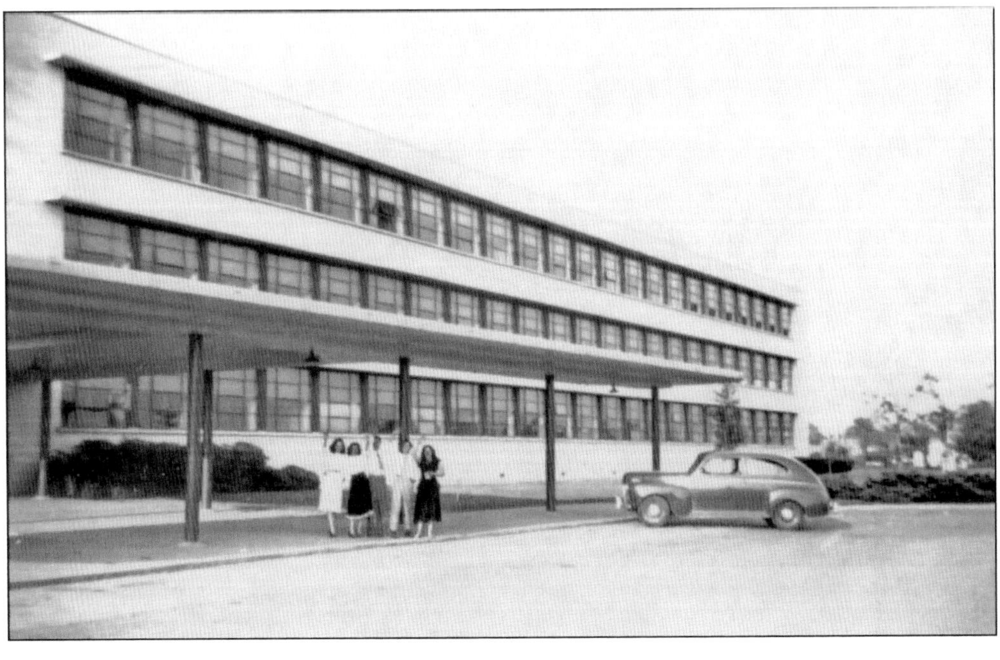

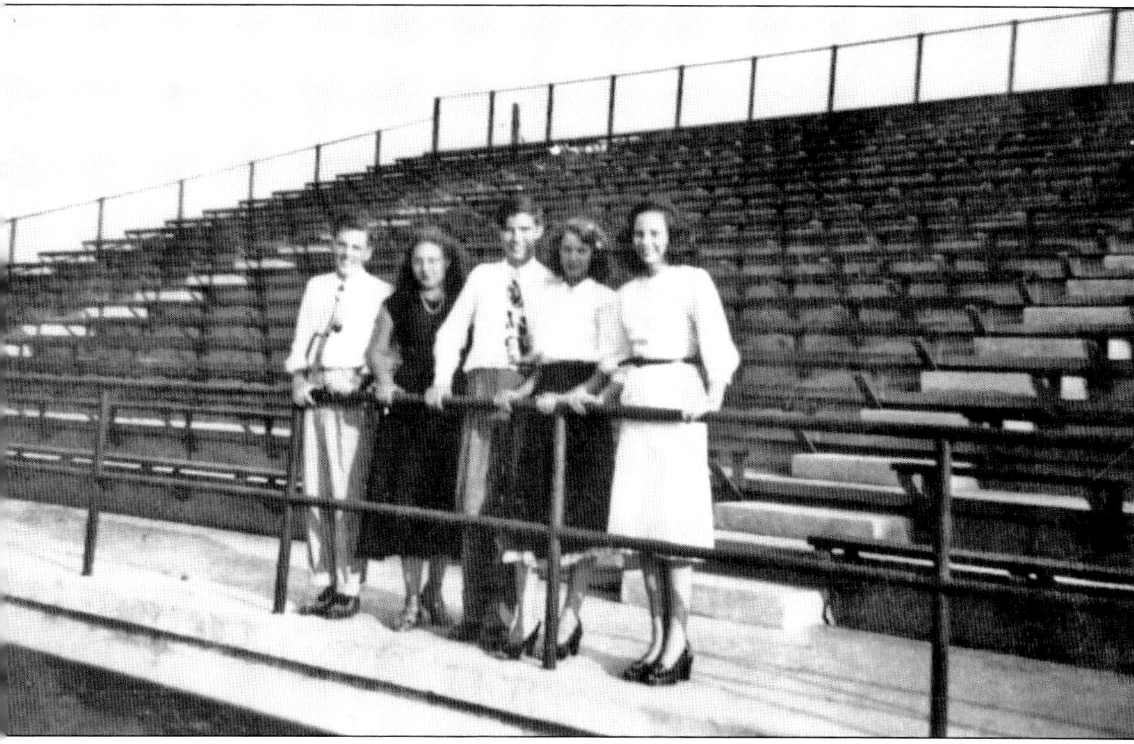

Taylor, McHalffey, Owens, Burt, and Knowles, the five students pictured on the previous page in front of Bossier High School, are shown from left to right here. This time, the group is standing by the railing inside the Bossier High School football stadium. All the bleachers are empty; this purposefully posed series must have been needed for some specific reason. (Courtesy Bossier Parish Historical Center and the Knowles-Skaggs family.)

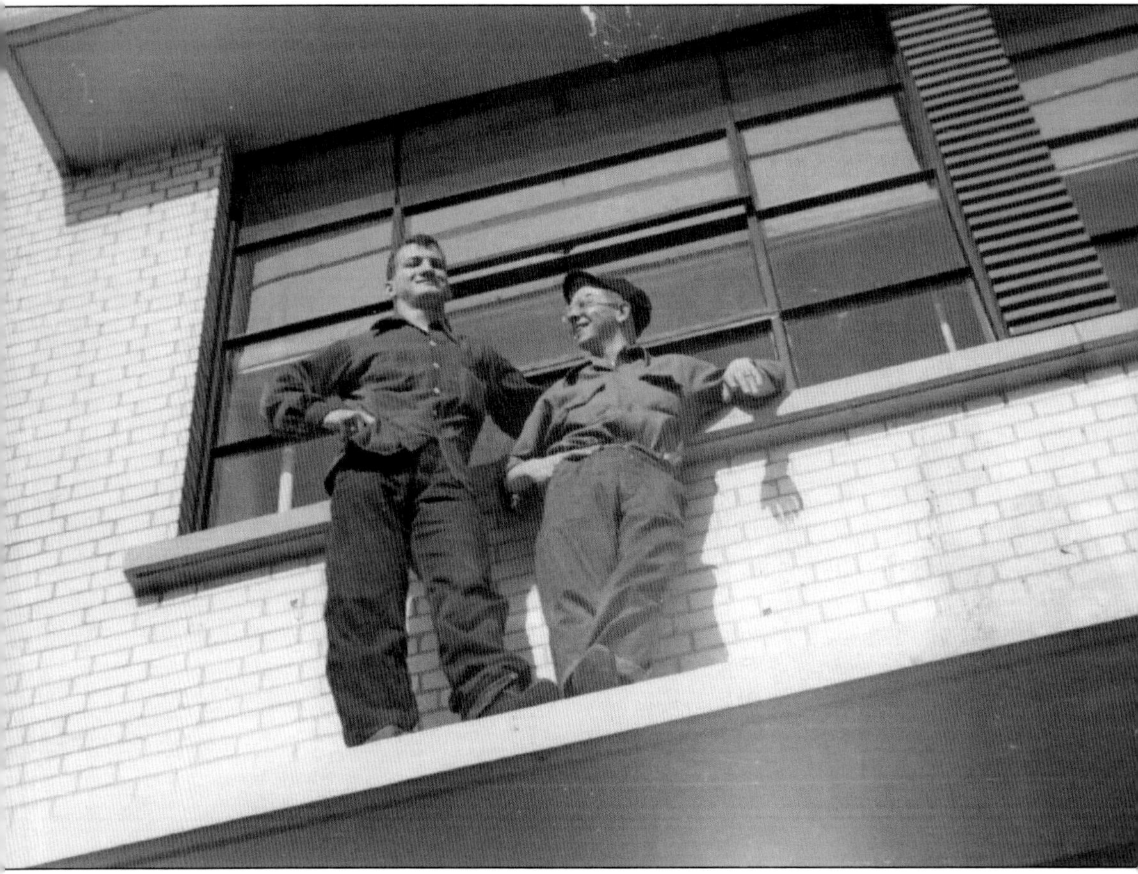

Two young men, Sammie Joe Green (left) and Darcy Hutto, stand on a ledge outside of Bossier High School around 1952. (Courtesy of Bossier Parish Library Historical Center.)

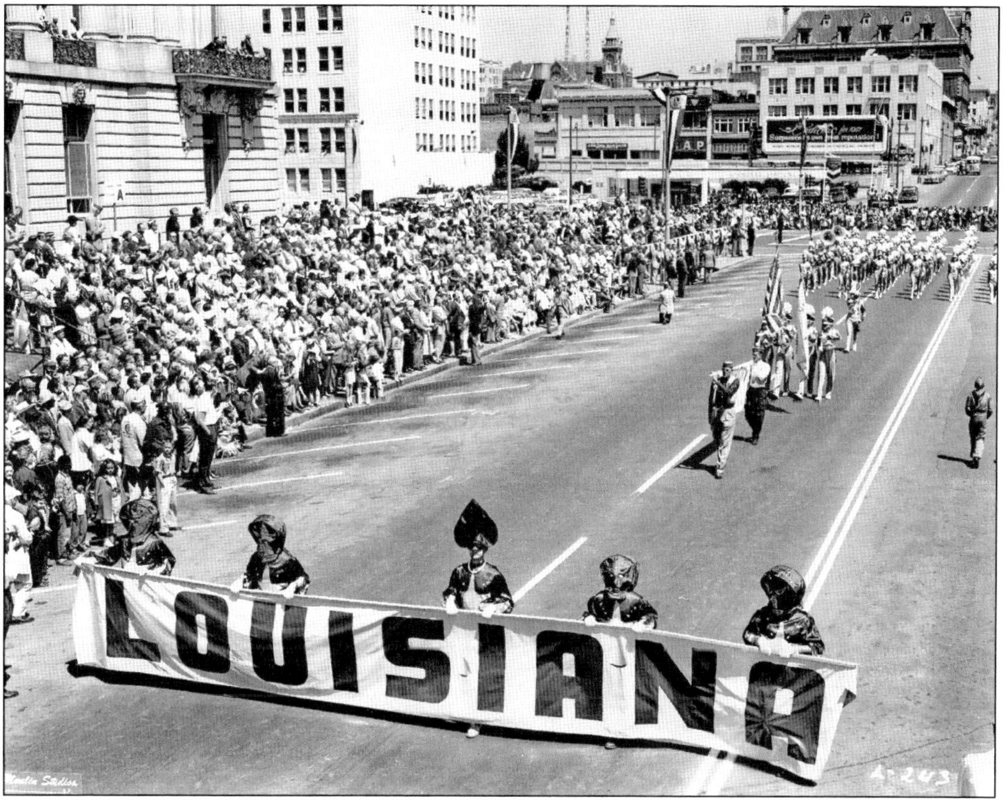

In 1957, the Bossier High School Marching Band traveled to San Francisco, California, and was sponsored by the Bossier City Lion's Club. There are five band members carrying a "Louisiana" sign, and the band is in the top-right corner. The band is continuing to march down the street past a Woolworth's store. (Courtesy of Mrs. Freddie Cherry.)

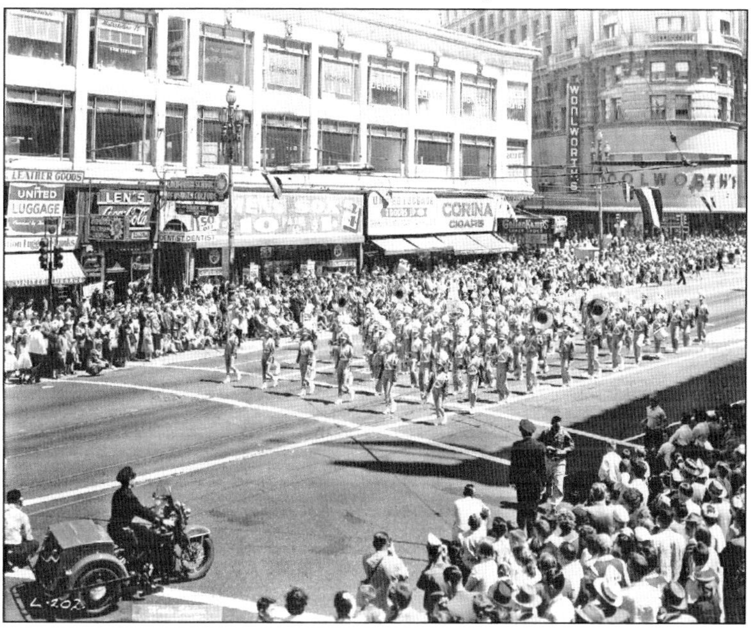

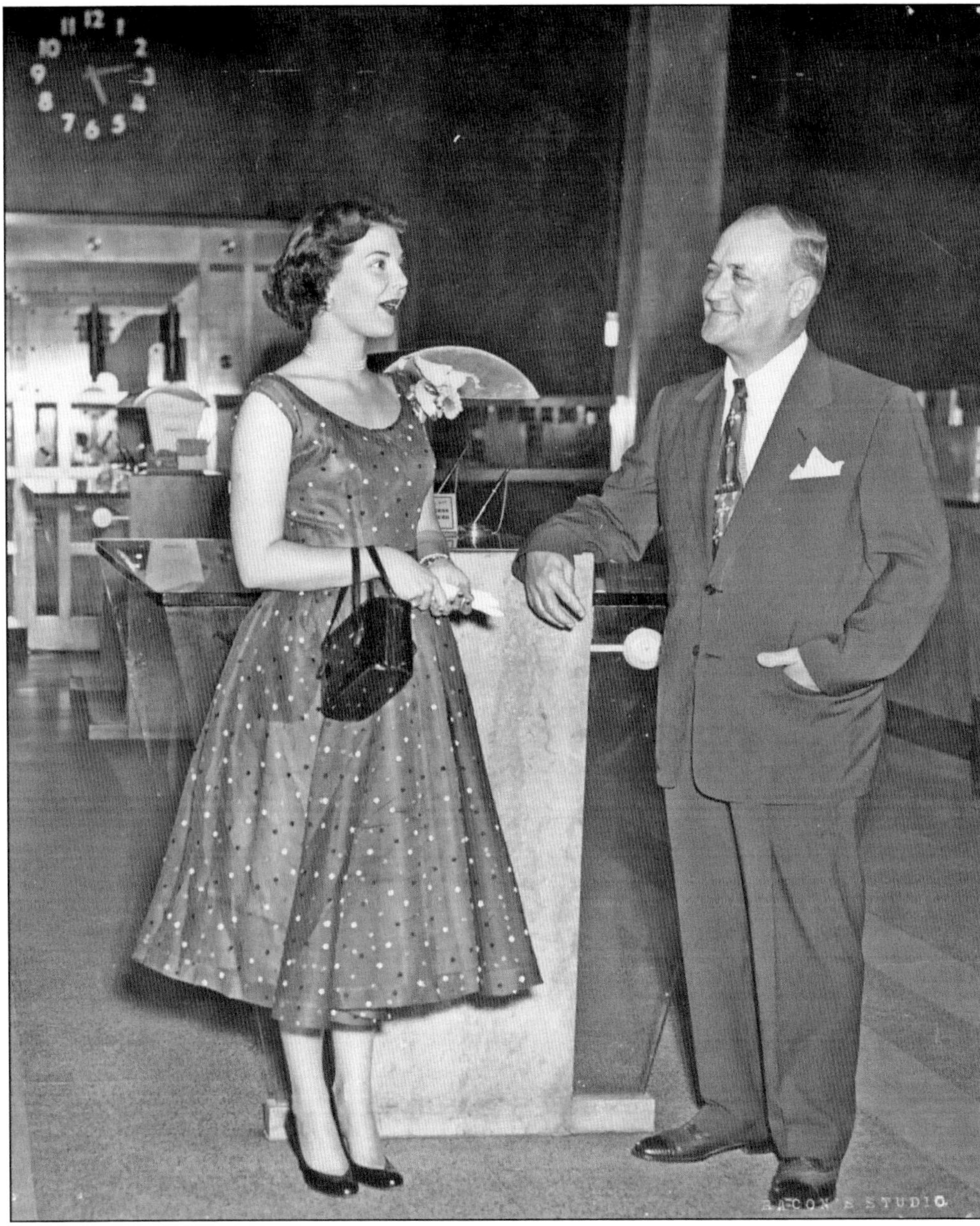

Bossier City mayor H.L. Fuller and the 1952 Maid of Cotton are pictured in the lobby of Bossier Bank and Trust. (Courtesy of the Bossier Parish Library Historical Center.)

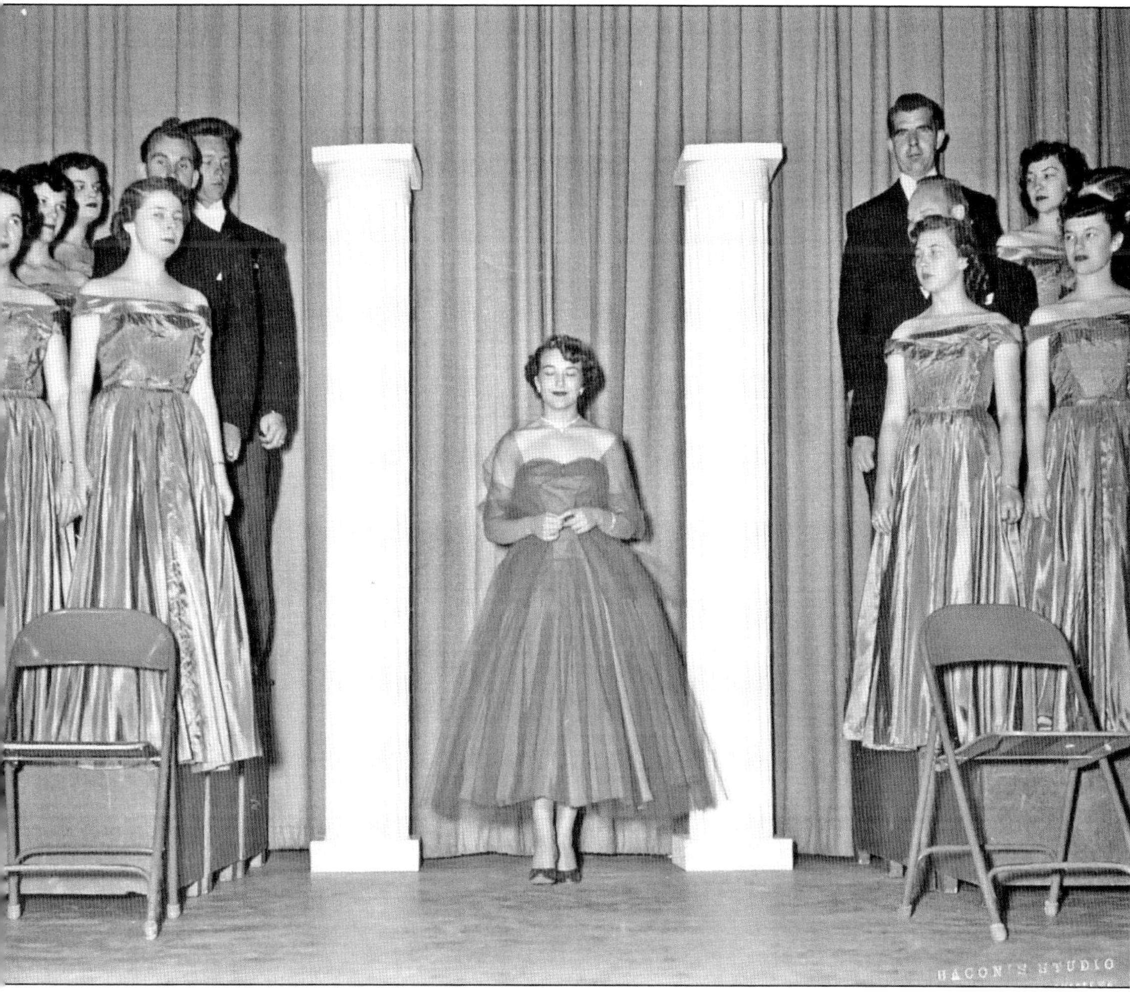

Margaret Ann Horton, a contestant and eventual winner in the 1952 Miss Bossier Contest, poses between two columns. (Courtesy of the Bossier Parish Library Historical Center.)

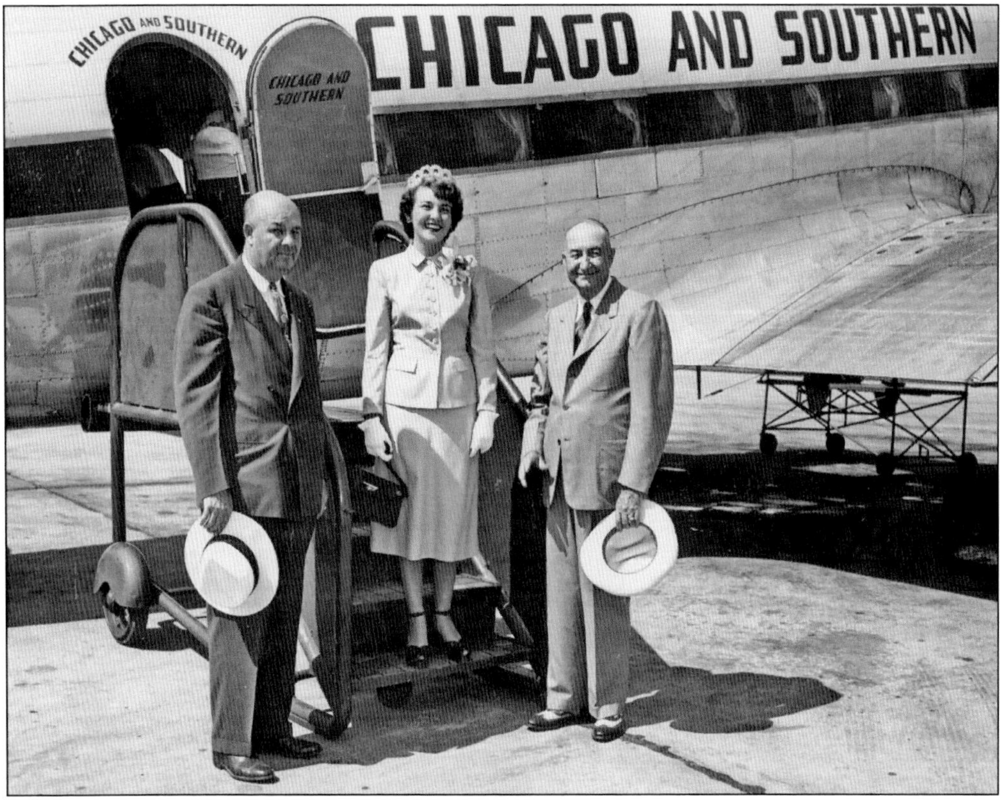

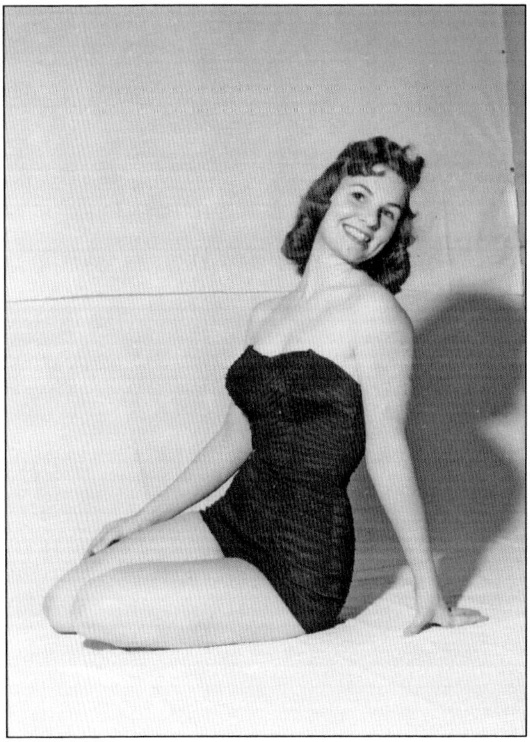

Miss Bossier City, Margaret Ann Horton, is pictured with V.V. Whittington (left) and an unidentified man just before she boards a plane to Cuba in 1952. (Courtesy of the Bossier Parish Library Historical Center.)

Anita Sue Thomasson, pictured here in 1960, won Miss Bossier City in 1958 and then won Miss Louisiana Tech in either 1959 or 1960. (Courtesy of the Bossier Parish Library Historical Center.)

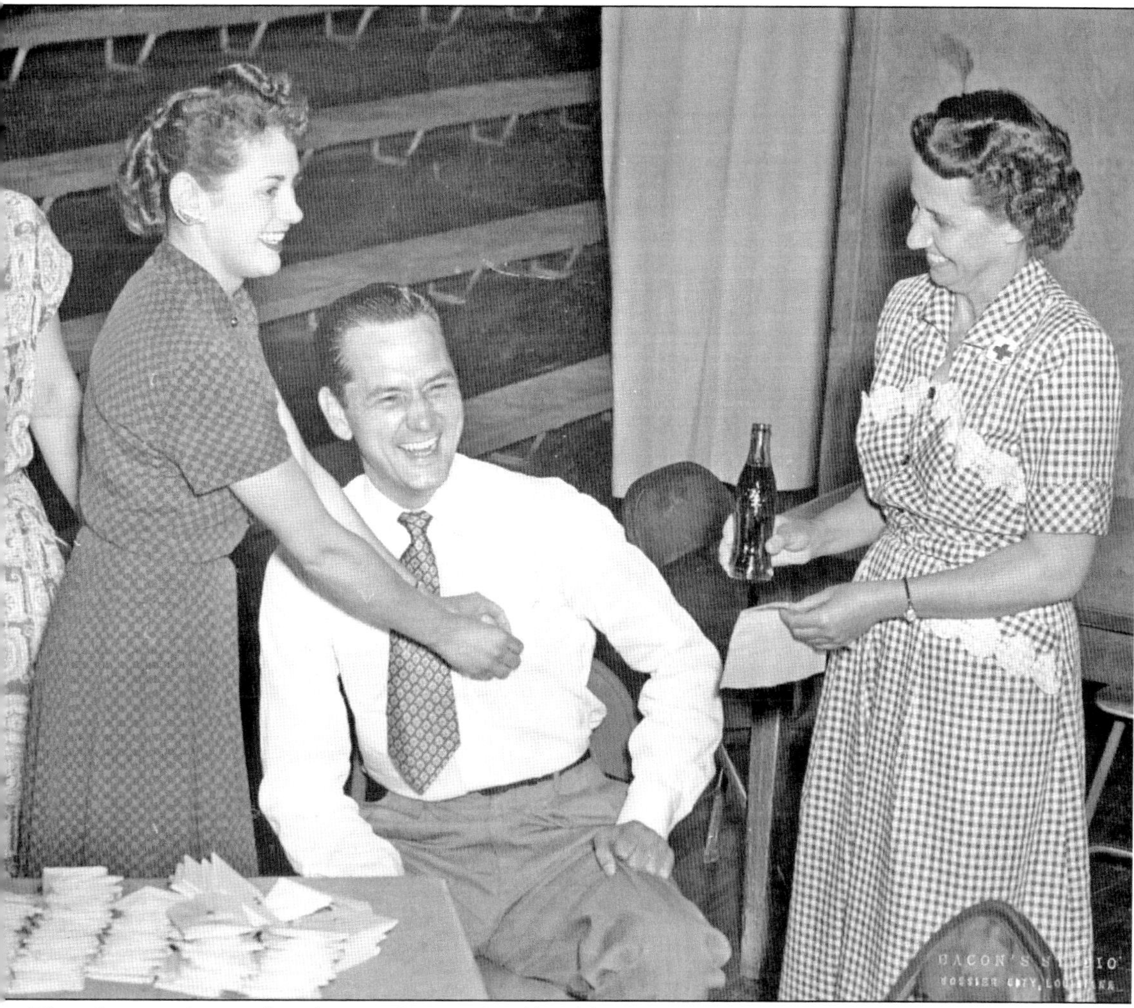

This photograph was taken during a Bossier City blood drive in 1952. Two unidentified women help Wayne Scwheitzer donate blood. (Courtesy of the Bossier Parish Library Historical Center.)

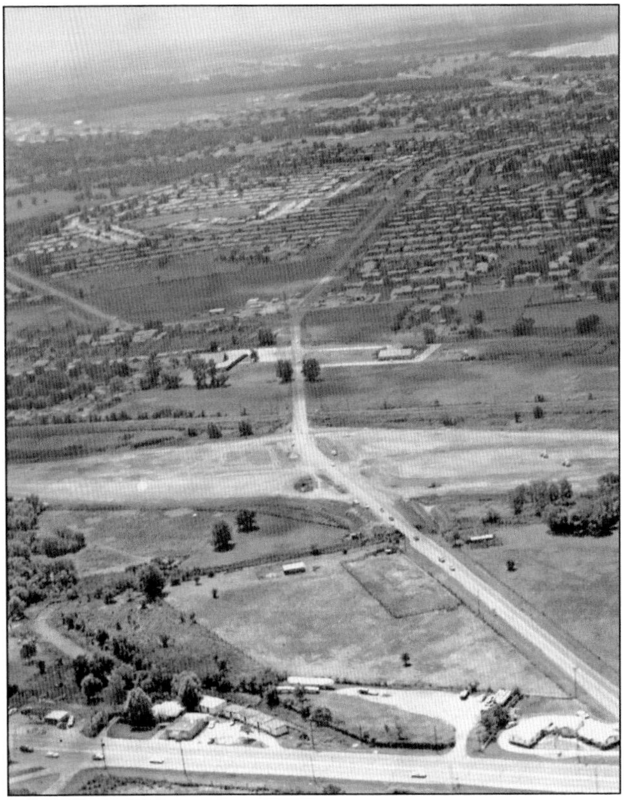

This image captures the view looking south above Airline Drive during the construction of I-20 in the early 1960s. John Knox Presbyterian Church is in the center. In the foreground, one can see Barksdale AFB and the Red River. (Courtesy of Trinity Presbyterian Church.)

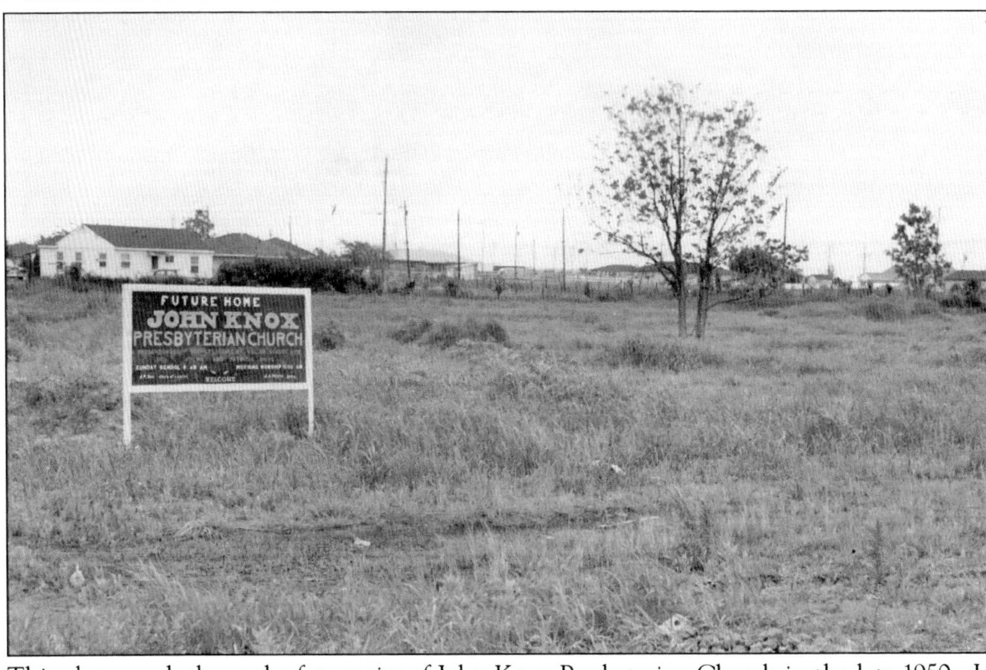

This photograph shows the future site of John Knox Presbyterian Church in the late 1950s. In the background is the Barksdale drive-in theater, located on the corner of Northgate and Old Minden Roads. (Courtesy of Trinity Presbyterian Church.)

In 1982, this stained-glass window was installed in John Knox Presbyterian Church. The stained glass, along with the blend of art deco and modernity of the church, makes the sanctuary one of the most beautiful rooms in Bossier City. (Courtesy of Trinity Presbyterian Church.)

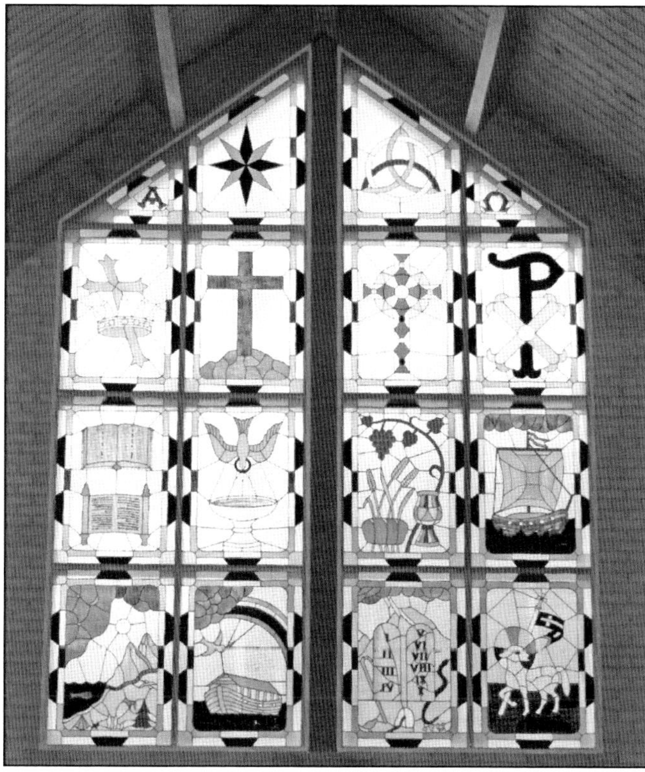

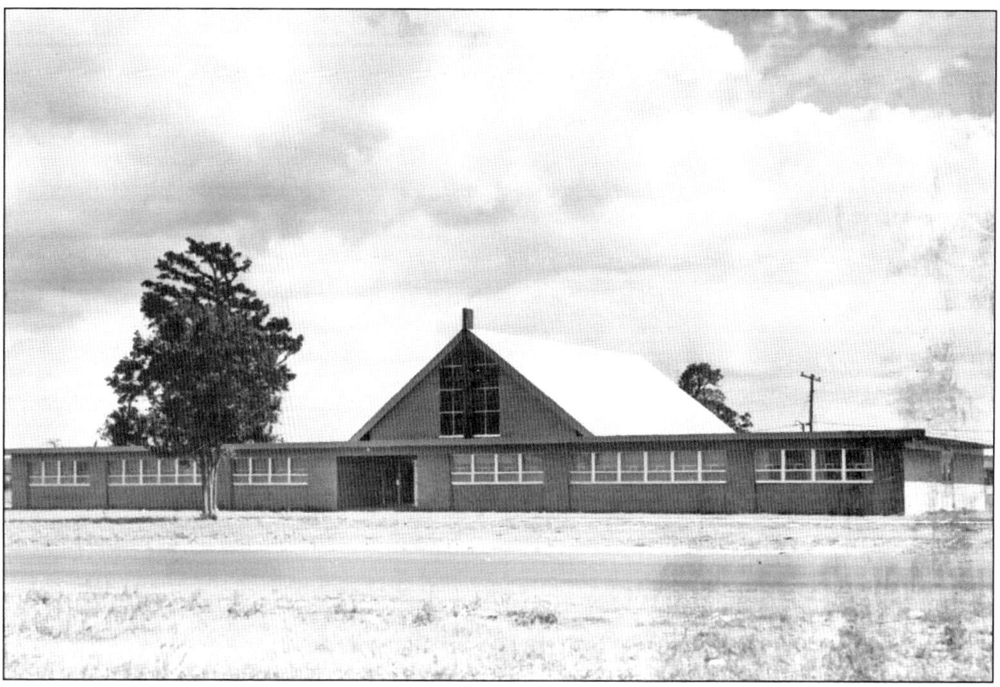

John Knox Presbyterian Church is located on Airline Drive and offers services on Sundays. In 2005, the church merged with the congregation of First Presbyterian and became Trinity Presbyterian Church. (Courtesy of Trinity Presbyterian Church.)

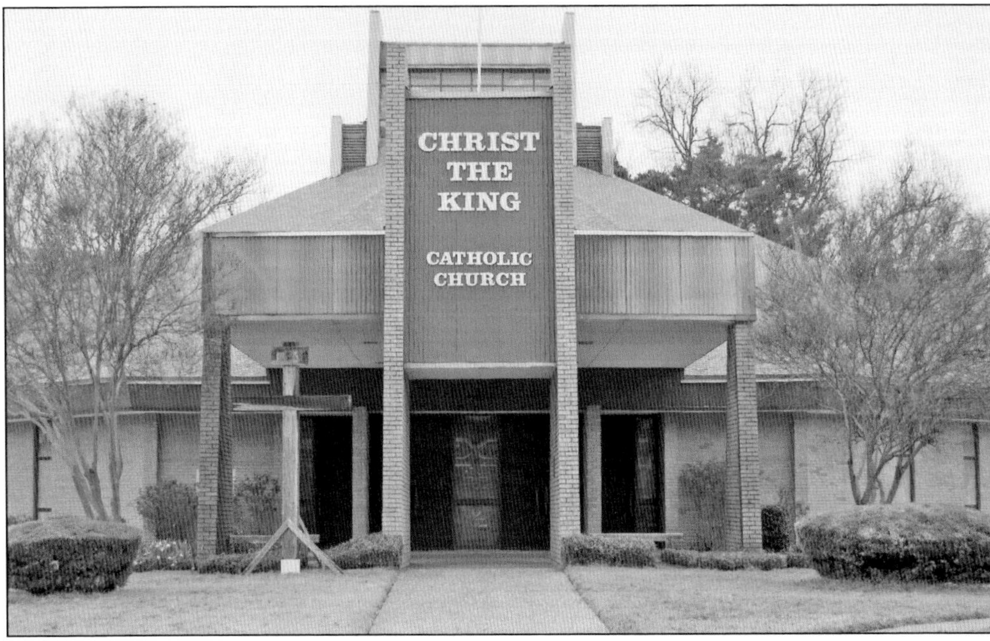

For many decades, the Catholic families in Bossier City had to cross the river to worship. In 1941, Christ the King Catholic Church was dedicated at its current location on Ogilvie Street. The church opened its own elementary school in 1954. (Courtesy of Robin Jones.)

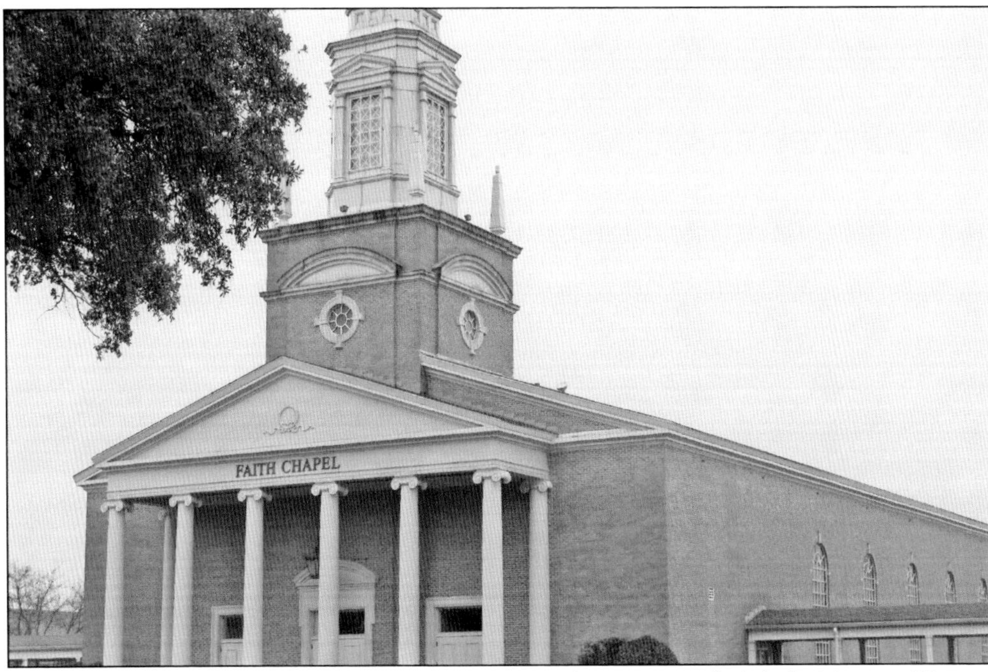

First Baptist Church can trace its roots back to 1903, when it was called Ardis Memorial Baptist Church after one of its charter members. In 1939, it was renamed First Baptist Church of Bossier City, and the congregation moved to their current location on East Texas Street in 1961. The church has continued to grow and now has over 7,000 members. (Courtesy of Robin Jones.)

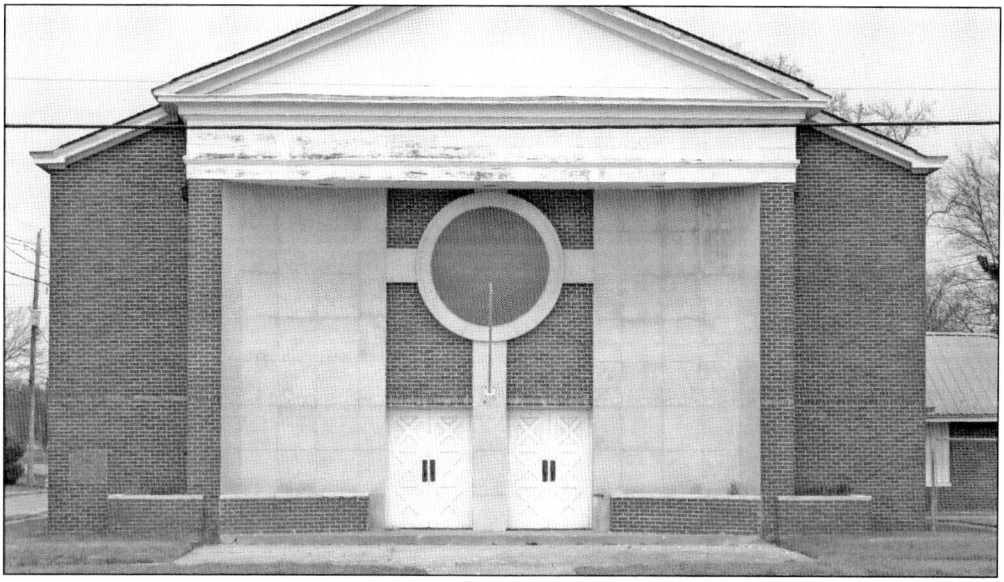

First United Methodist Church began in a store on Traffic Street in 1908. It then began to meet in the old Bossier schoolhouse on the site of the current Bossier Elementary School. The congregation established their own church building in 1921 in the same area of Bossier. Eventually, in 1948, they constructed a new building that still stands on the corner of Arcadia and Ogilvie Streets. The image above shows that building, which is now vacant. In 1973, the congregation moved to their current location on John Wesley Boulevard. (Courtesy of Robin Jones.)

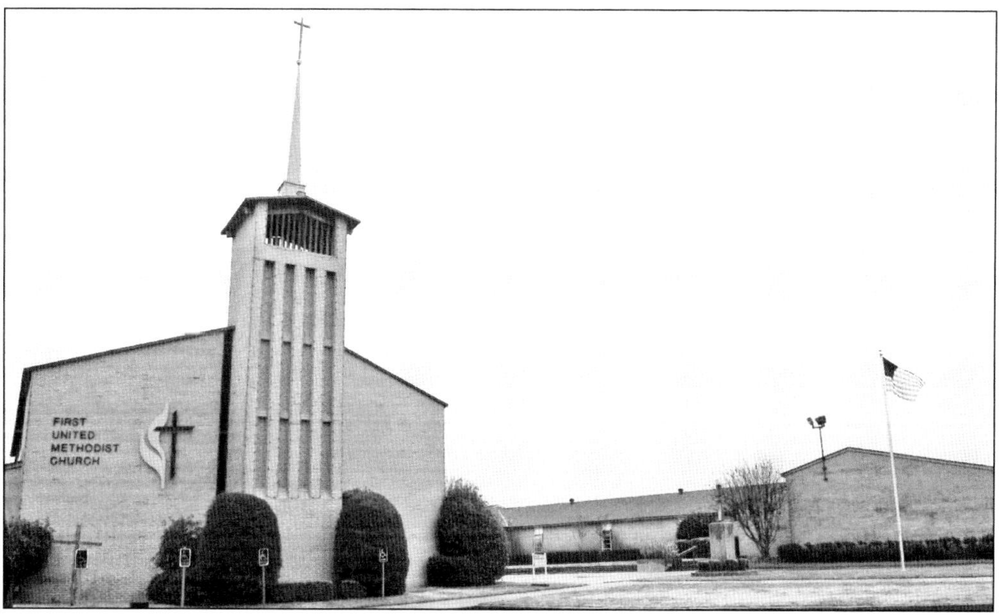

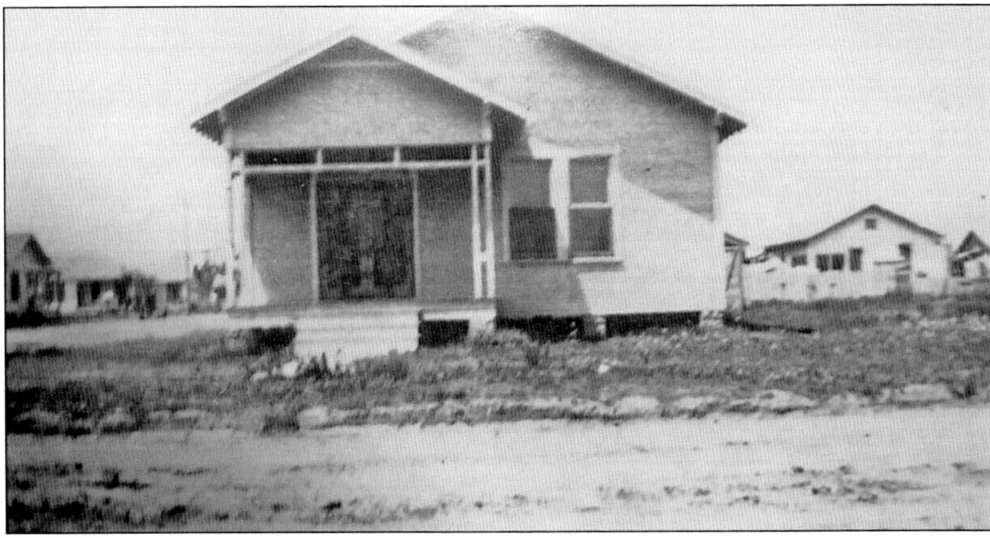

The First Presbyterian Church of Bossier City was organized on April 27, 1924, with 27 charter members. The first Sunday school was held on the same day with 55 pupils and teachers. The lots used for building the church were located on the corners of Delhi and Bennett Streets in downtown Bossier City. The original building was destroyed by fire, and the image below shows the second building. (Courtesy of Trinity Presbyterian Church.)

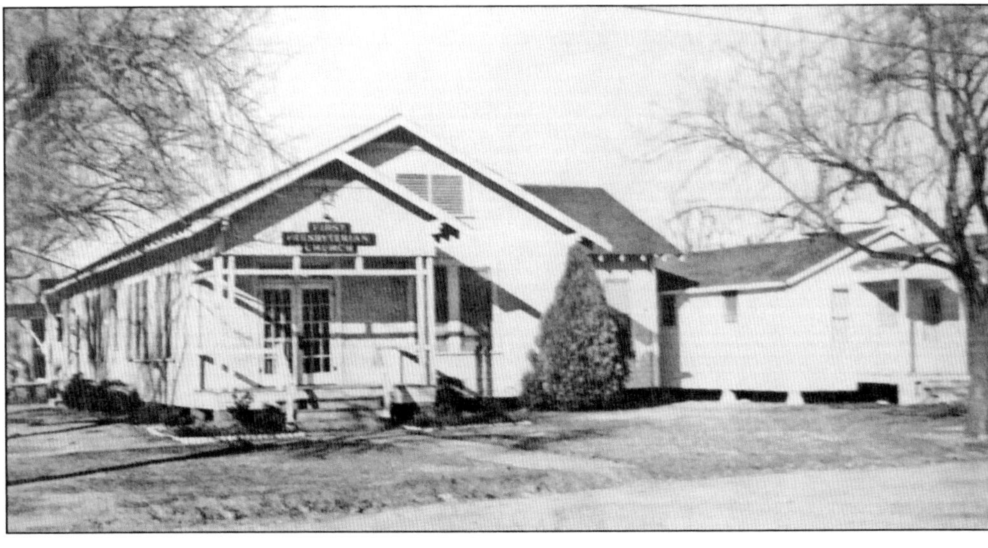

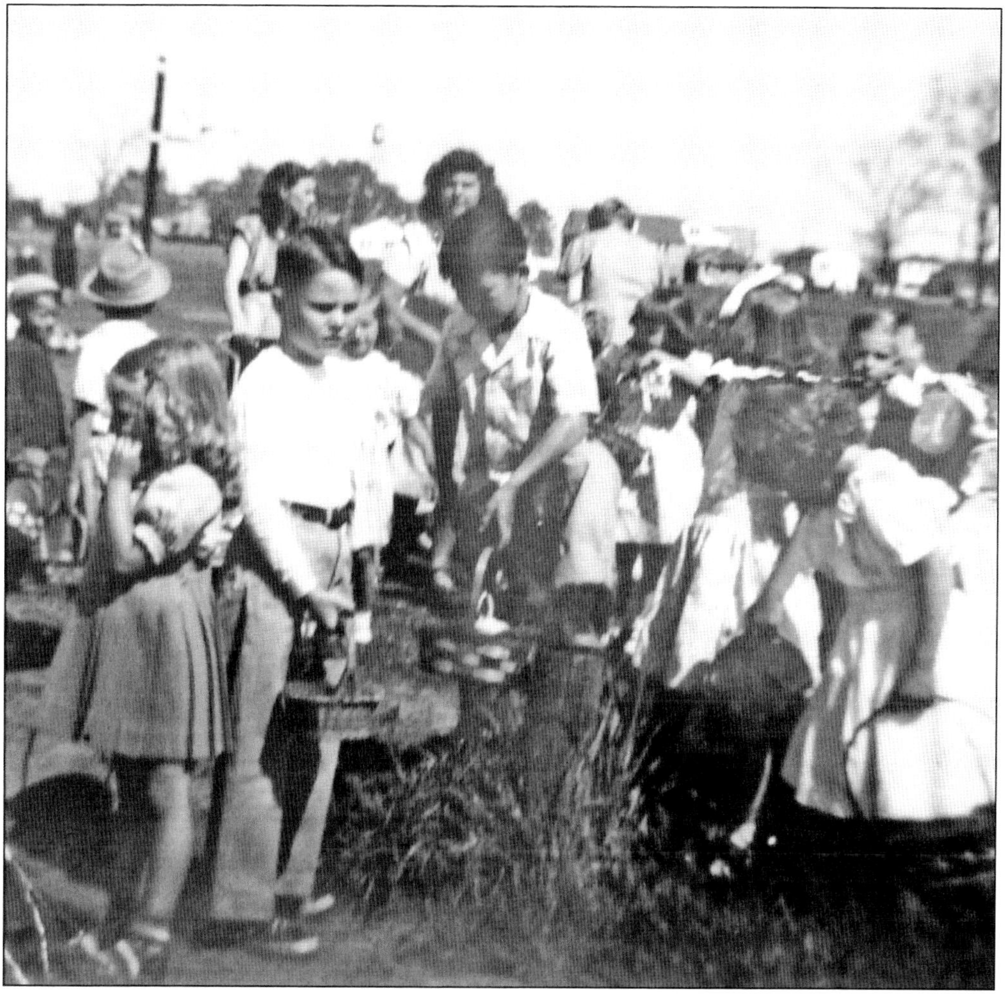

These images from 1942 show an Easter egg hunt and a potluck dinner attended by the congregation of First Presbyterian Church. It was about this time that the church's congregation had grown so large that they required a new building for worship. (Courtesy of Trinity Presbyterian Church.)

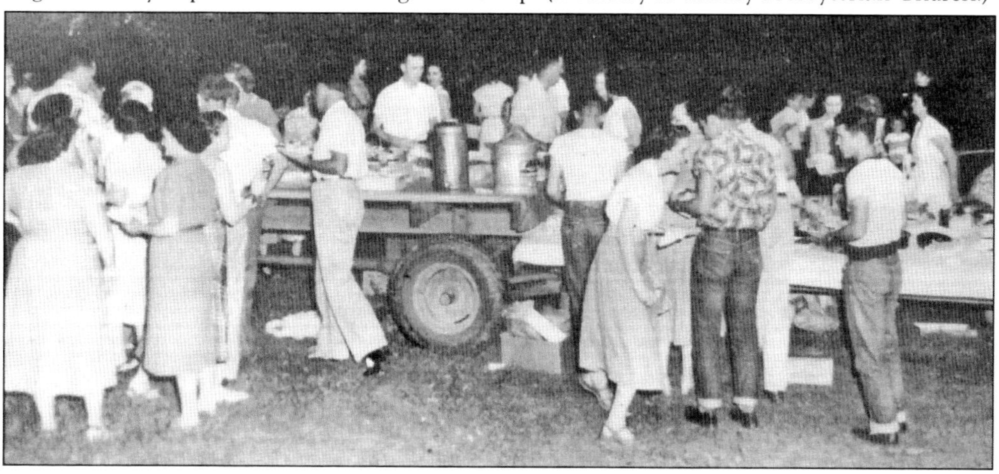

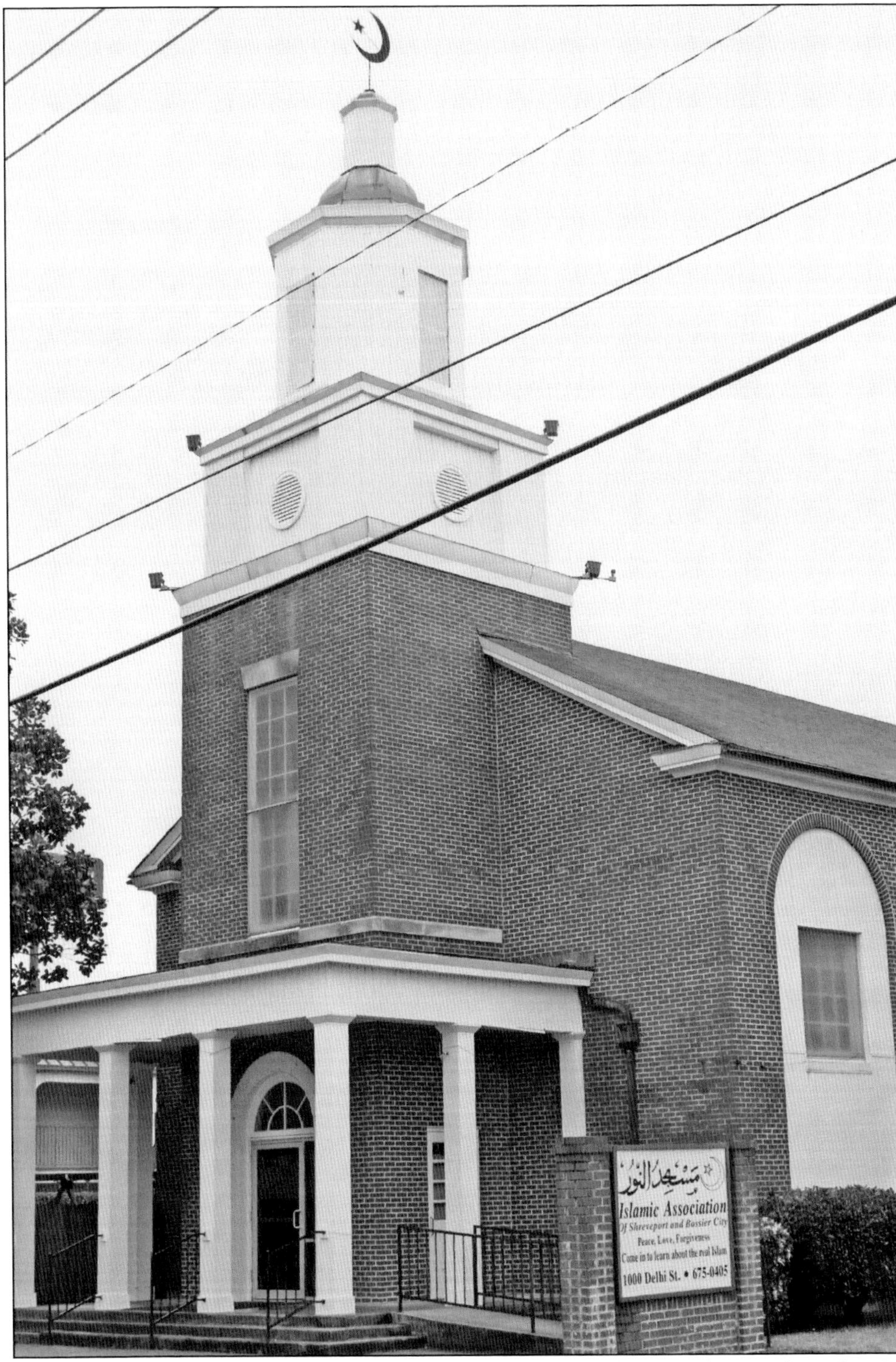

This is the third building that the First Presbyterian Church used for worship. Built in the 1940s, it housed the congregation until 2002 when they merged with John Knox Presbyterian Church to form Trinity Presbyterian Church. The building now serves Bossier City's Muslim population as a mosque. (Courtesy of Robin Jones.)

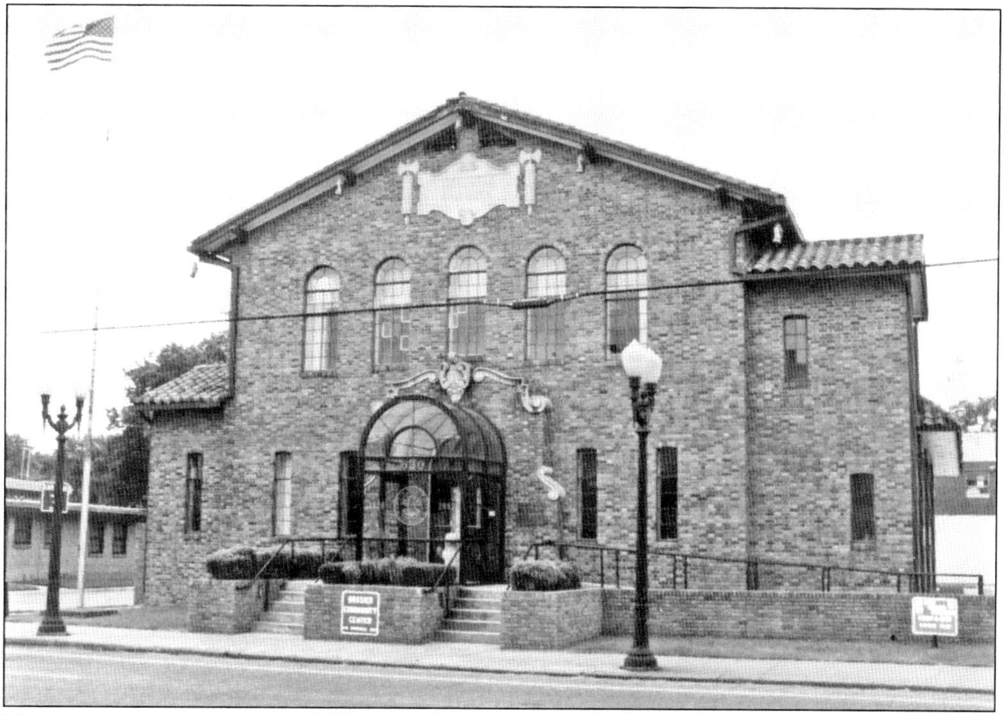

The Bossier City Municipal Building was constructed in 1929. It originally served as courthouse, fire department, police station, jailhouse, city hall, and sometimes even the library. The structure served as the primary city building for over 40 years. The police station and jailhouse expanded around it to where the parking lots and Bossier Arts Council Annex are now located. The fire station moved next door. In the 1970s, it split duties with the old Bossier Bank and Trust building as the municipal buildings in Bossier City. In 1985, the current municipal complex was built off of Benton Road, and the building turned into a community center. In 2000, it was renovated and transferred to the Bossier Arts Council, and it now serves as an art gallery, community theater, and space for local artists to work. (Courtesy of the Bossier Arts Council.)

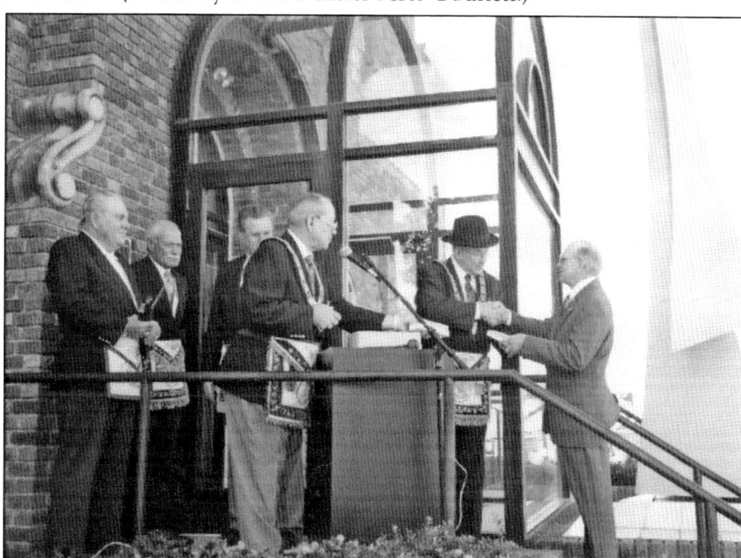

Local Masons from the McClanahan Lodge help to dedicate the Bossier Arts Council during its opening ceremony in 2000. There is a Masonic cornerstone placed in front of the building. (Courtesy of the Bossier Arts Council.)

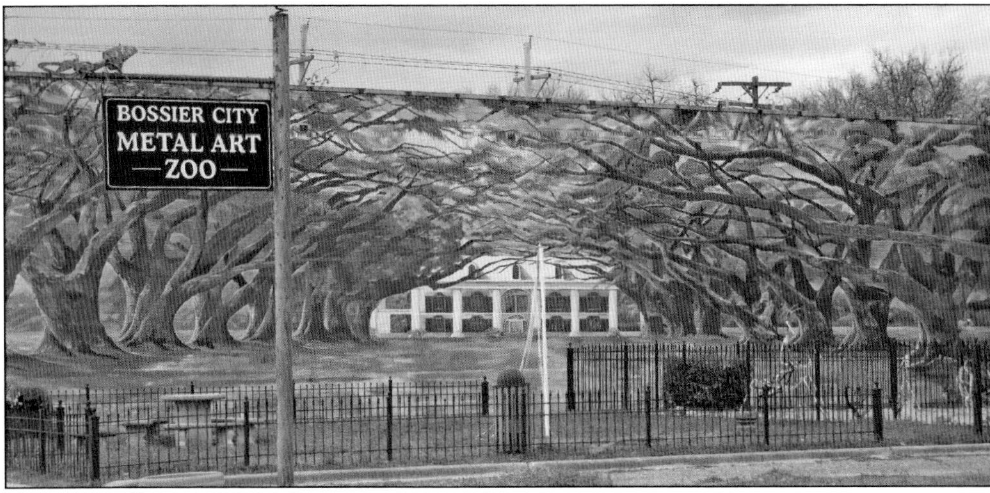

The image above shows the Bossier City Metal Art Zoo and a mural painted by artist Buddy West, both located in downtown Bossier City. The image below shows a mural on the south wall of the Bossier Arts Council painted by artist Chris Opp in 2011. It was designed by student Ashley Schaffer as part of the Bossier Arts Council annual student art show. (Courtesy of Robin Jones.)

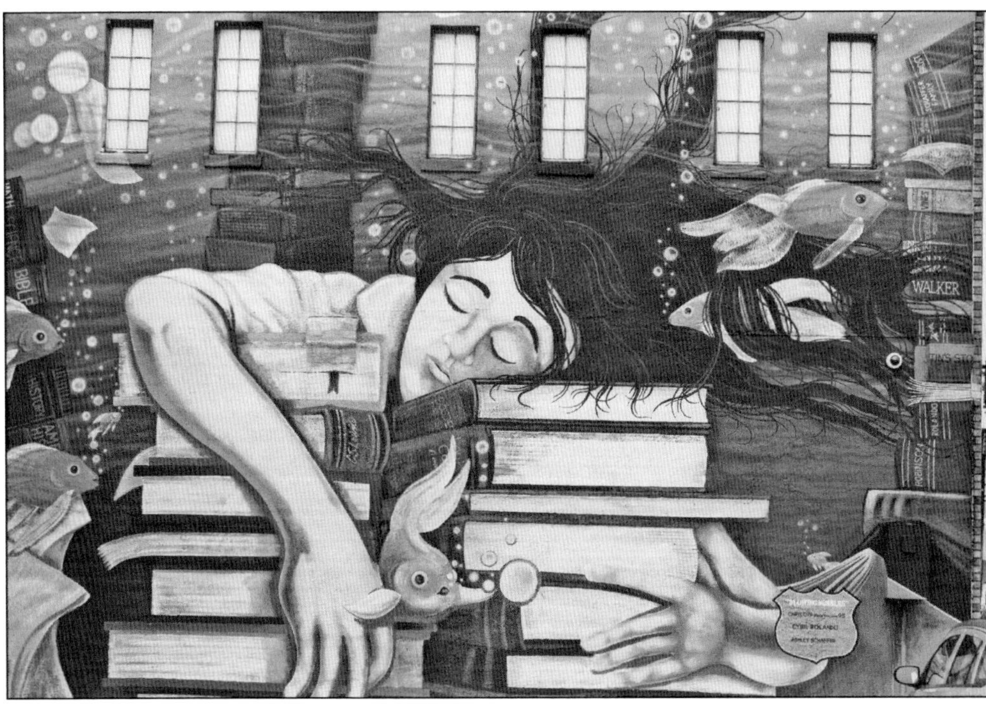

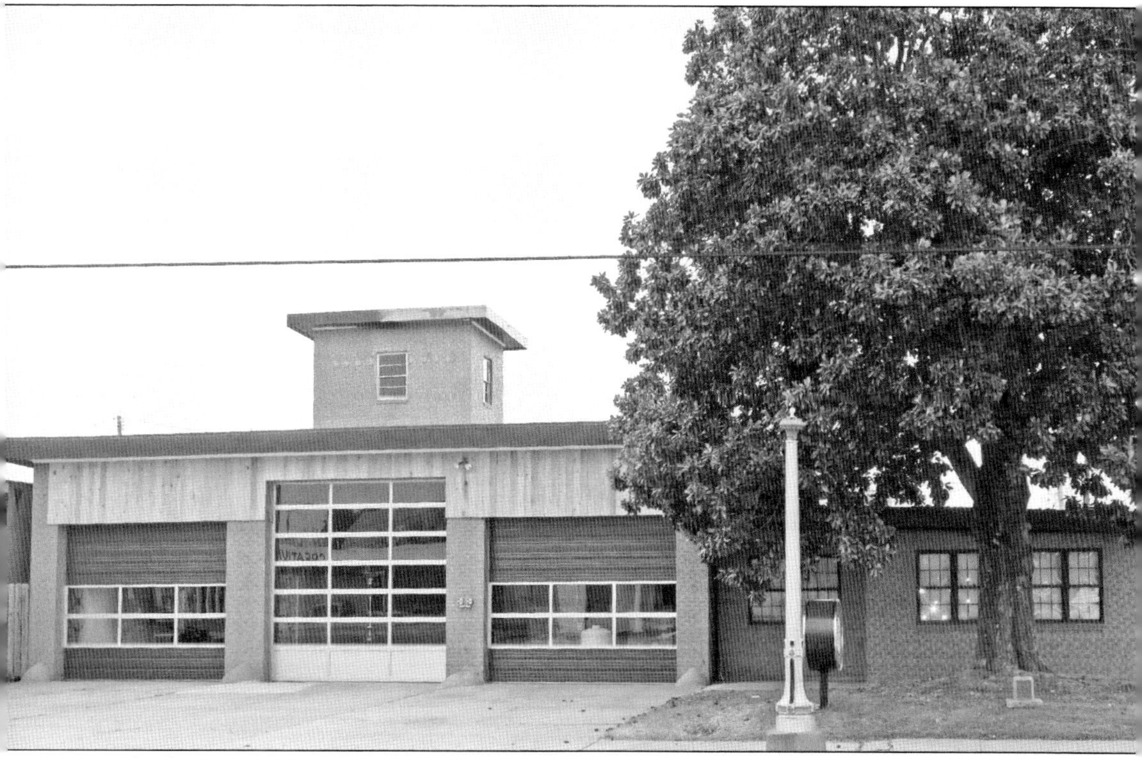

In 2015, the fire station next door to the Bossier Arts Council was purchased and remodeled into the Flying Heart Brewery. Its construction is part of a larger effort to revitalize downtown Bossier City. (Courtesy of Robin Jones.)

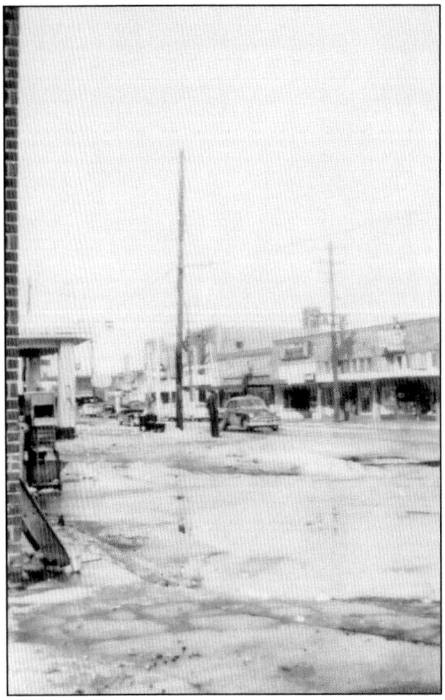

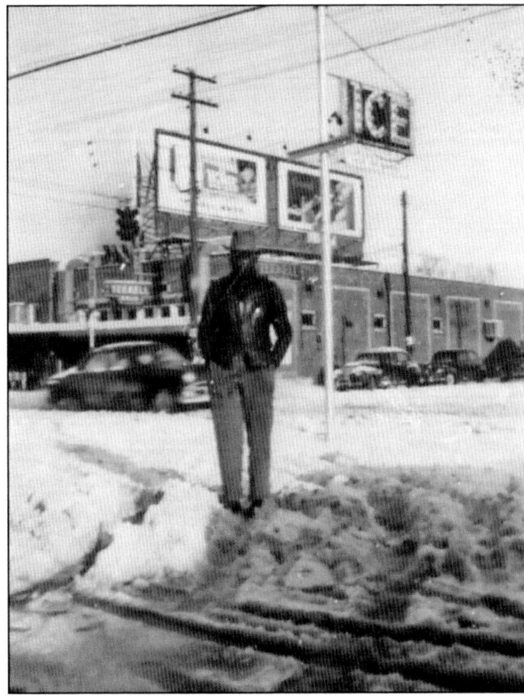

Snow is always an exciting event. These are two views of a snow-covered Bossier Ice Company in the late 1940s or early 1950s: facing west of Barksdale Boulevard (left) and the front of the icehouse (right). Bossier Ice operated into the 1960s. The building was torn down in the 1980s and is now a parking lot on the west side of the Bossier Arts Council. (Courtesy of Noel Memorial Library.)

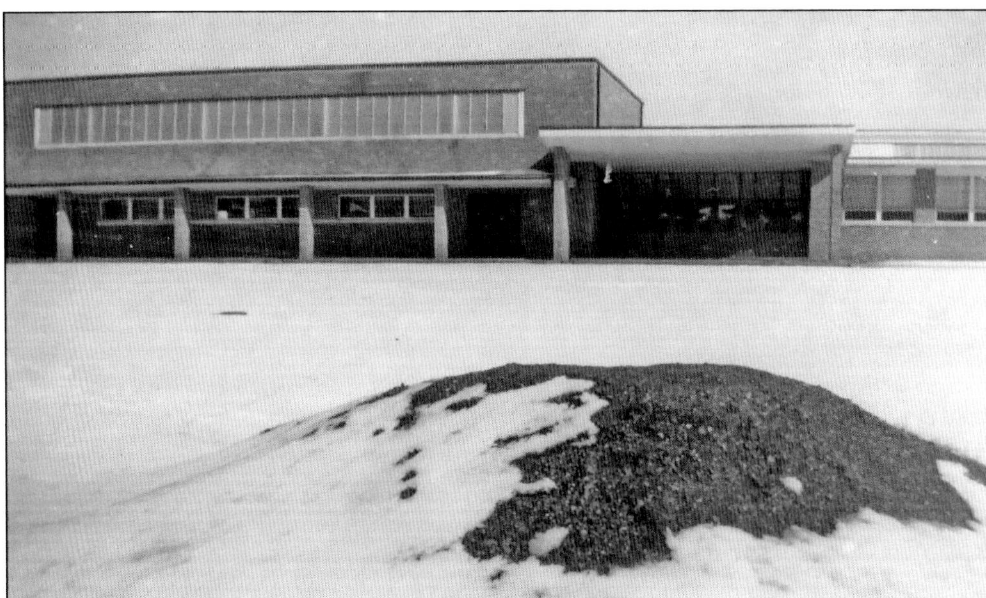

A snowstorm hit Bossier City in 1948. Many residents whipped out their cameras and snapped photographs of the winter wonderland. This is the front of the recently opened Bossier High School. (Courtesy of Bossier Parish Library Historical Center.)

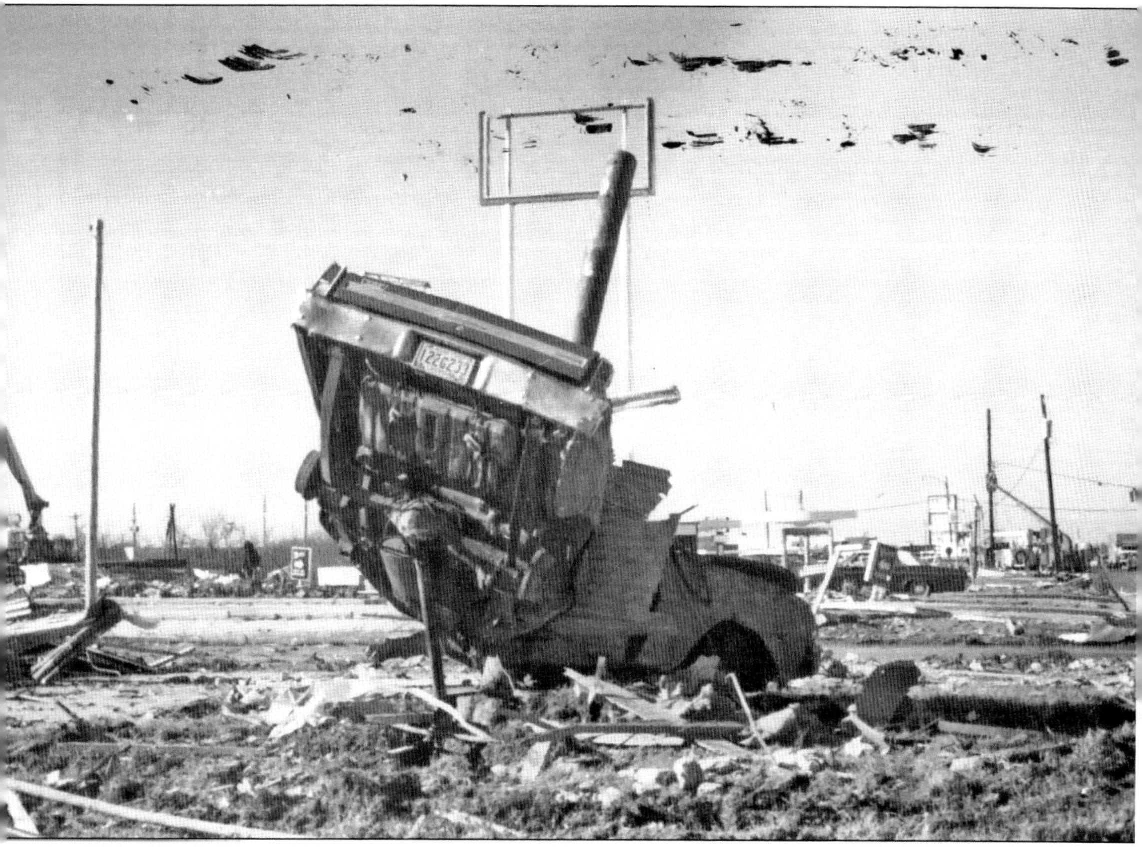

One of the biggest natural disasters in Bossier City's history was the tornado that came through in 1978. This is a photograph of the Pizza Inn that sat on Airline Drive near East Texas. (Courtesy of Bossier Parish Library Historical Center.)

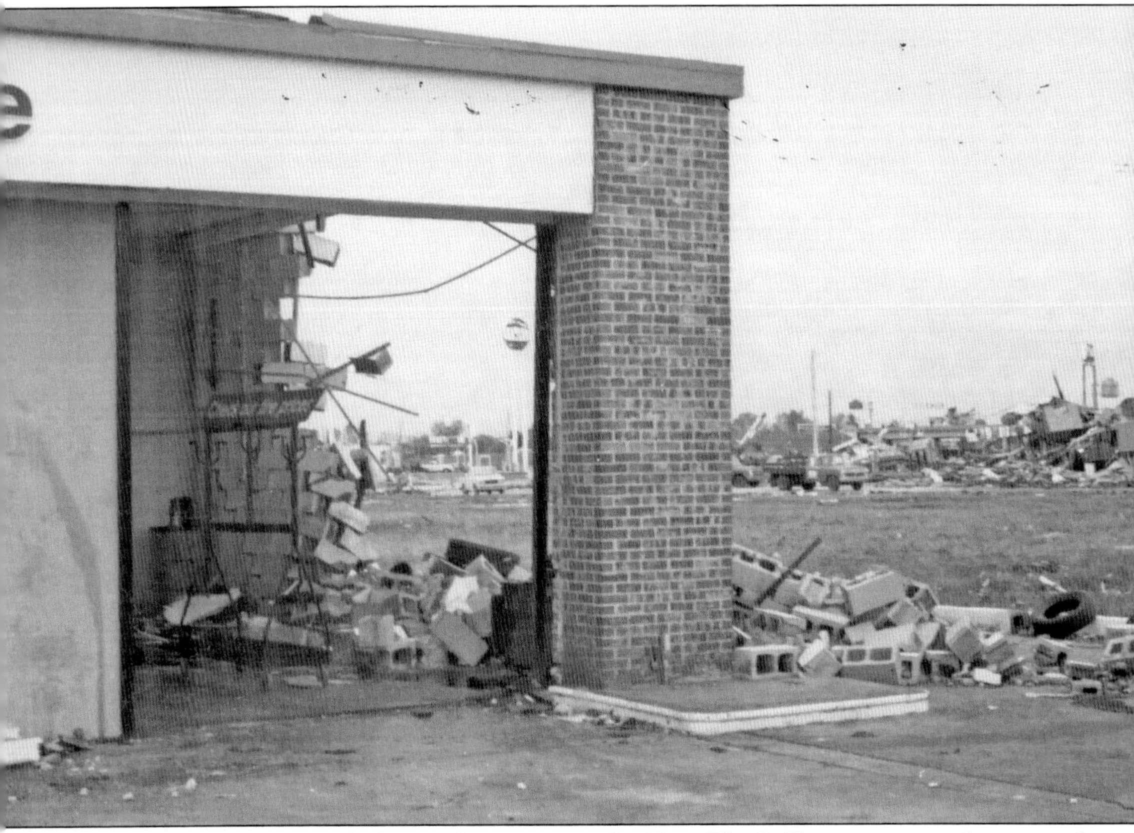

Pictured here is a tornado-damaged service center building. The Gulf station sign can be seen in the background, along with piles of debris. (Courtesy of Bossier Parish Library Historical Center.)

The substation near Preston Boulevard was significantly damaged by the tornado, and the storm leveled the Port Au Prince Apartments in the same part of town. (Courtesy of Noel Memorial Library.)

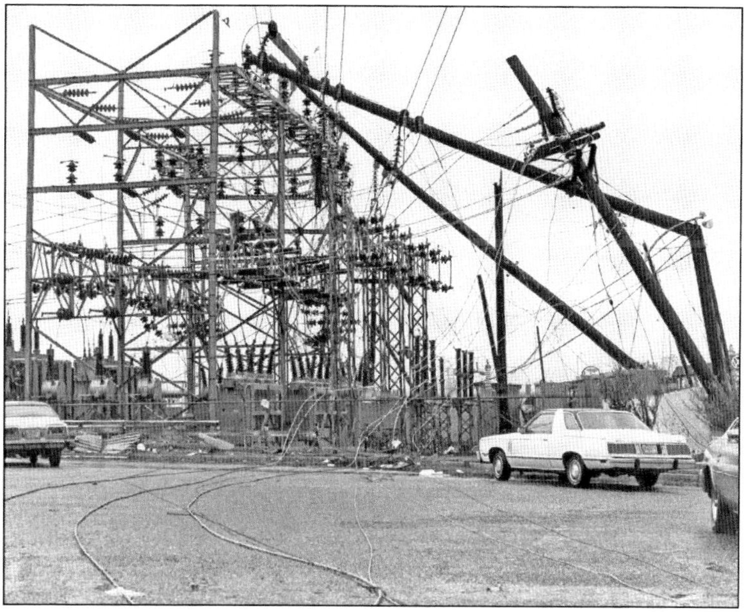

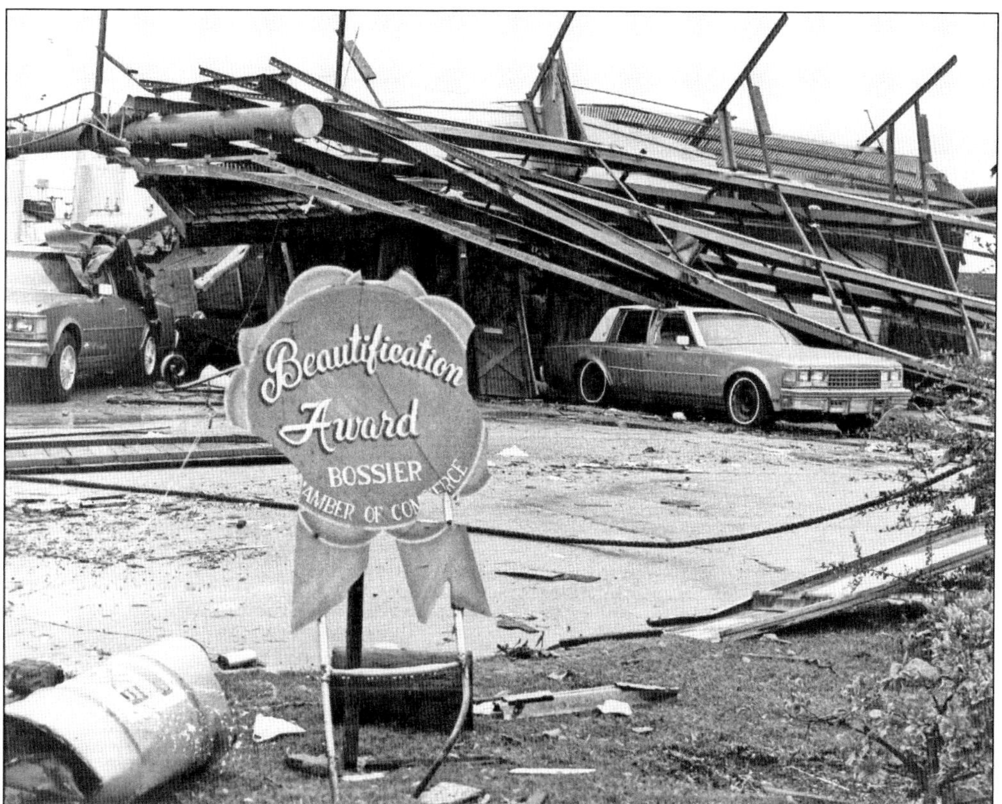

The irony of a beautification award in front of a collapsed billboard on top of a business in Bossier City after the tornado is palpable. (Courtesy of Noel Memorial Library.)

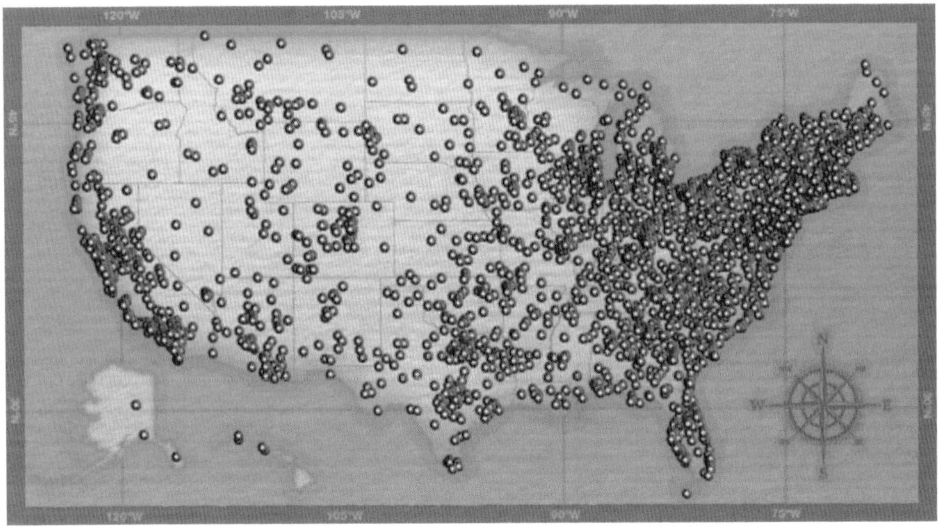